M000233586

The Multicultural Southwest

The Multicultural Southwest

A READER

edited by

A. Gabriel Meléndez
M. Jane Young
Patricia Moore
Patrick Pynes

the university of arizona press   tucson

The University of Arizona Press
© 2001 The Arizona Board of Regents
All rights reserved

www.uapress.arizona.edu

Library of Congress Cataloging-in-Publication Data
The multicultural Southwest : a reader / edited by A. Gabriel
Meléndez . . . [et al.].
ISBN 0-8165-2217-0 (alk. paper) —
ISBN 0-8165-2216-2 (pbk. : alk. paper)
1. Southwest, New—Ethnic relations. 2. Southwest, New—Social conditions.
3. Southwest, New—History. 4. Pluralism (Social sciences)—Southwest, New.
5. Indians of North America—Southwest, New—Social conditions. 6. Hispanic
Americans—Southwest, New—Social conditions. 7. Human geography—Southwest,
New. 8. Ethnicity—Southwest, New. I. Meléndez, A. Gabriel (Anthony Gabriel)
F790.A1 M85 2001
979'.033—dc21   00-012930

Manufactured in the United States of America on acid-free, archival-
quality paper containing a minimum of 30% post-consumer waste and
processed chlorine free.

14   13   12   11   10   7   6   5   4   3

Contents

Introduction

Scarcely a week into the year marking the four hundredth anniversary of the European presence in what today is the American Southwest, a group of unknown vandals entered the grounds of the Oñate Monument and Visitors' Center at Arcade, New Mexico, and marred a twelve-foot bronze sculpture of the Spanish conqueror and colonizer Juan de Oñate by severing the right foot of the image. This act of protest, carried out by individuals claiming to represent the people of Acoma Pueblo, may eventually come to be known as the first salvo in the battle surrounding the public commemorations planned for the Cuarto Centennial of Spanish and Mexican settlements in the Southwest. The director of the Oñate Center, Juan Estevan Arellano, a native of Embudo and a longtime community activist, had not discovered the vandalism before he was contacted by the *Albuquerque Journal*. Reporters at the *Journal*'s northern bureau in Santa Fe pressed Arellano for a comment after receiving a typed note from the perpetrators explaining why the foot had been removed and what they intended to do with it: "We will be casting small medallions to be sold to those who are historically ignorant" (*Albuquerque Journal*, January 8, 1998).

Northern New Mexico, in the heart of the American Southwest, is a complex region. Hispanos, the descendants of Spaniards, Indians, and Mexicans, are literally next-door neighbors to the ten northern Pueblos (Sandia, Santa Ana, San Felipe, San Ildefonso, Santo Domingo, Cochiti, Santa Clara, San Juan, Picuris, and Taos). Arellano pointed out to reporters that the two peoples maintain close and good relations. He suggested that "people who have recently arrived in northern New Mexico and who don't know the history of Oñate might be behind the act of vandalism." If that turns out to be true, these vandals will have no problem selling the recast medallions to the legions of recent immigrants who have come to New Mexico and the greater Southwest in search of high-tech employment, wide-open spaces, and a lower cost of living.

The incident behind this controversy is quite straightforward, however, and few dispute the facts of history that have shaped the region as we know it today. Despite valid criticisms of his actions, Juan de Oñate is still an integral part of that history. He is credited with establishing the Spanish capital, San Gabriel, at El Yunque, just across the river from the Pueblo of San Juan, in 1598; and he is charged with waging a war of conquest the following year against the people of Acoma. (This is a minor detail, but the monument protestors were actually a year early.) In 1599, Oñate laid siege to Acoma, cut off the water and food supply to the Sky City, and, eventually, subdued its people. At the end of the siege, Oñate ordered that the right leg of each Acoma man over the age of twenty-five be severed. Men under twenty-five, along with women and children, were sentenced to twenty years of servitude to the Spanish. Oñate was brutal, even for the violent times in which he lived. Nor were his victims the only ones aware of his cruelty; other Europeans censured his abuses and removed him from power. For his part in the siege of Acoma, Oñate was brought to trial in Mexico, forced to resign as governor, and was barred from ever returning to New Mexico.

The area we now know as the Southwest has produced awe and admiration in nearly everyone who has attempted to capture its distinctiveness in words. In compiling our reader, we have included writers whose work reveals the tremendous impact that everyday and common occurrences can have in a region diverse in its people and its ecology. We hope to create in students and other readers an awareness of the complex social, cultural, and ecological dynamics and to account for how these forces affect life in the Southwest. We have also been careful to include a discussion of the region's historical development and to explain the ways in which the past shapes life at present here.

Today, the United States is engaged in a national debate over what it means to be a multicultural and multiracial society. As the editors of this anthology, it is our belief that such redefinition is best achieved by looking to the failures and successes of intercultural relationships in regions like the Southwest where distinct cultures and peoples have coexisted over long periods. Carey McWilliams noted of the Southwest that "here identities change slowly; the spacing between peoples gives differences a chance to survive; and what survives has value for it has been severely tested" ([1948] 1968, 11). We agree, adding that difference has survived in the Southwest as it has in few other parts of the nation.

Memory in the Southwest is very often the fuel of human imagination, creativity, and possibility. Often, the southwestern experience sparks powerful, sometimes conflicting memories. For us, a people's memory is the "deep grammar" of the human story. It is a grammar we need to learn because it brings forth alternative views of environment, landscape, human social interaction, conquest, dispossession, technological change, and the survival of cultures.

We have organized our reader around seven themes, each occupying a corresponding section of our text: I. Southwestern Views, Ethnic Angles; II. Perceptions of the Other; III. Native America; IV. Hispano-Mestizo America; V. Borderlands America; VI. Environment, Technology, and the Peoples of the Southwest; and VII. Making Culture: The Future Southwest. These seven topics do not exhaust the possibility of perspectives that might be brought to bear in any study of the Southwest. Nonetheless, we see them as windows from which to consider essential aspects of the region. As a way to expand that field of vision we have added newspaper articles of a topical and timely nature.

The compiling and editing of this anthology has been a collaboration between two professors, Meléndez and Young, and two doctoral students, Moore and Pynes. All four of us are affiliated with the Department of American Studies at the University of New Mexico. We initially took on this task because we all had shared the experience of teaching the undergraduate course "Introduction to Southwest Studies," and variously had come to the conclusion that a satisfactory introductory reader on the Southwest was unavailable on the market. Thus, we decided to design one that engaged multiple aspects of the southwestern experience. The process of working as a group has at times been cumbersome. All four of us selected articles, voiced our opinions about what should be included in the anthology, and contributed to the section introductions. Working under the illusion that tenured professors have more time than graduate students, Meléndez and Young wrote the general introduction. We had never before coauthored any sort of written work and found that we enjoyed the exchange of ideas and share a passion for our subject and for writing. We wish, however, to acknowledge Moore and Pynes, whose voices appear throughout this volume. Their teaching experience, writing skills, and insight have been invaluable to developing this reader.

A. Gabriel Meléndez
M. Jane Young
University of New Mexico, Albuquerque, 2000

References

McWilliams, Carey. *North from Mexico: The Spanish-Speaking People of the Southwest.* New York: Greenwood Press, [1948] 1968.

"Statue of Spaniard Loses Foot." *Albuquerque Journal.* January 9, 1998.

The Multicultural Southwest

PART I

Southwestern Views, Ethnic Angles

We base the first section of our anthology on the idea that the Southwest defies absolute and categorical definitions. The geographer D. W. Meinig perceptively asks readers to consider whether the Southwest should best be thought of as a quarter of the nation or as a cultural border zone, a north to Mexicans, a west to Americans. Meinig's question challenges the certainty of the social scientist, and by posing it, he acknowledges that there is a limited utility to the geographer's maps, measures, quadrants, and geographical delineations in describing the region. The fullest answer to the geographer's question is not contained in any one article, nor can it be understood from any single perspective. The Southwest is a place on the map, but it is also an idea held in the mind. Thus, it is crucial to account for the ways its human, cultural, ethno-geographic, spiritual, political, and ecological features have fueled the human imagination.

Part I brings together the writings of geographers, cultural critics, early travelers, and historians, each of whom adds to the definition of the Southwest. Here, and in each section that follows, we have included the work of poets, novelists, and essayists because we feel that the language and vision of the creative writer are our best hope of communicating real, lived experience. We expect that each assessment of the Southwest offered in our compilation will encourage readers to explore new and far-reaching questions. Further inquiry may cause them to consider whether the region is reducible to essences, or whether it can be viewed from multiple and overlapping perspectives.

The Southwest

a definition

D. W. Meinig

The Southwest is a distinctive place to the American mind but a somewhat blurred place on American maps, which is to say that everyone knows that there is a Southwest but there is little agreement as to just where it is. Some would write it so broadly across the continent from the Pacific Ocean to the Gulf of Mexico as to include Nevada, Utah, Colorado, and Oklahoma as well as California, Texas, and the states directly between, a full quarter or more of the entire nation. Others would define it more narrowly, but still with little general agreement as to its proper bounds. It is thus incumbent upon those who use the term to offer a clear definition and rationale at the outset. That such regional delineations should emanate from the purpose of the study is axiomatic.

If in a work of social geography we might logically begin by making our definition dependent upon the presence of certain peoples, we are quickly brought into at least general focus upon a particular region. The term "Southwest" is of course an ethnocentric one: what is south and west to the Anglo-American was long the north of the Hispano-American, and the overlap of the colonizing thrusts of these two continental invaders—the one approaching west from the Atlantic Seaboard, the other north from central Mexico—suggests a first element in the definition of a distinctive cultural border zone. Whether based upon the historic patterns of the several specific thrusts of the Spanish and Mexicans or the presence in significant numbers today of Spanish-Americans, that zone is an extensive one, reaching from the vicinity of San

Francisco Bay to Galveston Bay. But if we add the continued presence of the American Indians as a significant part of the regional scene, our concern is narrowed from the whole breadth of these Anglo-Hispanic borderlands to that portion lying between Texas and California, for neither of these famous states has more than a few tiny reservations and a very few Indians remaining. The major non-reservation Indian area in Oklahoma lies well beyond the Hispanic zone and is quite separated in position and in specific Indian cultures from New Mexico and Arizona.

The physical character of the area thus defined by the general juxtaposition of these three peoples is by no means uniform, though it is dominated by mountain-and-bolson, or high plateau country, and a relatively dry climate. More significant to the search for a workable regional definition is the fact that it has tended to be set apart on the west, north, and east by broad zones of difficult country—the Mohave-Sonoran Desert, the Colorado River Canyonlands, the Southern Rockies, and the Llano Estacado—lands which long were and mostly still are thinly populated.

On the south the international boundary, now more than a century old, and antedating many of the major population movements and settlement developments, is so decisive to all modern relationships that it may be taken as a precise edge even though it cuts directly across the grain of the country and severs some of the Indians and Hispanos from their cultural kin and older connections farther south.

During the American era the development of California and Texas on either side as two areas strongly self-conscious of being, and widely acknowledged to be, very distinct parts of the nation has tended to accentuate the separateness of the area in between, just as Mormon-dominated Utah and, in a much vaguer way, the common image of mountainous Colorado have helped to define a regional border along the north. Such patterns have been strongly reinforced in modern times by the emergence of metropolitan "fields." Thus as measured by basic metropolitan services, such as newspapers, banking, and wholesaling, the combined reach of Los Angeles, Salt Lake City, Denver, and the several large Texas cities leaves a large area in between served by its own centers.

But although this Anglo-Hispano-Indian combination of peoples living within this rather detached area defines the Southwest as a general region relevant to our purpose, it is also apparent that within those gross bounds there has been relatively little close unity in developments and the area has never had a single focus. Historical movements, though often quite parallel in kind, have tended to be fixed in two quite distinct areas which, if in some ways similar in character, are not only distant from one another but have been separated by formidable barriers. Each of these nuclear areas is served by a major stream, the Rio Grande on the one hand, the Gila on the other; each is the home of agricultural Indians; and each was a salient of the Spanish frontier, but the two were separated through several centuries by the Apache-held highlands in between. The Anglos were the first to initiate any significant moves to bind these parts together but they never succeeded in making it a cohesive whole. While many Anglo developments have given the area some greater integrity as a region, other actions and consequences, most notably the political definition of an Arizona and a New Mexico and the rise of the metropolitan centers of Albuquerque and El Paso along the Rio Grande and Phoenix and Tucson in the Gila Basin, have powerfully reinforced this historic dualism.

The establishment of these political boundaries has further complicated the problem of regional definition, for although Arizona and New Mexico encompass in general not only the two main historically nuclear areas but the wider areas ultimately developed by extensions from them, they do not delimit such areas precisely, embracing rather more in some sectors and less in others. The largest anomaly is along the eastern border where the New Mexican boundary includes the western margins of the Great Plains, areas eventually colonized and developed by contiguous expansions westward from Kansas and Texas rather than eastward from the Rio Grande Valley. We cannot, however, simply exclude that area from our concern, for despite a different heritage and combination of peoples, it profoundly affects the social relations and balance of power within the state as a whole. An equally important but smaller discordance lies just to the south, where the western promontory of Texas extends to the El Paso district, an area historically and currently more closely bound to the Southwest as here defined than to its political unit. Some lesser discordances along the northern border will be noted later.

The Southwest thus defined—in general, Arizona, New Mexico, and the El Paso district—despite a persistent dualism and more internal diversity and less focus than such a single term suggests, has nevertheless a sufficiently common set of people and problems enmeshed in a common heritage and is sufficiently set apart by physical and cultural differences from its neighbors to make it a reasonable regional unit for the purpose and scale of this interpretation. It has the further merit of conforming rather closely with the view of many of its own residents. For as Oliver La Farge, a highly qualified regional interpreter, has noted, "If you ask a New Mexican what constitutes the Southwest, he will name New Mexico and Arizona; after hesitation, he may add the adjacent portions of Colorado, Utah and Nevada. California, Texas, and Oklahoma he rejects . . ." (La Farge, p. 216). That suggests a basic area, an ambiguous border zone on the north and a distinct separation on the east and west. It seems evident that most any Arizonan would offer a similar view.

Why there is such a "Southwest" in the minds of such people should become clear from the chapters that follow.

Reference

La Farge, Oliver. 1947–60. "New Mexico." In *American Panorama*, pp. 216–29. Garden City, N.Y.: Doubleday and Company, Inc.

The Golden Key to Wonderland

Charles Lummis

"Sun, Silence, Adobe—New Mexico in three words." So I wrote in 1890, after six years' exploration of this "Land of Poco Tiempo." Plainly, these three imply more—Restfulness—Romance—Beauty—Mystery—Room and Peace.

Now that I have studied 36 years longer, let's say: "Sun—Silence—Adobe—Wonder—Finality—New Mexico in five words." For the Southwest *(all of which was once New Mexico)* is the very Land of Wonder among the lands of Earth; and in our own country, it is the Serene Elbow-Room the hand of Man can never spoil. Its oases shall swell and blossom, its little cities grow bigger; but its mighty day-wide reaches shall endure unplowed and unabashed, unprettied and silent and free. It will always be a land where you can't make a noise "stick":

> That sky-full bowl of Silence
>   No fuss of Man can spill—
>   A hundred Indians whoop and sing,
> And still the Land is Still.

It is like to be the last place left in our country where one may find real Rest. Other lands we have fussed and frivoled and improved on God. But man will never make a fool of the Southwest.

There is no other such diagrammatic Picture-book of the Earth-building processes. We may know and care nothing about Geology—but we do care about Scenery, which is its flower. And for variety of noble Scenery, the Southwest has no rival. The Grand Canyon, the Petrified Forest, the Mesa Country, the fantastic mass and columnar and sculptural erosions of the Navajo Sand-stones, after the whaleback granite of the Continental Divide came humping up under their level keel, and shattered them at right angles, and "jointed" them for leagues either way with invisible fractures which the rains and frost found and wrought enchantments with—these are unique in the world. So are the monumental canyons gnawed by erosion in these same blanket strata. There are many mountain countries, but none like the Southwest.

There is no other State in the Union of such centuried Romance as New Mexico; nor other town so venerable as Santa Fe, nor other road with half the history or a tenth the tragedies of the old Santa Fe Trail. There are ten times as many prehistoric ruins in New Mexico as old ruins along the Rhine. No two other Rocks in the world are comparable, in picturesqueness and historic fascination and romance, with Acoma and Inscription Rock; nor in all the New World other inhabited towns of such mystery and wonder as Acoma, or Taos or the Moqui Pueblos. Nor is there elsewhere in all North America another Aristocracy so ancient, so poised, so rich in ritual and drama and spirituality as that of the Pueblos.

The student-explorer must feel some pang at seeing his Unknown Land thrown open and easy to the multitude, none of whom would pay a tenth so much in hardship and danger to see it as he paid to make it known. But one cannot be a historian who has not grown past narrow vanities. He winces, maybe, when a visiting convention of American Bankers elbows noisy into Pueblo home and temple alike; but so far from wishing to put a barbed fence around our Wonderlands, he would rather make it compulsory by Federal Statute that every American voter visit as many Lands as possible. Despite Babbitts and vandals, Americans *Need* to know the Southwest. It is "Good For What Ails Them"—part of which is smug, blank ignorance of their country. Over 35 years ago I invented the slogan "See America First!" I believe in it more profoundly than ever. Americans ought to see the Southwest, the most wonderful of all our Lands of Wonder. They are seeing it!

The keenest satisfaction I have had in this matter in these 42 years, is that now they can see it Sympathetically—which means Intelligently. It does a tourist little good to see the Southwest through the glazed eyes of those who have "lived among Indians and Mexicans all my life," and still disprize them—that is, know nothing whatever about them; and as little of the archaeology, the geology, the history, the Romance.

The Indian-detour is not merely a magnificent Pullmanizing of an incomparable wilderness; historically I see it as the most vital sociologic and educational enterprise ever launched in this country by a transportation company. My name went into the Advisory Board of the Indian-detour only on condition that I actually *advise*. For five months, in office and field, I have studied, suggested, learned, with officials, employees, tourist patrons. I have accompanied Detour trips covering two thousand miles—enough for analysis in a region so familiar to me. No one could fool me long as to his attitude toward my Southwest. The ideals, the insight, the actual sanity—on top of the Harvey efficiency—which motivate this gallant plan, make it not only the happiest thing that ever happened for the traveler, but perhaps also for the Southwest.

Today the laziest traveler can not only see, in Pullman comfort, many of the wildest and noblest sceneries on this continent, and the most picturesque and fascinating types of humanity—but he can see *comprehendingly*, with guides so charming and so authentic as were never available before.

I know of no other such corps of Couriers as the Indian-detour has trained to this service. Fine, clean, thoroughbred, lovely young women of old families, inheriting love and comprehension of their native State, and put through a schooling in its history and nature—they give the tourist such insight and understanding as not one traveler in 500 ever got before. Through their trained and sympathetic eyes the tourist sees in the Pueblos not "funny mud houses" and "savage dances," but the immemorial architecture and dramatic rituals of the oldest American Aristocracy. And in the Mexican towns the quiet, high-bred heirs of the oldest Aristocracy in Europe—heirs whose own unbraggart heroism tamed this remote wilderness a generation before the Pilgrims landed, and has held it against vastly greater odds through the three centuries since; with their architecture, so sane and logical for the Southwest that it is eagerly copied by the intelligent among us. The Babbitt sneers at the adobe house; the artist or cultured millionaire buys an old one if he can, and fixes it up; or next-best, builds him a new one, near to the art of the old as possible—and never quite equals it!

If you sit in the gallery through a session of the U.S. Senate, you may or may not deem the day well spent. But suppose you go with some one who introduces you to a dozen Senators, and six of them separately invite you out to lunch! The comparison is not exaggerated; you see as much more of New Mexico under the conduct of the Indian-detour than by your lonesome, as of the Senate if you were guest of a dozen Senators, instead of a mere dot in the gallery.

A thousand years from now it would be better if New Mexico could have been locked today, to stay forever as it is, an immortal butterfly, embalmed in its own amber. Then the Future (which we pretend to worship, and are busiest to destroy) would have some chance to learn for itself from the Past, which we spurn and forget, though it is the only foundation, measure, guide, and standard we have (or ever can have) for Today and Tomorrow.

But while no one would have cared, forty years ago, if you had put New Mexico in a vault, it can't be shut up today! People have heard of it! They are going to see it! *How* they see it—well, I would say it may make a whole century's difference in the conservation to posterity of this incalculable asset, whether visitors in this day see it intelligently, sympathetically, reverently, or with the old superficiality, rudeness and intolerance which injure visitor and visited alike. The marvelous Flower of Ancient Cultures in the Southwest can be kept alive only by appreciation; if it finds an atmosphere only of ignorant contempt, it must wither fast. And God knows we need to keep alive, somewhere among us, the Breeding and the Faith of our Mexican pioneers; the Art and Religious and Social Sense of our Pueblo Indians!

We Americans are wondrous smart—but we cannot create Antiquity. We can make money, but we cannot make Aristocracy. If we have a trace of real intelligence—or Humor—we shall keep, cherish and study the unsurpassed examples of Antiquity and of Aristocracy which we have here in our National heritage—the two things really best worth while that we can hand on securely to our children's children.

The Chicano Homeland

John Chávez

To the Anglo-American majority of the United States, the Southwest is vaguely identified as that group of states located at the corner of the country toward Mexico. Whether laymen or scholars, few Anglo-Americans agree on exactly which states the region comprises or what its characteristics are.[1] Chicanos, however, the region's Spanish-surnamed population, have a clearer image of the Southwest: To them, the Southwest is home, a land including California, Arizona, New Mexico, Texas, and Colorado, the states where 85 percent of U.S. citizens of Mexican descent reside.[2] But to Chicanos the Southwest is more than just their place of residence; it is their homeland, their lost homeland to be more precise, the conquered northern half of the Mexican nation.

Before the war between the United States and Mexico, which ended in 1848, present-day California, Texas, Nevada, Utah, Arizona, New Mexico, more than half of Colorado (the southern and western portions of the state), the Oklahoma Panhandle, and the southwestern corners of Wyoming and Kansas were all parts of Mexico's national territory. In the mind of the Chicanos, this immense territory remains their patrimony although they inhabit in significant numbers only five of the states mentioned.[3] Because of Mexico's prior possession of the Southwest, Chicanos consider themselves indigenous to the region. Their claims are supported by the fact that their ancestors not only explored and settled parts of the Southwest as early as the sixteenth century, but thousands of years earlier permanently occupied the region or migrated through it on their way south. The belief that the Southwest (especially the areas long settled by Mexicans) is the Chicano homeland and the belief that Mexicans are indigenous to and dispossessed of the region are beliefs that have had a formative and continuing influence on the collective Chicano mind.[4]

Within the individual Chicano mind the image of the Southwest is in the most literal sense a picture of a particular barrio street, of a specific rural adobe, of a particular brown child, or any number of other sensory perceptions that are peculiar to the Chicano's Southwest. This factual picture almost always possesses an emotional quality, a quality that often makes the perception to an extent fictitious. Thus, the picture of the child may include a smile that suggests happiness when in fact he may be sad. Every Chicano has at least such a perception of the Southwest. Of course, among the more experienced, the more traveled, the more educated, the image of the Southwest becomes more complex and abstract; it becomes a myth; yet its essence can always be translated into a picture, albeit of greater detail.[5] Thus a Chicano professor might picture a wall map of Mexico in the 1830s, a map suggesting Mexican control over territory dominated by Apaches. At its most sophisticated, the collective Chicano image of the Southwest and other ideas concerning such matters as race and culture together form a guiding myth that has affected Chicano history from earliest times to the present. Aspects of this myth can be traced from the chronicles of the Aztecs, through the Spanish-language newspapers of the 1850s, to the literature and social thought of Chicanos in the 1980s.

Because Chicanos have a distinct myth of the Southwest, many differences have arisen with Anglo-Americans (whites) concerning the character of the region. Anglos see the Southwest within a larger picture, the image of the American West or, as Henry Nash Smith has named it, the myth of the Virgin Land. "One of the most persistent generalizations," wrote Smith in 1950, "concerning American life and character is the notion that our society has been shaped by the pull of a vacant continent drawing population westward through the passes of the Alleghenies, across the Mississippi Valley, over the high plains and mountains of the Far West to the Pacific Coast."[6] Clearly this myth contradicts the Chicano view of the Southwest in several respects. First, of course, is the Anglos' image of the West as vacant before their arrival; Chicanos can hardly accept this since their predecessors had already founded such cities as San Antonio, Santa Fe, Tucson, and Los Angeles well before the appearance of Anglo-Americans. Second, such regional designations as "Far West," and, of course, "Southwest" itself, are applied from the perspective of the Anglo-American cultural centers on the Atlantic Seaboard. These designations certainly do not correspond to the Chicano picture since Chicanos view their region (despite their practical use of the term "Southwest") from the perspective of their cultural center in Mexico City. Furthermore, the current of their history has flowed south and north, not east to west.

As a result of this perspective, Chicanos view the Southwest as an extension of Mexico and Latin America, a Mexican region spreading beyond what is regarded as an artificial international boundary. Geographically, in fact, the Southwest does resemble the Mexican deserts and highlands more closely than it does the plains and woodlands of the eastern United States. To this familiar southwestern terrain the cultural influence of Mexico City has radiated for over three hundred years. Coastal California from San Diego to San Francisco, Arizona's Santa Cruz Valley from Tubac to Tucson, the Rio Grande Valley from El Paso to the New Mexico–Colorado state line, and South Texas including the lower Rio Grande and San Antonio—these four areas, formerly composing the far northern borderlands of New Spain, have been continuously Mexican in culture and population since before the United States imposed the present boundary on Mexico. And despite the invasion of the Anglos and their subsequent cultural dominance, Mexican culture today extends to other parts of the Southwest, wherever Chicanos have pushed out the margins of the old borderlands. In California, Chicanos have taken their culture into the Central and Imperial valleys; in Arizona, to Yuma and Phoenix; in Texas, to Houston and Dallas; and in Colorado many Chicanos have even settled in Denver beyond the lands of the Mexican Cession of 1848. Given this geography, it is small wonder that Chicanos and Anglos perceive the Southwest differently.[7]

The Chicano myth, however, does bear important similarities to the Native American image of the United States. Both Indians and Chicanos see themselves as indigenous to and dispossessed of their homelands, which in the Southwest means they claim the same territory. Nevertheless, in the twentieth century these overlapping claims have caused little conflict, for Anglos have simply possessed the land; instead these claims have led the two minorities to recognize that they have common backgrounds. In 1971 Armando Rendón, a Chicano journalist, acknowledged just that point:

> We maintain that there exist blood and cultural bonds to the land of the Southwest; we do not deny the Indian peoples' claims to the land. We believe we have had at least a share in its perpetuation through the hands of those who originally worked the land and who have historical claims to it. This issue of land and its relationship to the Chicano should be discussed with Indian tribesmen. . . . Chicanos have a blood relationship to our Indian forebears. Descen-

dants of early Spanish colonists who reject such an alliance with the Indian natives of the Americas also reject the most obvious claim to the retribution for the misdeeds committed by the Anglos who stole the land.[8]

That knowledgeable Native Americans recognize such Chicano claims is evident from the following statement made in 1973 by Jack D. Forbes, a Native American scholar:

> The Aztecas del norte (an Azteca is a person of Aztlán or the "Southwest") compose the largest single tribe or nation of Anishina-beg (Indians) found in the United States today. . . . Some call themselves Chicanos and see themselves as people whose true homeland is Aztlán.
>
> Since Chicanos are racially 70 to 80 percent Indian, they do indeed have much in common with Native Americans, a fact that must be considered in discussions of claims to the Southwest.[9]

Along with race, culture, and historical experience, the Chicanos' image of the Southwest is an important element in the overall self-image, the self-identity, of that people. Interacting with other elements of their self-identity, the Chicanos' regional myth not only distinguishes that minority from Anglos, but separates them from Mexicans south of the border. Unlike Mexican nationals, Chicanos see the Southwest more readily than Mexico as their homeland, and consequently picture themselves more readily as a people of that region than of Mexico. While they generally remain the same mestizo (racially mixed Indian and Spanish) people as Mexicans to the south, the Chicanos' view of themselves as distinct has merit because their residence in the Southwest has greatly modified their history and culture. Even though the boundary between the United States and Mexico is artificial in many respects, that boundary does make the Southwest a predominantly Anglo cultural region. This fact has led Chicanos to incorporate so many Anglo traits into their basic Mexican culture that a distinct way of life has emerged. While Mexico remains the homeland in the sense of a motherland—a cultural source and a nation of origin (be that the present republic or the republic at its greatest extent)—the Southwest is the present home of Chicanos, a home that since 1848 has helped make them what they are.

The Chicanos' present view of the Southwest had its beginning in 1848, as did their current self-image. In that year, on signing the Treaty of Guadalupe Hidalgo, Mexico surrendered the region and most of its inhabitants to the United States. Before that the Mexican view of the region, as far back as the sixteenth-century Aztec chronicles, had been focused on the feature of the homeland; the earliest Spanish conquistadores had, of course, seen the border-lands as foreign conquests, but their mestizo descendants came to call the region home. After the Anglo-American invasion, however, the Mexican image of the region incorporated the feature of the lost land, and Mexicans in the Southwest soon viewed themselves as a conquered people. Thus, though modified with time, the picture of the lost homeland came into being and was handed down to the present.

Over the last 130 years the myth of the lost land has served as a focus for Mexican nationalism in the Southwest. Though sometimes evoking defeatism, the myth has more often roused the pride of Southwest Mexicans, reminding them of their long history in and prior rights to the region.[10] Indeed these rights have formed the foundation for claims of many kinds against U.S. society. Over the decades the region's Mexicans have defended their language, customs, prop-erty, freedom of movement, and their very dignity on the basis of their rights as a native people, as well as their rights as citizens. Those Mexicans living outside the region, both in the rest of the United States and in Mexico, have also made legitimate claims against U.S. society based on the seizure of the Southwest from the Mexican nation as a whole. Yet the greatest significance of the myth of the lost land has been the recurring hope for the recovery of that territory in one form or another. In the late 1960s, this deep wish reappeared in repeated Chi-cano allusions to the ancient Aztec homeland of Aztlán, traditionally located in the Southwest. Noting this phenomenon, Armando Rendón commented: "The concept of Aztlán is undergirded by a desire for restitution of the land of Aztlán. The Chicano does not wish to have merely an empty dream. Just as for other displaced peoples in the world's history, the cry of the land is keen in our ears; we, too, have had title to the land which was violently taken from us. Geography and culture make the vision of a new state for the Chicano not quite so wild an idea; the direct roots we have sunk into the land can burgeon once more."[11]

The desire of Southwest Mexicans for recovery of the region has always been tied to their desire for cultural, political, and economic self-determination, a self-determination they believe can only be achieved through control of the space they occupy. The story of the struggle for that environment is central to Chicano history.[12]

Aztlán, Cíbola, and Frontier New Spain

The distant ancestors of Chicanos and other indigenous American peoples arrived in the Western Hemisphere in small groups beginning from forty to seventy thousand years ago. Since by that time human beings had existed in the Old World for millions of years already, the discovery of the Americas was clearly the finding of a "New World," and the discoverers would certainly have been justified in viewing it as a "Virgin Land." Over the millennia the descendants of the first arrivals spread south from the point of entry, at what we now call the Bering Strait, to the tip of South America, where they arrived about 11,000 B.C.[13] During this migration, of course, countless groups broke off from the general movement south to establish themselves in local areas, which in time became their homelands. Despite the occurrence of these events in prehistoric times, this migration through and occupation of the Americas would later form an important part of the Chicanos' image of themselves as a native people of the Southwest, their ancient, as well as modern, homeland. Because Chicanos would know their Native American ancestry by the color of their own skin, they could be sure that their forefathers had in the distant past crossed over from Siberia and moved south. And on their way south generations of these ancestors would necessarily have entered the Southwest, inhabited it permanently, or occupied it temporarily before moving on to Mexico proper.

These early ancestors probably had no conception of the Southwest on the scale visualized by their descendants. Southwestern cultures from earliest times until after the coming of the Europeans undoubtedly regarded their particular territories as sacred lands that provided sustenance as well as space,[14] but these homelands were always local areas corresponding to specific tribes. Since the Indian tribes of the Southwest were never united,[15] they most likely perceived the region as a whole about as much as modern man would perceive the world as a whole. The conception of the region as such began from a distant perspective, from central Mexico after the arrival of Cortés in 1519. Even though the history of Chicanos already lay deep in the Southwest itself, their modern image of the region would develop from the perspective of Mexico City.

After taking Tenochtitlán (Mexico City) in 1521, the Spanish looked to the north for new lands to conquer and projected their own myths onto the unknown region that was to become the Southwest. They imagined that to the north there was a rich land of warrior women, that in that direction there were silver cities, or that at the very least the unexplored region touched on a waterway that would link Europe to the wealth of the Orient. All these myths manifested Edenic aspects which when viewed together formed the first general myth of the Southwest as a whole—the myth of the region as a land of golden promise. While this image was the invention of the foreign Spaniards, it soon influenced and was influenced by Indians both in the north and in central

Mexico. The Indians on the northern frontier, probably to encourage the Spanish to move on to other areas, sometimes agreed with the invaders' conceptions of the region and elaborated on them. In this way the European legend of the Seven Cities of Silver, which led to Spain's exploration of the Southwest, became the native legends of the Seven Cities of Cíbola and the riches of Quivira.

In central Mexico the Spanish myth of the golden northern land aroused interest in the legend of Aztlán, the Edenic place of origin of the Mexica (the Aztecs). Aztlán, meaning either "land of the herons" or "land of whiteness," was an old name by Cortés' arrival. According to their own histories, the Aztecs had left that homeland, located somewhere in the north, in 1168 and journeyed to the lakes where in 1325 they founded Tenochtitlán.[16] After the Spanish conquest Indian, mestizo, and Spanish chroniclers, relying on native informants, recorded the legend of Aztlán along with the rest of the history of the Aztecs. However, in their histories the chroniclers, influenced by the myth of the golden north, placed Aztlán in the Southwest; in fact it was probably in Nayarit, only four hundred miles northwest of Mexico City. This error would later lead Chicanos to refer to the Southwest as Aztlán, an application of the name that would, nevertheless, be paradoxically appropriate.

By the middle of the seventeenth century the Edenic picture of the north had disappeared at least from the minds of the authorities in Mexico City. By then the region was seen as a series of frontier outposts established to defend central New Spain from northern intruders. On the other hand, Spanish missionaries still viewed the borderlands as golden areas of opportunity for spiritual conquest and agricultural development. But most significant for the future Chicano image of the Southwest was the increasingly popular belief among the settlers that the region was their homeland. To be more exact, the *descendants* of the first settlers apparently came to perceive the land in that way—especially by the late eighteenth century. Since most of the settlers from the very beginning had been Indians and mestizos from central New Spain and had intermarried with the northern natives, it was not surprising that they eventually pictured the borderlands as home, much as their indigenous ancestors had perceived their own northern tribal lands.

The oldest evidence of these ancestors in the Southwest has been found in Texas and dates back to about 35,000 B.C. Some of the earliest evidence of a clearly distinguishable culture has been found in southern Arizona and dates back to about 8000 B.C.[17] Significantly, according to anthropological studies of Indian languages, social organization, material culture, and origin myths, the Cochise culture of southern Arizona was the parent culture of peoples as far apart as the Ute of Colorado and the Aztec of the Valley of Mexico.[18] The ancestral Cochise people apparently spoke the language from which the Uto-Aztecan linguistic family derives. In addition to the Ute, the Gabrielino of California, the Pima of Arizona, some of the Pueblo peoples of New Mexico, the Comanche of Texas, and many other southwestern tribes have spoken Uto-Aztecan languages and probably descend from the Cochise people. In Mexico, besides the Aztec, Uto-Aztecan tribes include the Opata of Sonora, the Tarahumara of Sinaloa and Durango, the Huichol of Jalisco, and many others, forming an almost unbroken line from the Southwest to Mexico City. This together with other cultural evidence indicates that at about 1000 B.C. descendants of the original Cochise people migrated south and became the direct ancestors of many of the Mexican people.[19] Thus, while Aztlán, the Aztecs' homeland of 1168, was relatively close to Mexico City, their more distant homeland in both time and space was in the Southwest.

Contact between the Southwest and the Valley of Mexico increased after 1000 B.C. because just as Uto-Aztecan speakers were moving south, the technology of maize cultivation was moving north. The introduction of maize to the Southwest from Mexico led to the replacement of the hunting-and-gathering Cochise culture by the sedentary cultures of the Mogollon, Hohokam, Anasazi, and Pueblos. These cultures, which overlapped a great deal in time and space from about 300 B.C., existed largely in Arizona and New Mexico but also across the present border in Sonora and Chihuahua. As time passed, communication in the form of indirect trade became common throughout the Southwest and Mexico, and the cultural influence of the civilizations of central Mexico became dominant. After introducing squash, beans, and irrigation methods to the Southwest, the peoples of central Mexico—especially the Teotihuacanos, Toltecs, and Aztecs, from A.D. 200 to 1520—had an important impact on cloth making, pottery, architecture, and government in the region to the north.[20] Interestingly, the Indians of both the Southwest and Mexico reached their cultural high points at roughly the same time, between A.D. 900 and 1520. Clearly even in ancient times the Southwest was an extension of Mexico.

This interconnection became more pronounced with the capture of Tenochtitlán by the Spanish under Hernán Cortés in 1521. Though the Southwest had felt the effects of the rise and fall of Mexican cultures for two thousand years, the founding of New Spain would lead to closer ties than ever before between that northern region and the Valley of Mexico. While many of these new ties would be provided by a foreign European power, many others would be renewals of ties that had already existed for thousands of years. The most important of the renewed bonds would be racial, for as the Spanish expanded toward the north, they would be accompanied by central Mexican Indians more numerous than the conquerors themselves.

The importance of Spain's Indian allies for the expansion and unification of New Spain can hardly be exaggerated since it was as much they as the Spaniards who toppled the Aztecs. Anthropologist Eric Wolf has convincingly argued the importance of these allies to the capture of Tenochtitlán:

> [Cortés] enlisted on his side rulers and peoples who had suffered grievously at the hands of their Mexica enemies. . . . Spanish fire-power and cavalry would have been impotent against the Mexica armies without the Tlaxcaltec, Texcocans and others who joined the Spanish cause. They furnished the bulk of the infantry and manned the canoes that covered the advance of the brigantines across the lagoon of Tenochtitlán. They provided, transported, and prepared the food supplies needed to sustain an army in the field. They main-tained lines of communication between coast and highland, and they policed occupied and pacified areas. They supplied the raw materials and muscular energy for the construction of the ships that decided the siege of the Mexica capital. Spanish military equipment and tac-tics carried the day, but Indian assistance determined the outcome of the war.[21]

Just as the demolition of the Aztec state had been accomplished by an alliance of Spaniards and Indians, the creation of New Spain, racially and cul-turally, would be the accomplishment of these two groups and their descendants, the mestizos. This would be as true in the northern borderlands as in the center of the viceroyalty. Later this fact would lead to much uncertainty in the Chicanos' image of themselves in both Mexico and the Southwest, for being descendants of both conquered Indians and conquering Spaniards and Indians, Chicanos would vacillate between a self-identity as foreigners and a self-identity as natives.

Endnotes

1. See Rupert Norval Richardson and Carl Coke Rister, *The Greater South-west: The Economic, Social, and Cultural Development of Kansas, Oklahoma, Texas,*

Utah, Colorado, Nevada, New Mexico, Arizona, and California from the Spanish Conquest to the Twentieth Century (Glendale, Calif.: Arthur H. Clark Co., 1934), pp. 13–15.

2. Leo Grebler, Joan W. Moore, and Ralph C. Guzmán, The Mexican-American People: The Nation's Second Largest Minority (New York: Macmillan, Free Press, 1970), p. 15.

3. The National Atlas of the United States of America, p. 140; and Richard L. Nostrand, "The Hispanic-American Borderland: Delimitation of an American Culture Region," Annals of the Association of American Geographers 60 (December 1970): 657.

4. Cf. Henry Nash Smith, Virgin Land: The American West as Symbol and Myth (Cambridge: Harvard University Press, 1950), p. 4.

5. Ibid., p. vii.

6. Ibid., p. 3.

7. D[onald] W[illiam] Meinig, Southwest: Three Peoples in Geographical Change, 1600–1970 (New York: Oxford University Press, 1971), pp. 4–5.

8. Armando B. Rendón, Chicano Manifesto (New York: Macmillan, 1971), p. 295.

9. Jack D. Forbes, Aztecas del Norte: The Chicanos of Aztlan (Greenwich, Conn.: Fawcett Publications, Premier Books, 1973), pp. 13, 183; and Eric R. Wolf, Sons of the Shaking Earth (Chicago: University of Chicago Press, Phoenix Books, 1959), p. 32.

10. For general discussions of territoriality and nationalism, see Robert D. Sack, "Human Territoriality: A Theory," Annals of the Association of American Geographers 73 (March 1983): 55–74; and Hans Kohn, The Idea of Nationalism: A Study in Its Origins and Background (New York: Macmillan, Paperbacks, 1961), pp. 4–9.

11. Rendón, p. 309.

12. For criticism of the general historical approach and interpretations used in the present work, see Arthur F. Corwin, "Mexican-American History: An Assessment," Pacific Historical Review 42 (August 1973): 270–73; Bruce Kuklick, "Myth and Symbol in American Studies," American Quarterly 24 (October 1972): 435–50; and Manuel A. Machado Jr., Listen Chicano! An Informal History of the Mexican-American, with a foreword by Barry M. Goldwater (Chicago: Nelson Hall, 1978), pp. xii–xvi.

13. Victor Barnouw, An Introduction to Anthropology, vol. 1: Physical Anthropology and Archaeology, The Dorsey Series in Anthropology, 3rd ed. (Home-

wood, Ill.: Dorsey Press, 1978), pp. 128, 139, 186; and Richard E. Leakey, *The Making of Mankind* (New York: E. P. Dutton, 1981), pp. 213, 6.

14. Edward H. Spicer, *Cycles of Conquest: The Impact of Spain, Mexico, and the United States on the Indians of the Southwest, 1533–1960* (Tucson: University of Arizona Press, 1962), pp. 576–77.

15. Robert F. Berkhofer Jr., *The White Man's Indian: Images of the American Indian from Columbus to the Present* (New York: Alfred A. Knopf, 1978), p. 3.

16. Lowell Dunham, trans., introduction to *The Aztecs: People of the Sun*, by Alfonso Caso, The Civilization of the American Indian Series (Norman: University of Oklahoma Press, 1958), p. xiv.

17. Barnouw, p. 186; and Lynn I. Perrigo, *Our Spanish Southwest* (Dallas: Banks Upshaw & Co., 1960), p. 1.

18. Florence Hawley Ellis, "What Utaztecan Ethnology Suggests of Utaztecan Prehistory," in *Utaztekan Prehistory*, ed. Earl H. Swanson Jr., Occasional Papers of the Idaho State University Museum, no. 22 (Pocatello: Idaho State University, 1968), p. 96.

19. James A. Goss, "Culture-Historical Inference from Utaztekan Linguistic Evidence," in Swanson, pp. 3, 5, 14; see also Eric R. Wolf, *Sons of the Shaking Earth* (Chicago: University of Chicago Press, Phoenix Books, 1959), pp. 34–41.

20. C. W. Ceram [Kurt W. Marek], *The First American: A Story of North American Archaeology*, trans. Richard Winston and Clara Winston (New York: Harcourt Brace Jovanovich, 1971), p. 165; Carroll L. Riley, "Early Spanish-Indian Communication in the Greater Southwest," *New Mexico Historical Review* 46 (October 1971): 286–87; and Matt S. Meier and Feliciano Rivera, *The Chicanos: A History of Mexican Americans*, American Century Series (New York: Farrar, Straus & Giroux, Hill & Wang, 1972), pp. 4–5; see also William C. Sturtevant, gen. ed., *Handbook of North American Indians*, 20 vols. (Washington, D.C.: Smithsonian Institution, 1978–), vol. 9: *Southwest*, ed. Alfonso Ortiz, pp. 26–30, 48–49, 174.

21. Wolf, pp. 154–55.

Dry Root in a Wash

Simon Ortiz

The sand is fine grit
and warm to the touch.
An old juniper root
lies by the cutbank of sand;
it lingers, waiting
for the next month of rain.

I feel like saying,
It will rain, but you know
better than I these centuries
don't mean much
for anyone to be waiting.

Upstream, towards the mountains,
the Shiwana work for rain.

They know we're waiting.
Underneath the fine sand
it is cool
with crystalline moisture,
the forming rain.

Sky Looms

texts of transformation and sacred worlds

Marta Weigle
and Peter White

Oh our Mother the Earth; oh our Father the Sky,
Your children are we, and with tired backs
We bring you the gifts that you love
Then weave for us a garment of brightness;
May the warp be the white light of morning,
May the weft be the red light of evening,
May the fringes be the falling rain,
May the border be the standing rainbow.
Thus weave for us a garment of brightness
That we may walk fittingly where birds sing,
That we may walk fittingly where grass is green,
Oh our Mother the Earth, oh our Father the Sky!

—Herbert Joseph Spinden, trans., *Songs of the Tewa*, 1933.

New Mexicans have always lived in what they believe to be a sacred world, a center set apart from all Other. Whether they call their world the Middle Place or the land between the sacred mountains, whether they name it the Land of the Seven Cities of Cíbola or simply *"mi placita,"* or whether they designate it the Well Country, the Land of Enchantment, or "our claim," New Mexico becomes through singing, telling, and celebrating a place of tremendous spiritual power and peril. New Mexicans have danced and sung, chanted and processed, narrated and prayed in their search for *salvus* and salvation. Through their lore, drama, and ritual they have created the expressive means of renewal and regeneration.

Native New Mexican Erna Fergusson, defining *Our Southwest* in 1940, wrote: "The arid Southwest has always been too strong, too indomitable for most people. Those who can stand it have had to learn that man does not modify this country; it transforms him, deeply. . . . It is magnificence forever rewarding to a man courageous enough to seek to renew his soul."[1]

In Native American songs and mythology of emergence and healing, this courage is expressed by the first people, who move upward into this world, and by the culture heroes and heroines who journey through unfamiliar domains, learning to protect and enrich their peoples. Hispanic colonists raised crosses throughout the harsh new land and annually disciplined themselves in symbolic reenactments of the sorrowful Passion and heroic journey of their savior-protector. Those who navigated the Great Plains by wagon and rail sought revitalization in new fields under boundless skies and found strength in the fellowship of work and worship. Such journeys are mythic in their affective and imaginative scope and voice an archetypal experience that runs thematically through all New Mexicans' lore.

Emergence and the Heroics of Culture

Pueblo, Apache, and Navajo peoples share a belief in this world as one of several. The present world is a mediator between one or more underworlds within the earth mother, from whom the first people emerged, and the upper worlds of the sun, moon, and stars. These celestial realms are inhabited by deities of thunder, lightning, and other transformative, creative powers. Journeying between these worlds is perilous and usually undertaken with the help of guides.

In an Acoma Pueblo version of the emergence myth, both the tutelary deity Tsichtinako and the first human beings in the underworld of Shipapu are female. Their long pilgrimage up into this world of light is one of uncertainty and anxiety, as shown in the following telling recorded by Matthew W. Stirling from a group of Acomas visiting the Smithsonian Institution in 1928.

> In the beginning two female human beings were born. These two children were born underground at a place called Shipapu. As they

grew up, they began to be aware of each other. There was no light and they could only feel each other. Being in the dark they grew slowly.

After they had grown considerably, a Spirit whom they afterward called Tsichtinako spoke to them, and they found that it would give them nourishment. After they had grown large enough to think for themselves, they spoke to the Spirit when it had come to them one day and asked it to make itself known to them and to say whether it was male or female, but it replied only that it was not allowed to meet with them. They then asked why they were living in the dark without knowing each other by name, but the Spirit answered that they were *nuk'timi* (under the earth); but they were to be patient in waiting until everything was ready for them to go up into the light. So they waited a long time, and as they grew they learned their language from Tsichtinako.

When all was ready, they found a present from Tsichtinako, two baskets of seeds and little images of all the different animals (there were to be) in the world. The Spirit said they were sent by their father . . . and that he wished them to take their baskets out into the light, when the time came. . . .

[The women planted unseen seeds from their baskets, and the trees grew slowly toward the light. Before their emergence, when, thanks to their helpers Badger and Locust, they could see the light above, Tsichtinako "taught them the prayers and the creation song, which they were to sing," and the animals helped them to the surface.] . . .

The earth was soft and spongy under their feet as they walked, and they said, "This is not ripe." They stood waiting for the sun, not knowing where it would appear. Gradually it grew lighter and finally the sun came up. Before they began to pray, Tsichtinako told them they were facing east and that their right side, the side their best aim was on, would be known as *kū'ā'mē* (south) and the left *ti dyami* (north) while behind at their backs was the direction *puna'me* (west) where the sun would go down. They had already learned while underground the direction *nuk'um'* (down) and later, when they asked where their father was, they were told *tyunami* (four skies above). . . .

They now prayed to the Sun as they had been taught by

Tsichtinako, and sang the creation song. Their eyes hurt for they were not accustomed to the strong light. For the first time they asked Tsichtinako why they were on earth and why they were created. Tsichtinako replied, "I did not make you. Your father, Uchtsiti, made you, and it is he who has made the world, the sun which you have seen, the sky, and many other things which you will see. But Uchtsiti says the world is not yet completed, not yet satisfactory, as he wants it. This is the reason he has made you. You will rule and bring to life the rest of the things he has given you in the baskets." The sisters then asked how they themselves had come into being. Tsichtinako answered saying, "Uchtsiti first made the world. He threw a clot of his own blood into space and by his power it grew and grew until it became the earth. Then Uchtsiti planted you in this and by it you were nourished as you developed. Now that you have emerged from within the earth, you will have to provide nourishment for your-selves. I will instruct you in this." Then they asked where their father lived and . . . why Tsichtinako did not become visible to them. . . . And they asked again how they were to live, whether they could go down once more under the ground, for they were afraid of the winds and rains and their eyes were hurt by the light. Tsichtinako replied that Uchtsiti would take care of that and would furnish them means to keep warm and change the atmosphere so that they would get used to it.

At the end of the first day, when it became dark they were much frightened, for they had not understood that the sun would set and thought that Tsichtinako had betrayed them. "Tsichtinako! Tsichti-nako! You told us we were to come into the light," they cried. "Why, then, is it dark?" So Tsichtinako explained, "This is the way it will always be. The sun will go down and the next day come up anew in the east. When it is dark you are to rest and sleep as you slept when all was dark." So they were satisfied and slept. They rose to meet the sun, praying to it as they had been told; and were happy when it came up again, for they were warm and their faith in Tsichtinako was restored.[2]

Navajo accounts of their emergence dramatically portray the long and arduous upward journey of primordial beings through subterranean domains numbering anywhere from two to fourteen. As the emerging beings move from a lower platter or hemisphere to one above, they repeatedly fall into a pattern of transgression and failure, followed by destruction and flight into the next world. Each vertical movement represents another of their desperate attempts to flee the omnipotence of powers who live in the four directions and who become thoroughly disgusted and exasperated with the first beings' inability to live peacefully and harmoniously. They ascend to escape great walls of water or sometimes to avoid the fire converging upon them. In short, the people are initially well intentioned, then they become disorderly and violent, only to see their subterranean worlds, one after another, wracked by flood or conflagration.[3]

With the birth of Changing Woman a more lasting order and blessing begins to be possible. Her children, twin gods fathered by the Sun, travel to the Sky to obtain instruction and protection from their father and Grandmother Spider. Upon return to this world, they embark on their mission to tame the malevolent forces which imperil yet-to-be-created Navajos. Changing Woman's twin sons thus stand as models for the culture heroes and heroines whose courageous journeys to other worlds provide knowledge of new ways of healing and protection for the Navajos of this world.

Among these other worlds is the Land-beyond-the-sky, where dwell "extra-powerful storm elements—Winter, Pink and Spotted Thunders, Big Winds, and Whirl-winds, [who] run a school for novices learning the ritual of the Male Shooting, Hail, Water, and Feather chants; the pupils are conducted thither and back by other gods."[4] The hero of the Navajo Windway myth, in a version recorded by Father Berard Haile from Black Mustache in 1929, disregards ritual injunctions and comes face to face with these devastating otherworld forces:

Then [the hero] left for that place of which it had been told him, "You must not go there," toward the Black Range (Jemez Mountains). He reached that mountain and walked along a slope. There was a heavy stand of pine mixed with spruce, they say. Then it happened that above him a cloud appeared which began to spread out, and it was almost midday at the time. . . .

And so it seems, that when the rain began to splash this way he was thinking, "Under which one shall I run, shall I go under a pine perhaps, perhaps under a spruce?" he thought to himself. And then he ran toward a tall spruce which stood there, which alone (happened to have) thick boughs, to this he ran. But it seems that it might not have happened if he had placed the arrows, which he was carrying, with their tips upward, but in matter of fact he leaned them with their pointed ends downward. At that instant a flash of lightning struck him, even the messenger who had been given to him had not warned him in time, they say. Thunder had shattered him, his former flesh had been scattered about in small pieces. He did not return home at sunset, and that night he was missed. "Where can he have gone to!" they were saying as they discussed this all night long, they say.[5]

The Way of the Cross: Passion and Penance

The heroic journey of the Christian culture hero is commemorated in the Stations of the Cross, a processional devotion nurtured in New Mexico by the Franciscan missionaries who acted as spiritual guides for the early Spanish colonists. In later years, when fewer clergy shepherded a growing diocesan population, lay Penitente brotherhoods carried on the Franciscan tradition in communal Holy Week observances of the Way of the Cross, the Encuentro, or Encounter, between Jesus and His Mother on the path to Calvary, the simulated Crucifixion, and the evening Tenebrae or "earthquake" services marking the cosmological disruptions which followed the death of Jesus.

During Holy Week, the most significant transformational time of the Roman Catholic Church calendar, worshippers in New Mexico pray and sing long and mournful *alabados*, or hymns, of the Passion. The following stanzas are from an alabado collected by Reyes N. Martínez in Arroyo Hondo during the late 1930s. It was "sung at any procession of the Via Crucis, during Lent, and at the wakes held during that season of the year, [or at] a wake of a deceased person who was a member of the fraternity of the Penitentes."

On that dolorous way,	En la calle amarga,
With Dimas and Jestas, [sic]	Con Dimas y Jestas [sic]
He fell three times,	Tres veces cayó,
With the cross uphill.	Con la cruz acuestas.
With gall and vinegar	Con hiel y vinagre
They strengthened Him,	Le fortalecieron,
It was when on the cross	Fue cuando en la cruz
Hanging there they saw Him.	Pendiente lo vieron.
Adore the cross	Adora la cruz
That He drags along	Que lleva arrastrando,
Splashed with His blood	Pinta con su sangre
That He goes shedding.	Que va derramando.

Adore the garments	Adora el rofrage
With which He is dressed,	Que lleva vestido,
With His own blood	Con su misma sangre
I saw him dyed.	Yo lo vi teñido.
O precious blood!	O preciosa sangre!
Alleviate my suffering	Alivia mis males
And let me drink	Y dadme a beber
From your precious chalice.	De tu precioso cáliz.[6]

Devotion to the Blood of Christ was especially important to Hermanos, or Brothers, of the Penitente Brotherhood, a lay religious society whose members pledged themselves to year-round acts of Christian charity and to performing the rituals and disciplines of Holy Week. Some of their public practices included penitential processions of flagellants and cross-bearers. In many Hispanic communities a Penitente Brother was chosen to participate in a symbolic re-enactment of the Crucifixion, the quintessential moment of Christ's heroism and the supreme confirmation of Christian belief.

During the 1920s, Santa Fe poet Alice Corbin Henderson and her husband, artist William Penhallow Henderson, were invited to join the villagers at Abiquiú and witness this penitential sacrifice. They stood before the Brothers' *morada* (meetinghouse) and watched as two Hermanos dug a hole to receive the cross.

For some time nothing happened. Then, finally, a group of men came out carrying a small wooden platform on which stood the almost life-sized Cristo in a red dress. Again the door opened, and the heavy cross, with a living man bound upon it, was carried out, with its cross-beam upward, through the door and laid upon the ground with its foot on the edge of the hole made ready to receive it. Slowly and carefully the cross was raised into place, turned facing the Morada, and made firm; and on the cross hung the supreme penitent, in imitation of his Savior. Facing the penitent on the cross stood the red-robed Cristo, who, with eyes no longer blindfolded, thus acknowledged His living disciple. At the foot of the cross, the Hermano Mayor and other leaders of the Brotherhood knelt praying. The black-cowled figure on the cross wore only the white cotton drawers rolled up as a loincloth. His wrists and arms were bound to the main timber by a horse-hair rope. Around his chest, a band of linen supplemented the rope, and eased the strain somewhat.

For ten, fifteen, seventeen minutes—and they seemed ages long as we waited—the figure hung on the cross; then the black-cowled head suddenly fell forward, the body slumped, and the men slowly lowered the cross and carried it into the Morada with the limp figure hanging upon it. The men with the Cristo followed singing and the door closed upon them.

Meanwhile, the sun sinking at our backs had turned the cliffs across the valley into splendid cathedral shapes of rose and saffron beauty—a beauty that is touched here in this country with a some-times terrible sense of eternity, loneliness, and futility. For all the gay laughter of youth on the hillside, the stark parable of the Crucifixion is close to the country's soul. It eats into the heart, this terror; and it is not difficult to imagine how the early Franciscans felt, as they gazed upon this terrible afternoon light on bare mesa and peak, and felt the thorns of this eternal loneliness pressing into their souls. Actual mortification of the flesh is perhaps less poignant. What, one won-dered, in such a stark primeval landscape, could call for an artificial terror—for a theatrically induced tragic sense of life and death? Yet we were to have this too, presently, in the symbolic Tinieblas.[7]

Las Tinieblas, the so-called earthquake or Tenebrae service of Good Friday night, is the Brothers' last public ritual during Holy Week. Together with most villagers and often a fair number of outsiders, the Brothers gather in the church or morada for a devotion similar to the official church ritual that commemorates the chaos following Jesus's death. This tumult is evoked in a verse from the alabado "Salve de Dolores," or "Hail, Lady of Sorrows," sung at Arroyo Hondo for wakes and during Lent, from a version collected by Reyes N. Martínez in 1940:

The rocks break in two	Las piedras se parten
And the winds howl	Y braman los aires
Children become frightened	Tortubean los hijos
Sepulchres break open.	Los sepulcros se abren.[8]

At the beginning of the Tinieblas, the only light comes from thirteen to seventeen candles which are placed in a triangular, white, standing candela-brum; in a special, black, *tenebrario* holder; or on the altar. Each candle or pair of candles, which symbolizes the desertion of the apostles, is extinguished following the singing of an alabado verse. Lorin W. Brown describes what happens in Córdova when the last light, representing the dead Lord, is removed or covered:

> Suddenly, a voice calls out "Ave María," whereupon a deafening tumult breaks out. It is the clapping of hands added to the clattering racket of the *matracas* [ratchets] in the hands of the Brethren. When the noise dies down, someone is heard saying: "*Un sudario en el nombre de Dios por l'alma del difunto José——.*" (A prayer for the repose of the soul of the deceased José——, in the name of God.)
>
> A subdued murmur is heard as most of the assembly join in the semi-whispered response to the request.
>
> Another name is called out, and the request is complied with. Perhaps three or more requests for prayers are called out and complied with when the same voice again calls out "Ave María," and the clapping of hands is resumed with the accompanying sounds as before . . . [including] the rattling of heavy chains.[9]

The alternating cacophony and prayer lasts nearly an hour before the single remaining light is returned and the others relighted from it. If the service is held in a church, the Brothers leave first, facing the altar and walking backward until out of the door; if at a morada, non-members depart immediately.

The Tinieblas is a dramatic high point in the village year. Families and neighbors literally huddle together in the din-filled, disorienting darkness—in the midst of chaos. At the same time, they symbolically take a stand in the face of this disintegration and are, in a sense, "heartened." In calling out the names of their beloved departed, they vividly recall the foundations and human history of their community.[10]

Wind and Fire: Sacrifice on the Plains

Both Hispano and Anglo settlers on the vast eastern grasslands, known as the Llano Estacado or Staked Plains, recalled the beginnings of their lonely communities in poignant songs and tales of the culture hero buffalo hunters and cowboys who had discovered the water sources that made later ranch and homestead life possible. These accounts commemorate the sacrifice of legendary figures who confront their destiny in dramatic encounters on the open plains. Such stories give transcendent meaning to an otherwise harsh existence wrested from inhospitable, desolate territory. Singers, storytellers, and their audiences participate in the discipline of *ciboleros*, or buffalo hunters, like the tragic Manuel Maes from

Galisteo, who died on the Llano in 1873 and whose last words are imaginatively re-created in a *corrido*, or ballad, collected by Lorin W. Brown in 1937:

Oh my sorrel colored horse,	Caballo alazán tostado
That you should have been my death!	Que tú la muerte me dites
I found that I was tired	Me vide tan fatigado
And lost my hold on my lance	Saltar la lanza me hicisteis
And so the prairie sod is drenched	El suelo quedó regado
With my blood. You dyed it . . .	Con mi sangre lo tiniesteis . . .
Near the shores of a lake	A orillas de una laguna
Where they are going to bury me	De ande me iban enterrar
Like a prickly pear plant without its fruit.	Como al nopal sin la tuna.
Youth! here you'll remain.	Joven te vas a quedar.
"Cañon de l'Agua" to all well known	Cañon del agua mentado
You'll be my resting place	Tú fuistes mi habitación
And of my beloved parents	Y de mis padres amados
I wish their blessing	Espero su bendición
I hope they will commend	Que me haigan encomendado
That my soul should have absolution.	Que mi alma tenga perdón.
My heart had warned me	Mi corazón me avisaba
That death was imminent	La muerte se te apoderá
On this Staked Plain	En este llano estacado
I will leave my skeleton.	Vienes a hacer calavera.[11]

Both Spanish and Anglo buffalo hunters were followed by trailblazers of another sort—the cowboys who herded cattle over dangerous terrain along the Goodnight-Loving Trail. The perils of cowboy life are expressed in "Little Joe, the Wrangler," one of America's most famous cowboy songs, which Jack Thorp composed on the trail from Chimney Lake, New Mexico, to Higgins, Texas, and first performed in Uncle Johnny Root's saloon in Weed, New Mexico. Folklorists Austin and Alta Fife call Little Joe "one of a constellation of heroes who, as a group, make up the mythical image of the cowboy—in this particular case the image of an abused youth whose loyalty in the crisis of a cattle stampede leads to a hero's death."[12]

Thorp opens his 1908 collection, *Songs of the Cowboys*, with "Little Joe, the Wrangler," whom he portrays as "a little 'Texas Stray'" who wanders into camp "all alone."

The trail boss, who "sorter liked the little stray somehow," guides him in the lore of the cow camp, but disaster intervenes:

We'd driven to red river and the weather had been fine;
We were camped down on the south side in a bend
When a norther commenced blowing and we doubled up
our guards
For it took all hands to hold the cattle then.

Little Joe the wrangler was called out with the rest
And scarcely had the kid got to the herd
When the cattle they stampeded; like a hail storm, long
they flew
And all of us were riding for the lead.

'Tween the streaks of lightning we could see a horse far
out ahead
'Twas little Joe the wrangler in the lead;
He was riding "old Blue Rocket" with his slicker 'bove
his head
Trying to check the leaders in their speed.

At last we got them milling and kinder quieted down
And the extra guard back to the camp did go
But one of them was missin' and we all knew at a glance
'Twas our little Texas stray poor wrangler Joe.

Next morning just at sunup we found where Rocket fell
Down in a washout twenty feet below
Beneath his horse mashed to a pulp his horse had rung
the knell
For our little Texas stray—poor wrangler Joe.[13]

The ranchers and farmers who followed their culture heroes onto the "great American desert," as the Llano Estacado was known in the nineteenth century, settled first near old water sources and later sought others, drilling into the "desert" and harnessing the power of the omnipresent wind. May Price Mosley, who was raised in Lea County, speaks of her hunter and rancher neighbors as shrewd and even visionary individuals who first established themselves beside life-giving springs and then dug wells and built in ever-expanding radii. She recounts their emergence as a mythic penetration of the apparently barren earth:

> Thus did a few ex–buffalo hunters with their pick-axes and "din-imite" explode the long accepted theory of the Llano Estacado being a part of the "great American desert," and bit by bit uncover the fact that it was and is underlaid with one of the most remarkable and inexhaustible water supplies known to the continent. Sheet water, which at the few depressions of the plains reached to the surface in slight seeps, or very near the surface in shallow water spots. Water all through the centuries, for man's taking in exchange for a few mo-ments' or a few hours' labor. Water beneath all its prairies, which but awaited the perfection of the well drill, the windmill, and the pump-ing plant to make this desert bloom.[14]

Roland Dickey remembers the sound of the windmills, "those Martian flowers that once sucked subsurface water from the plains," in eastern New Mexico:

> In those days, long before the deep primordial water table was being drained by electric pumps and circular irrigation systems, our lives centered around the windmill, a veritable polestar. We kept one ear on the wind, and although the big wheel and tail of the mill machin-ery would yaw automatically—that is, turn sideways in rising wind and reduce speed—it could be ripped apart like a loose sail.
>
> At the first sound of pump rods plunging up and down at a suicidal rate, we would rush to draw down the cable that furled the long fletched tail against the wheel, narrow-edge to the wind. During a gale this called for the weight and strength of two people on the 2-by-4 cutoff brake. The steel wheel would squawk and groan as it fought the wind, turning this way and that like an animal cornered.[15]

The same winds that helped turn desert into garden could transform Eden into an apocalyptic inferno, as in Curry County:

> But here ill winds do blow, and about November 15, 1906, a prairie fire started west of Melrose. The people in the Grady and Belleview country saw it coming for two nights and one day before it struck them about sunrise after the second night. Four hours more put this fire in Hereford [Texas]. Then the wind changed. The fire [was]

going south to north side of the Santa Fe R.R. A slight wind change sent the fire west traveling along the railroad to a plowed field west to Melrose where the settlers gathered with water to wet sacks with which to fight it. They won.

In 1938, Mrs. Lena S. Maxwell collected old-timers' stories like the one above and told Mrs. Belle Kilgore her own reminiscences of that catastrophe and "hard times" around her hometown of Grady:

> I remember about the prairie fire that swept everything from the face of the earth reaching from the southwest of Grady and Belleview to the northwest and as far as Clayton, New Mexico. One boy was caught out with his mules. The child's face was burned so badly and only his teeth on one side was left. The mules were so badly burned that they had to be killed.
>
> Storms! An electric storm where we lived, four miles south of Grady and six miles directly south of the edge of the caprock. It was sometime in August. A big cloud stretched from east to west which was the blackest and angriest that I have ever seen. . . . When we went into the house and closed the doors there were little sparks of electricity all through the room just like sassafras wood sparks from an open fireplace popping from the fire. The lightning got continually worse. We took the metal hairpins out of our hair and I took off my corset which had steel staves in it. We put on our night dress and crawled into a fifty-pound feather bed. My daughter put her arms around me. I said, "Do not do that dear, if I am struck and killed it will kill you too." She cried, "Mama if you are killed I do not want to live." So we lay clasped in each other's arms until the electrical display had passed over, which seemed at least an hour. That is the most terrible experience that I have ever gone through with. That was perhaps in 1914 or '15.[16]

Trinity Site: Initiation into the Nuclear Age

A pinprick of a brilliant light punctured the darkness, spurted upward in a flaming jet, then spilled into a dazzling cloche of fire that bleached the desert to a ghastly white. It was precisely 5:29:45 A.M.

Across the test site everything suddenly became infinitely tiny. Men burrowed into the sand like ants. Oppenheimer in that blinding instant thought of fragments from the sacred Hindu epic, *Bhagavad-Gita:*

If the radiance of a thousand suns
Were to burst at once into the sky,
That would be like the splendor
of the Mighty One. . . .
I am become Death,
The shatterer of worlds.

For a fraction of a second the light in that bell-shaped fire mass was greater than any ever produced before on earth. Its intensity was such that it could have been seen from another planet.[17]

Thus journalist Lansing Lamont describes July 16, 1945, the "Day of Trinity," when all people of this world emerged into the terrible light of the nuclear age. Acutely aware that this thunderous explosion of the world's first atomic bomb portends both deliverance and destruction, Lamont portrays the instant of transformation as one of awesome descent and ascent, of sublime terror, majesty, and fear:

For a split second after the moment of detonation the fireball, looking like a monstrous convoluting brain, bristled with spikes where the shot tower and balloon cables had been vaporized. Then the dust skirt whipped up by the explosion mantled it in a motley brown. Thousands of tons of boiling sand and dirt swept into its maw only to be regurgitated seconds later in a swirling geyser of debris as the fireball detached itself from the ground and shot upward. As it lifted from the desert, the sphere darkened in places, then opened as fresh bursts of luminous gasses broke through its surface.

At 2,000 feet, still hurtling through the atmosphere, the seething ball turned reddish yellow, then a dull blood-red. It churned and belched forth smoking flame in an elemental fury. Below, the countryside was bathed in golden and lavender hues that lit every mountain peak and crevasse, every arroyo and bush with a clarity no artist could capture. At 15,000 feet the fireball cleaved the overcast in a bubble of orange that shifted to a darkening pink. Now, with its flattened top, it resembled a giant mushroom trailed by a stalk of radioactive dust. Within another few seconds the fireball had reached 40,000 feet and pancaked out in a mile-wide ring of graying ash. The air had ionized around it and crowned it with a lustrous purple halo. As the cloud finally settled, its chimney-shaped column of dust drifted northward and a violet afterglow tinged the heavens above Trinity.[18]

Endnotes

Epigraph: Herbert Joseph Spinden, trans., *Songs of the Tewa* (1933; reprint, Santa Fe: Sunstone Press, 1976), pp. 94, 9, 120. Sky looms are the small desert rains that resemble a loom hung between the sky and the earth. They appear as symbolic decorations on Pueblo Indian pottery and on the white cotton mantle of ceremonial dress.

1. Erna Fergusson, *Our Southwest* (New York: Alfred A. Knopf, 1940), pp. 18–19.

2. Matthew W. Stirling, *Origin Myth of Acoma and Other Records*, BAE Bulletin 135 (Washington, D.C.: Government Printing Office, 1942), pp. 1, 3– 4. Stirling explains that this version "was learned by the chief informant during his initiation in youth into the Koshari, the group of sacred clowns to whom theoretically all religious secrets are divulged. . . . The tradition is couched in archaic language so that in many places the younger interpreters were unable to translate and the elderly informant would have to explain in modern Acoma phraseology. . . . Other paraphrases may have been made for the benefit of the White man or as interpretation of Acoma religion by one who is an exceptionally good Catholic and no longer a participant in the ceremonial life of Acoma" (p. vii). C. Daryll Forde worked with Stirling in the early stages of recording this myth and published a version of it, "A Creation Myth from Acoma," in *FolkLore* 41 (1930): 370–87. Paula Gunn Allen frames her novel, *The Woman Who Owned the Shadows* (San Francisco: Spinsters, Ink, 1983), with a literary version of this Keres Pueblo emergence myth. See also Allen, *The Sacred Hoop: Recovering the Feminine in American Indian Traditions* (Boston: Beacon Press, 1986), pp. 13–29.

3. Sam D. Gill, "Navajo Views of Their Origin," in *Handbook 10*, pp. 502– 5. See also Washington Matthews's dated paper on Navajo and other emergence myths, "Myths of Gestation and Parturition," *American Anthropologist* 4 (1902): 737–42; and Erminie Wheeler Voegelin and Remedios W. Moore, "The Emergence Myth in Native North America," in *Studies in Folklore*, ed. W. Edson

Richmond, Indiana University Publications in Folklore 9 (Bloomington, 1957), pp. 66–91.

4. Gladys A. Reichard, *Navaho Religion: A Study of Symbolism*, Bollingen Series 18, 2d ed. in one vol. (Princeton, N.J.: Princeton University Press, 1974), p. 17.

5. Leland C. Wyman, *The Windways of the Navaho* (Colorado Springs, Colo.: Taylor Museum of the Colorado Springs Fine Arts Center, 1962), pp. 106–7.

6. Reyes N. Martínez, coll. and trans., "Venid Pecadores (Come, Ye Sinners)," n.d., New Mexico Federal Writers' Project, 5-5-5 #125, History Library, Museum of New Mexico; diacritical marks added. See also *"Venir, pecadores,"* the five versions collected by Juan B. Rael, *The New Mexican "Alabado,"* with transcription of music by Eleanor Hague, Stanford University Publications University Series, Language and Literature, vol. 9, no. 3 (Stanford, California, 1951), pp. 44–48, 142.

7. Alice Corbin Henderson, *Brothers of Light: The Penitentes of the Southwest* (New York: Harcourt, Brace, 1937), pp. 46–49.

8. Reyes N. Martínez, "Salve de Dolores (Hail, Lady of Sorrows)," coll. from Mrs. Alcaria R. Medina, Arroyo Hondo, March 18, 1940, New Mexico Federal Writers' Project, 5-5-5 #29, History Library, Museum of New Mexico. Diacritical marks added.

9. Lorin W. Brown, "Lent in Córdova," n.d., New Mexico Federal Writers' Project, revised version reprinted in Lorenzo de Córdova, *Echoes of the Flute* (Santa Fe: Ancient City Press, 1972), p. 43.

10. Marta Weigle and Thomas R. Lyons, "Brothers and Neighbors: The Celebration of Community in Penitente Villages," in *Celebration: Studies in Festivity and Ritual,* ed. Victor Turner (Washington, D.C.: Smithsonian Institution Press, 1982), pp. 246–47.

11. Lorin W. Brown, "Manuel Maes," October 11, 1937, New Mexico Federal Writers' Project, 5-5-50 #14, History Library, Museum of New Mexico (diacritical marks added); intro. only in Brown with Charles L. Briggs and Marta Weigle, *Hispano Folklife of New Mexico: The Lorin W. Brown Federal Writers' Project Manuscripts* (Albuquerque: University of New Mexico Press, 1978), p. 49.

12. Jim Bob Tinsley, *He Was Singin' This Song* (Orlando: University Presses of Florida, 1981), p. 86; Austin E. Fife and Alta S. Fife, eds., *Songs of the Cowboys,* by N. Howard ("Jack") Thorp (New York: Bramhall House, 1966), p. 28.

13. The text is from pp. 10–11 in the facsimile of the 1908 ed., reprinted in the Fifes' book following p. 257.

14. May Price (Mrs. Benton) Mosley, "Desert Water (Lea County)," New Mexico Federal Writers' Project, October 12, 1936, in her *"Little Texas": Beginnings in Southeastern New Mexico*, ed. Martha Downer Ellis (Roswell, N.M.: Hall-Poorbaugh Press, 1973), p. 6.

15. Roland F. Dickey, "Chronicles of Neglected Time: Windscapes," *Century Magazine*, March 16, 1983, p. 10.

16. Lena S. Maxwell, "As It Happened in Curry County," New Mexico Federal Writers' Project, 1938, reprinted in *New Mexicans in Cameo and Camera: New Deal Documentation of Twentieth-Century Lives*, ed. Marta Weigle (Albuquerque: University of New Mexico Press, 1985), pp. 158–59; Mrs. Belle Kilgore, "Mrs. Lena Kempf Maxwell, School Teacher and Museum Manager, Clovis, New Mexico," New Mexico Federal Writers' Project, June 26, 1937, reprinted in Weigle, ibid., pp. 169–70.

17. Lansing Lamont, *Day of Trinity* (New York: Atheneum, 1965), p. 235. See also Ferenc Morton Szasz, *The Day the Sun Rose Twice: The Story of the Trinity Site Nuclear Explosion, July 16, 1945* (Albuquerque: University of New Mexico Press, 1984), pp. 83–91. Szasz quotes William L. Laurence: "One felt as though he had been privileged to witness the Birth of the World—to be present at the moment of Creation when the Lord said: 'Let There Be Light' " (p. 89).

18. Lamont, ibid., pp. 238–39.

PART II

Perceptions of the Other

This section is comprised of essays that describe different perceptions of reality that inform the worldviews of those who reside in the Southwest, whether they be longtime residents or recent immigrants. Although such perspectives are frequently revealed in dramatic contrasts, they are sometimes fluid and subtle, indicating the dynamics of cultural change as well as the necessary stability of certain core beliefs and values. Romantic and inaccurate stereotypes often color perceptions of the "other," and this is certainly apparent in the Southwest, where divergent beliefs have sometimes led to violence, contestation, and controversy. Toelken and Sekaquaptewa trace the source of such conflict to differences in perceptions of time and space as viewed by Native Americans and Anglo-Americans. Even while the Native Americans tend to view time as cyclical as opposed to "Western" notions of time as linear and nonrepeatable, Southwesterners may also share attitudes about time and place that provide a basis for understanding and acceptance. One's location in the transitional zone can promote an understanding of the essential ambiguity, the "in-between" aspects of experience, especially for those who see their world of tradition and long-held ethnic customs being turned into myth. And yet, is not the notion of quaint and unchanging rural groups defined by race, religion, class, ethnicity, or occupation the myth? We ask ourselves, as do the authors in this section, Is there an overarching mainstream American society that is rapidly erasing all traces of difference? Or is this so-called melting pot only another stereotype that arises from the inability to perceive and understand that which is "other?"

Hopi Indian Ceremonies

Emory Sekaquaptewa

I do not intend here to make any claims about religion in a scholarly sense. I simply want to talk about a personal experience and what significance it has in my present world. As with most of us, I have become aware of the new interest in cultural pluralism. I find that in this new atmosphere of awareness many people, especially American Indians, are attempting to strengthen their identity within their cultural background. But this is responsible for some unfortunate results. There are many who have lost touch with their culture, and they are trying now to recapture what they have lost, unable to resort to something they already are and to strengthen it from within. I am concerned personally about how I have made my adjustment to the dominant society (which is the term we use). It is in this area that I have attempted to set down guidelines which might be of some help to those who find adjustment and adaptation difficult. I am going to try to illustrate my point of view by giving an impression and interpretation of some Hopi ceremonies. I have chosen to illustrate how it happens that attitudes are developed in the child. In particular, I want to talk about the kachina ceremony, with which I am most familiar. My remarks are of an autobiographical nature.

I was born and raised in a small Hopi village. My first language, of course, was Hopi. In the world I first came to know, I had various experiences which resulted in images by which I knew the world around me. One of these very significant and prominent images, as I recall my early childhood, is the kachina doll. It developed particular meaning for me.

In Hopi practice the kachina is represented as a real being. From the time children are able to understand and to verbalize, until they are eight or ten years old, they are taught that the kachina is real. Every exposure the child has to the kachina is to a spiritual being which is real. There are a variety of ways in which the Hopis attempt to demonstrate this realism to the child. The kachina is all goodness and all kindness. The kachina also gives gifts to children in all of its appearances. Thus it is rather difficult for me to agree with the descriptions of the kachina that often appear in literature. The kachina is frequently described as being grotesque, but the Hopi child does not perceive the kachina as grotesque.

By his conduct toward the child, the kachina demands good behavior. As children we were taught that all things that come from the Kachina hold certain spiritual gifts of reproduction. That is to say, when we received a bowl of fruit or something else, the gift was brought home and placed in the middle of the room. We were then given cornmeal and asked to go outside the house and pray in our childish fashion for an abundance of what we had received. And when we came back into the house, there was more than we had actually received from the hand of the kachina. This kind of practice builds in Hopi children the notion of the kachina as the symbol of ideal goodness.

Then there are times when the kachina is the symbol of admonition. When the child misbehaves he or she is threatened either with the idea that the kachinas will withhold their kindness from them, or even that the kachinas will come and deprive them of their person. There are various ways to dramatize this. I recall a little skit, which was performed to appease the kachina *soya*. The soya has been described as an ogre, but this is a misnomer. The soya is used to threaten the child because of bad behavior, but it certainly does not appear as an ogre to the child. So I prefer to say soya, which is the name of this kachina. He appears at a certain time of the year; and in preparation for his appearance certain children are given a warning. If they do not behave, straighten up, the kachina will come and take them. But threats as such are never effective unless there is some mechanism by which the child can appreciate and understand how one can get out of this predicament. So, in preparation for the appearance of the soya to the child, the parents plan or design a scheme by which they are going to save the child at the very last moment. The one which was used in the case I am talking about was this: the child, barely six years old, had misbehaved and was threatened with the appearance of the soya, who would come and take him away because he had misbehaved. So on the day of the arrival of the kachina, the parents had planned that when the kachinas came to the door, they would send the child outside, and the mother would appear with the child and inform the kachina in all seriousness that it was not right and timely for them to come after him, because he was going to be married. He was a groom and until this very important ceremony was completed he was not available. So the kachinas demanded some proof. They were very persistent, so after much drama and emotion the bride was brought out to show that there really was a marriage ceremony going on. The bride turned out to be the old grandmother, who was dressed in the full paraphernalia of a bride. Then bride and groom appealed as a pair to the kachinas that this was indeed an important ceremony. Obviously when there is a marriage, the relations on both sides are very interested in the preservation of the union. So all the relatives intervened, and soon they outnumbered the kachinas, and thus the child was saved. The child not only learned the importance of good behavior, but this drama also strengthened his security by showing him that there are people who do come to his aid.

This is just an attempt to point out the various ways the child is brought up to feel and know security. Security comes from knowing one's place within the prevailing kinship relationship; within the community. But it also involves learning the cultural norms or the community ethic.

Then comes a time when the child has demonstrated a certain degree of responsibility and understanding, when he or she shows the ability to comprehend a little more of the spiritual world. At this time they are ready to be initiated into the kachina ceremony. This ceremony is quite elaborate and is intended to expose the young person to what the kachina is in fact and in spirit, attempting to help him discern the difference between the spirit and the fact. He learns that he has become eligible to participate in the kachina dance like his father, his brothers, his uncles, whom he has held in high regard. Now he is going to participate as one of them. He learns to identify with the adult world in this fashion. Because this is done in such a dramatic way he has a good foundation. When it is revealed to him that the kachina is just an impersonation, an impersonation which possesses a spiritual essence, the child's security is not destroyed. Instead the experience strengthens the individual in another phase of his life in the community.

Since the kachina has been so prominent in the child's life, most of the child's fantasies involve the kachina. Before his initiation most of his fantasies have consisted in emulating the kachina. Children go around the corner of the house; they enact their feelings about the kachina, they dance and sing like the kachina. At this early age they begin to feel the sense of projection into this spiritual reality. When the child is initiated and becomes eligible to participate as a kachina, it is not difficult to fantasize now as a participant in the real kachina ceremony, and that is the essence of the kachina ceremony. The fantasizing continues, then, in spite of the initiation which seems to have the effect of revealing to the child that this is just a plaything, that now we are grown up and we don't believe.

This idea of make-believe continues with the Hopi man and woman as they mature, and as far as I am concerned it must continue throughout life. For the kachina ceremonies require that a person project oneself into the spirit world, into the world of fantasy, or the world of make-believe. Unless one can do this, spiritual experience cannot be achieved.

I am certain that the use of the mask in the kachina ceremony has more than just an esthetic purpose. I feel that what happens to a man when he is performer is that if he understands the essence of the kachina, when he dons the mask he loses his identity and actually becomes what he is representing. Of course there are various circumstances created to help him to make this projection: the circumstances connected with the ceremony itself, in addition to the individual's background of exposure to the kachina ceremony from childhood. The spiritual fulfillment of a man depends on how he is able to project himself into the spiritual world as he performs. He really doesn't perform for the third parties who form the audience. Rather the audience becomes his personal self. He tries to express to himself his own conceptions about the spiritual ideals that he sees in the kachina. He is able to do so behind the mask because he has lost his personal identity. He is less inhibited by the secular world and its institutions, all of which inhibit people. I think this is a very important element in the kachina ceremonies. The idea of performing to yourself is a rather difficult one for me to describe in terms of a theory. I would have difficulty were I asked to give concrete answers to questions about religious belief and experience. But the essence of the kachina ceremony for me as a participant has to do with the ability to project oneself into the make-believe world, the world of ideas and images which sustain that particular representation.

Now what does all this mean with reference to the issues we talked about earlier? What does it say about cultural backgrounds? How does it apply to identity questions? How can it prepare one for the modern world of technology and all the consequences of life in an affluent society? This is a particular area of concern to me. I have attempted to understand, first, for myself, what one can do when he knows himself to be an Indian in an Indian culture and then goes into an affluent society which operates according to very different values. Anthropologists have attempted to identify and understand the various means of assimilation and acculturation, such as incorporation, assimilation, diffusion, and, lately, compartmentalization. But the problem remains a difficult one.

I don't know how to offer clarification in scientific terms. But I do feel that a process of compartmentalization is necessary for an Indian coming out of his own cultural environment into another cultural situation. Compartmentalization—or keeping the two worlds separate and distinct—is necessary if the American Indian is to make the proper adjustments and adaptations. I think that many people who come from one cultural situation to another share this problem. The problem stems from the compulsion they feel to make the proper adjustments by becoming like the members of the dominant society. The notion of compartmentalization argues that one need not reject his cultural values to make an adjustment to an alien situation. Instead one tries to put his own cultural values in abeyance while he participates in the other culture, perhaps participating only in form and not in substance. But nevertheless his conduct and behavior fit the alien situation so that he himself becomes inconspicuous, while his values remain elsewhere. This is perhaps the layman's explanation of the theory of compartmentalization.

It is to this situation that I have attempted to address myself. I have done this because I know that, as Indian people, we have come to realize the importance of rediscovering ourselves or strengthening ourselves. And I have watched with great interest the way in which Indians across the country have manifested their own interest in their Indianness. This interest has manifested itself in a wide range of attitudes from the sort of disinterested, passive attitude to highly motivated militant aggressiveness. And there are a variety of possibilities in between. I have attempted to look at this situation and see why there is such a wide range of attitudes. I am sure that the goal is the same: it is to retain and preserve and strengthen the Indian culture. It is my belief that those Indians who have retained their own cultural values to the highest degree are not concerned with convincing anyone that they are Indians. Those who, for various reasons have not been able to retain their cultural values are quite concerned with convincing their audience that they are Indians. It is manifested through an aggressive attitude and an intense effort to prove to the world that "I am Indian."

As a result, we have come recently to see a development of pan-Indianism. This is something new to an Indian whose only experience is within his own tribal culture. "Indian" is certainly a term which was confusing from the beginning. To the non-Indian, "Indian" may have some validity. But it does not derive from a particular Indian culture. It is something which has been concocted by the non-Indian. He has put together various characteristics of Indians across the country and has produced a new image, which is a stereotype Indian. It is a stereotype, and not an accurate reflection of our empirical reality. It is something which has been created or constructed as a representation of the Indian. In terms of bringing awareness of the Indian to the non-Indian, it serves well. Once the non-Indian becomes aware of the existence of Indians and the richness of their cultures, then he is ready to become interested in a specific tribe of Indians. If this is what is happening, then it is a good thing.

I have often wondered, however, whether we should be convincing the white man that we are Indians. I feel that we should be convincing ourselves and strengthening ourselves in our own cultural values. I really get a little frustrated when I see Indians attempting to straighten out facts about Indians. They are attempting to destroy the stereotype, because they want the non-Indian to know the truth about the Indian. They are more concerned about that than about strengthening the cultural values that come from within the Indian culture. I think that the latter is the more important for us to be concerned about. We are certainly intimidated by the attitude that is taken by the non-Indian. The Indian has become a national symbol of certain things. For example, he has become a hero lately in our corporate concern for ecological balance. In our concern about environmental pollution, the Indian has become a symbol of conservation. This, I think, is good. However, if one were to ask an Indian (to whom is attributed a special knowledge about conservation and harmony with nature) some pointed questions on this subject, he cannot expect that the Indian will be able to explain harmony to you in analytical and scientific terms.

I recall a problem of this sort in a school operated under the Bureau of Indian Affairs. These days there are various programs either coming through the Bureau of Indian Affairs or funded through the bureau and contracted with other agencies, state and federal. These projects are presumably intended to help the child to understand and become better adjusted to the school system of the white man, thus to be in position to experience a little more success. One of these programs was a science project, a study of ecology. The teachers at the school implemented the project by means of the guidelines given them. It called for the children to bring various living things (insects, animals, etc.) into the classroom, putting them in a cage and accepting responsibility for their care while they watched what happened. It seems that the Hopi children were not interested in taking care of the animals while they studied them. It didn't matter to them whether the animals died or survived. The teachers became very concerned about how to teach the Hopi child about ecology if he didn't show any interest. He had no feeling for the animal.

We never resolved the problem as far as the teachers are concerned. But I would like to make the statement that perhaps ecology, or learning how to live with the environment, is not a matter of taking sides with one or some other living things; rather it is acceptance of the fact that if a certain living thing cannot survive on its own, that is a fact. Must we intervene with our special powers as human beings to control and bring about ways to help this poor thing to survive outside its natural ability to survive? And I talk about pets—cats and dogs— who are treated like human beings in the Anglo household and society. They are really deprived of their natural instincts; they become very dependent on the human beings. Indians don't keep their dogs in the house. The dog which becomes a pet of an Indian family really has a great responsibility to survive on his own, as well as on occasion to depend on his master for things. What I am trying to say is that learning to live with the environment is not a matter of taking sides, but of accepting facts. It seems to me that this attitude and the conduct of the Indian is the only way that he is able to communicate with the people who are concerned about conservation, but not always in verbal ways. We sometimes get overly scholarly about these things, and we tend to build up reputations about Indians in our own terms, rather than stopping and just listening for awhile, watching and seeing what happens, to see if we can make any sense of that kind of communication coming from the Indian.

Seeing with the Native Eye

how many sheep will it hold?

Barre Toelken

There are some things that one knows already if he or she has read very much about the Native Americans. One of the most important is that there is almost nothing that can be said about "the Indians" as a whole. Every tribe is different from every other in some respects, and similar in other respects, so that nearly everything one says normally has to be qualified by footnotes. What I am about to say here does not admit room for that. I propose, therefore, to give a few examples from the Navajo culture and make some small glances at other Indian cultures that I know a little bit about; that is simply a device to keep my observations from appearing as though they were meant to be generally applicable to Indians of the whole country.

It is estimated that there were up to 2,000 separate cultures in the Northern Hemisphere before the invasion of the Europeans. Many of these groups spoke mutually unintelligible languages. Anthropologists estimate that there were as many as eighty such languages in the Pacific Northwest alone. In terms of language and traditions these cultures were very much separated from each other; and although they have been lumped into one category by whites ever since (and that is the source of some of our problems), any given Indian will have a few things in common with some other tribes and many things not in common with others. My generalizations are made with this in mind from the start. But one must start *somewhere* in an attempt to cope with the vast conceptual gulf which lies between Anglos in general and natives in general, for it is a chasm which has not often been bridged, especially in religious discussion.

I do not claim, either, to be one of those rare people who *have* succeeded in making the leap—an insider, a confidant, a friend of the Red Man's Council Fire—in short, one of those Tarzans even more rare in reality than one would conclude from their memoirs. But I did have the good fortune to be adopted by an old Navajo, Tsinaabaas Yazhi ("Little Wagon"), in southern Utah in the mid-fifties during the uranium rush. I moved in with his family, learned Navajo, and lived essentially a Navajo life for roughly two years. Of course I have gone back since then on every possible occasion to visit my family, although my adopted father is now dead, as is his wife and probably 50 percent of the people I knew in the fifties. Anyone who has read the Navajo statistics knows why. This is not intended to be a tale of woe, however; I simply want it understood that I was not a missionary among the Navajo. Nor was I an anthropologist, a teacher, a tourist, or any of the other things that sometimes cause people to come to know another group briefly and superficially. Although, indeed, at one time I had it in my mind to stay with them forever, it is probably because my culture did not train me to cope with almost daily confrontation with death that I was unable to do so. I learned much from them, and it is no exaggeration to say that a good part of my education was gained there. It was probably the most important part. "Culture shock" attended my return to the Anglo world even though I left the Navajos as "un-Navajo" as when I arrived.

Based on that experience, though, I think I can say something about how differently we see things, envision things, look at things, how dissimilarly different cultures try to process the world of reality, which, for many Native American tribes, includes the world of religion. In Western culture, religion seems to occupy a niche reserved for the unreal, the Otherworld, a reference point that is reached only upon death or through the agency of the priest. Many Native American tribes see religious experience as something that surrounds us all the time. In fact, my friends the Navajos would say that there is probably *nothing* that can be called clearly non-religious. To them, almost anything anyone is likely to do has some sort of religious significance, and many other tribes concur. Procedurally, then, our problem is how to learn to talk about religion, even in preliminary ways, knowing perfectly well that in one society what is considered art may in another be considered religion, or that what is considered as health in one culture may be religion in another. Before we can proceed, in other words, we need to reexamine our categories, our "pigeonholes," in order to "see" things through someone else's set of patterns. This is the reason for the title: "Seeing with the Native Eye."

Through our study of linguistics and anthropology we have learned that different groups of people not only think in different ways, but that they often "see" things in different ways. Good scientific experiments can be provided, for example, to prove that if certain ideas are offered to people in patterns that they have not been taught to recognize, not only will they not understand them, they often will not even see them. We see things in "programmed" ways. Of course Benjamin Whorf was interested in demonstrating the pervasiveness of this theory with respect to language, and many anthropologists and linguists have had reservations about his theories. But the experimentation continues, and there is some interesting and strong evidence that a person will look right through something that he or she is not trained to see, and that different cultures train people in different ways. I will not get into the Jungian possibilities that we may be born with particularized codes as well; this is beyond my area of exper-tise. But it is clear that when we want to talk about Native American religion, we want to try to see it as much as possible (if it is possible) with the "native eye." That is to say, if we talk about Native American religions using the categories of Western religions, we are simply going to see what *we* already know is there. We will recognize certain kinds of experiences as religious, and we will ignore others. To us, for example, dance may be an art form, or it may be a certain kind of kinesis. With certain Native American tribes, dance may be the most religious act a person can perform. These differences are very significant; on the basis of this kind of cultural blindness, for example, Clyde Kluckhohn classified the Navajo coyote tales as "secular" primarily because they are humorous.

The subtitle of this paper comes from my adopted Navajo father. My first significant educational experience came when I was trying to educate him to what the outside world looked like. Here was an eighty- or ninety-year-old man in the 1950s who had never seen a paved road or a train; he had seen airplanes flying overhead and was afraid of them. He had seen almost nothing of what you and I experience as the "modern, advanced world." I decided I would try to cushion the shock for him by showing him pictures, and then I would invite him into town with me sometime when I went to Salt Lake City. I felt he needed some preparation for the kind of bombardment of the senses one experiences in the city after living out in the desert.

I showed him a two-page spread of the Empire State Building which ap-peared in *Life* that year. His question was, immediately, "How many sheep will it hold?" I had to admit that I didn't know, and that even if I did know, I couldn't count that high in Navajo; and I tried to show him how big a sheep might look if you held it up against one of those windows, but he was interested neither in my excuses nor in my intent to explain the size of the building. When I told him what it was for, he was shocked. The whole concept of so many people filed together in one big drawer—of course he would not have used those terms—was shocking to him. He felt that people who live so close together cannot live a normal life, so he expected that whites would be found to be spiritually impoverished and personally very upset by living so close together. I tried to assure him that this was not so. Of course I was wrong. Little by little one learns.

The next episode in this stage of my learning occurred about six months later, when I was at the trading post and found a magazine with a picture of the latest jet bomber on it. I brought that to him to explain better what those things were that flew over all the time. He asked the same question in spite of the fact there were lots of little men standing around the plane and he could see very well how big it was. Again he said, "How many sheep will it carry?" I started to shrug him off as if he were simply joking with me, when it became clear to me that what he was really asking was, "What is it good for in terms of something that I know to be valid and viable in the world?" (That, of course, is not his wording either.) In effect, he was saying that he was not willing even to try to understand the Empire State Building or the bomber unless I could give those particular sensations to him in some kind of patternings from which he could make some assessment. He was not really interested in how big they were, he was interested in what they were doing in the world. When I told him what the jet bomber was for, he became so outraged that he refused ever to go to town, and he died without ever having done so as far as I know. He said that he had heard many terrible things about the whites, but the idea of someone killing people by dropping a bomb and remaining out of danger was just too much!

The only other thing that shocked him, by the way, emerged as I explained to him about the toilet facilities in white houses. He could hardly believe that one. "They do that right in the house, right inside where everyone lives?" "No, no, you don't understand. There is a separate room for it." That was even worse—that there could be a special place for such things. A world so neatly categorized and put in boxes really bothered him, and he steadfastly refused to go visit it. At the time I thought he was being what we call primitive, backward—he was dragging his feet, refusing to understand the march of science and culture. What I "see" now is that, as a whole, he was simply unable to—it did not "compute" in the way we might put it today; he did not "see" what I meant. In turn, he was trying to call my attention to that fact, and I was the one who did not understand.

I bring these matters up not because they are warm reminiscences, but because difficulties in communicating religious ideas are parallel to these examples. When my adopted father asked, "How many sheep will it hold?" he was asking, "What is it doing here, how does it function? Where does it go? Why do such things occur in the world?" We might consider the Pueblo view that in the springtime Mother Earth is pregnant, and one does not mistreat her any more than one might mistreat a pregnant woman. I once asked a Hopi whom I met in that country, "Do you mean to say, then, that if I kick the ground with my foot in the springtime, it will botch everything up, so nothing will grow?" He said, "Well, I don't know whether that would happen or not, but it would just really show what kind of person you are."

One learns slowly that in many of these native religions, religion is viewed as embodying the reciprocal relationships between people and the sacred *processes* going on in the world. It may not involve a "god." It may not be signified by praying or asking for favors, or doing what may "look" religious to people in our culture. For the Navajo, for example, almost *everything* is related to health. For us health is a medical issue. We may have a few home remedies, but for most big things we go to a doctor. A Navajo goes to the equivalent of a priest to get well because one needs not only medicine, the Navajo would say, one needs to reestablish his harmonious relationship with the rhythms of nature. It is the ritual as well as the medicine which gets one back "in shape." The medicine may cure the symptoms, but it won't cure you. It does not put you back in step with things, back in the natural cycles—this is a job for the "singer."

I want to go a little further into this, because these patterns of balance, these reciprocations that we find so prominently in Native American religions, are things which for our culture are not only puzzling but often considered absolutely insane. It is the conflict or incongruency in patterning that often impedes our understanding. Let me give a few examples of this patterning. In Western culture—I suppose in most of the technological cultures—there has been a tremendous stress on lineal measurements, grid patterns, straight lines. I think one reason for this is that technological cultures have felt that it is not only desirable but even necessary to control nature. We know there are very few straight lines in nature. One of the ways people can tell if they are controlling nature is to see that it is put in straight lines—we have to put things "in order." And so we not only put our filing cases and our books in straight lines and alphabetical "order," we also put nature in straight lines and grid patterns—our streets, our houses, our acreage, our lives, our measurement of time and space, our preference for the shortest distance between two points, our extreme interest in being "on time."

Those who have read the works of Edward T. Hall and other anthropologists on the anthropology of time and space are familiar with these ideas. Each culture has a kind of spatial system through which one knows how close to stand to someone else, how to walk in public and in private, where the feet are supposed to fall, where things are supposed to go. These patterns show up in verbal expressions too—we have to "get things straightened out," "get things straight between us," make someone "toe the line." We also arrange classrooms and auditoriums in some sort of lineal order (other groups might want these to be arranged in a circle). To us, having things "in order" means lining things up, getting things in line. We talk about "getting straight with one another," looking straight into each other's eyes, being "straight shooters." We even talk about the "straight" people vs. the "groovy" people. Notice how we often depict someone who is crazy with a circular hand motion around the ear. Someone who does not speak clearly "talks in circles," or uses circular logic. We think of logic itself as being in straight lines: A plus B equals C. We look forward to the conclusion of things, we plan into the future, as though time were a sort of straight track along which we move toward certain predictable goals.

It should be obvious that I am choosing, intentionally, certain lineal and grid patterns which are virtually unmatched in Native American patterns. We learn to find each other in the house or in the city by learning the intersection of straight lines—so many doors down the hallway is the kitchen, or the bathroom, and we are never to confuse them. We separate them. One does not cook in the bathroom—it is ludicrous to get them mixed up. We have it all neatly separated and categorized. For most Native American groups, almost the reverse is true—things are brought together. Instead of separating into categories of this sort, family groups sit in circles, meetings are in circles, dances are often—not always—in circles, especially the dances intended to welcome and include people. With the exception of a few tribes such as the Pueblo peoples, who live in villages which do have straight lines, most of the tribes usually live (or lived) in round dwellings like the hogan of the Navajo, the tipi of the Plains Indians, the igloo of the Eskimo. The Eastern Indians and some Northwestern tribes sometimes lived in long houses, but the families or clans sat in circles within.

There is, then, a "logical" tendency among Native peoples to re-create the pattern of the circle at every level of the culture, in religion as well as in social intercourse. I think the reason for it is that what makes sense, what "holds sheep" for many tribes, is the concept that reciprocation is at the heart of everything going on in the world. I have had Pueblo people tell me that what they are doing when they participate in rain dances or fertility dances is not asking help from the sky; rather, they are doing something which they characterize as a hemisphere which is brought together in conjunction with another hemisphere.

It is a participation in a kind of interaction which I can only characterize as sacred reciprocation. It is a sense that everything always goes this way. We are always interacting, and if we refuse to interact, or if some taboo action has caused a break in this interaction, then disease or calamity or drought comes about. It is assumed that reciprocation is the order of things, and so we will expect it to keep appearing in all forms.

I think that it makes anthropological and linguistic sense to say that any culture will represent things religiously, artistically, and logically, the way its members "see" things operating in the world. But here is where the trick comes in. When we from one culture start looking at the patterns of another culture, we will often see what *our* culture has trained us to see. If we look at a Navajo rug, for example, we are inclined to say that Navajos use straight lines in their rugs. And yet if we talk to Navajos about weaving, the *gesture* we often see is a four-way back-and-forth movement; and they talk about the interaction within the pattern—a reciprocation. Most often the Navajo rug reciprocates its pattern from side to side and from end to end, creating mirror images. My adopted sister, who is a very fine weaver, always talks about this kind of balance. She says, "When I am thinking up these patterns, I am trying to spin something, and then I unspin it. It goes up this way and it comes down that way." And she uses circular hand gestures to illustrate. While we are trained to see the straight lines, and to think of the rug in terms of geometric patterns, she makes the geometrical necessities of weaving—up one, over one—fit a kind of circular logic about how nature works and about how she interacts with pattern. If we are going to talk about her beliefs with respect to rugs, we need somehow to project ourselves into her circles.

Let me give a couple of other examples. These, by the way, are not intended to be representative, but are just some things that I have encountered. They are simply illustrative of the way a Navajo might explain things. There is a necklace that one often finds in curio shops these days. They are called "ghost" beads by the whites, though I do not know any Navajos who call them that except when talking to whites (they feel they ought to phrase it the way the whites will understand it). The brown beads in these arrangements are the inside of the blue juniper berries, which the Navajo call literally "juniper's eyes." In the most preferred way of producing these necklaces, Navajos search to find where the small ground animals have hidden their supply of juniper seeds. Usually a small girl, sometimes a boy, will look for likely hiding places, scoop them all out and select the seeds that have already been broken open, so as not to deprive the animals of food. She puts all the whole seeds back, and takes only the ones that have a hole in one end. She takes them home, cleans them, punches a hole in the other end with a needle, and strings them together. I do not know any Navajo in my family or among my acquaintances who ever goes without these beads on him somewhere, usually in his pocket. Colored glass beads have been added to appeal to white buyers.

My Navajo sister says that the reason these beads will prevent nightmares and keep one from getting lost in the dark is that they represent the partnership between the tree that gives its berries, the animals which gather them, and humans who pick them up (being careful not to deprive the animals of their food). It is a three-way partnership—plant, animal, and man. Thus, if you keep these beads on you and think about them, your mind will tend to lead a balanced existence. If you are healthy by Navajo standards, you are participating in all the cycles of nature, and thus you will not have bad dreams. Bad dreams are a *sign* of being sick, and getting lost is a *sign* of being sick. So these beads are not for warding off sickness itself; rather, they are reminders of a frame of mind which is essentially cyclic, in the proper relationship with the rest of nature—a frame of mind necessary to the maintenance of health.

In an experiment by anthropologist John Adair and filmmaker Sol Worth, some young Navajos were given cameras and encouraged to make their own movies. One girl made a movie called *Navajo Weaving*. It lasts, as I recall, almost forty-five minutes, but there are only a few pictures of rugs in it. Most of the film is about people riding horseback, wandering out through the sagebrush, feeding the sheep, sometimes shearing them, sometimes following them through the desert, sometimes picking and digging the roots from which the dyes are made. Almost the entire film is made up of the things that the Navajo find important about making rugs: moving human interactions with nature. That is what rug-making is for the Navajos. Something which for us is a secular craft or a technique is for these people a part or extension of the active reciprocations embodied in religion.

Religious reciprocity extends even into the creation of the rug's design. My Navajo sister wove a rug for me as a gift, the kind which the traders call *yei* (*yei* means something like "the holy people"). The pattern in this particular rug is supposed to represent five lizard holy people. The two on opposite ends are the same color, and the next two inward the same color, and the one in the middle a distinctly different color. The middle one is the dividing line, so that the pattern reciprocates from end to end of the rug. When my sister gave it to me, she said, "These represent your five children." Of course I was moved to inquire why she should represent my five children as lizards. I wondered what her reasoning was, and I certainly knew children are not "holy people"—far from it. She pointed out, "Your oldest and youngest are girls, and they are represented by the two opposite figures on each end. Then you have twin boys—they are the two white ones, because they are alike. Then there is another boy, who doesn't have a mate in your family, so he is the center point of the family, even though he isn't that in terms of age." She made the pattern reciprocate from one end to the other not only in terms of representing my family but also in terms of color. All the dyes were from particular medicinal plants which are related to good health. Lizards represent longevity, and by making my children congruent with the lizard people, she was making a statement of, an embodiment of, their health and longevity. This is a wish that any Navajo might want to express, because, as noted above, health and longevity are central to Navajo religious concerns. If I knew more about the symbolic function of certain colors in the rug, or the use of the dye-producing plants in Navajo medicine, I have no doubt that I would have still more to say about the religious expression intended therein.

Also central to Navajo religion is the restoration of health when it has been lost. The hogan is the round dwelling the Navajos live in. The fire is in the middle of the floor, and the door always faces east. One of the reasons for this, as my adopted father told me, was to make sure that people always live properly oriented to the world of nature. The door frames the rising sun at a certain time of the year. The only light that comes in is either through the smoke hole on the top, or through the door, if it happens to be open. Healing rituals involving "sandpainting" are usually held inside the hogan, and are oriented to the four directions. When the patient takes his or her place on the sandpainting, ritually they are taking their place within the world of the "holy people," related to all the cycling and reciprocation of the universe.

That orientation is, in itself, a powerful aspect of the psychological curing that is to take place. Everyday living in a hogan of course calls to mind the rituals that have been held—or might take place—in that space. Moreover, the more common round ("female") hogan is said to be a physical rendering of Changing Woman's womb, with the smoke hole representing her navel, and the doorway representing her vagina, through which we emerge, metaphorically reborn, after every sing and every morning before dawn. The same representation is found on the Navajo wedding basket as well, and both seem to have developed as the Navajos became more female-centered after their arrival among the Pueblos over the past 600 years. Correspondingly, the older "male" hogan, which resembles an erect teepee covered with mud, has all but disappeared from Navajo use.

To complicate religious discussion further, Natives and Europeans do not necessarily agree on what is "real," or what is spiritual, or what is holy or sacred. People from Western cultures that use "noun-heavy" languages tend to discuss issues—even quite abstract ideas—as "things." Navajos, using a verb-heavy language (which has over 350,000 conjugations of the verb "to go," according to anthropologist Gary Witherspoon), tend to classify by motion or sound. Thus, the words for "car," "Spaniard," "bird," and "witch" (to name only a scattered few) are verbs, not nouns. The Siouan languages can handle very abstract ideas by using only adjectives (thus the term *wakan tanka*, literally "holy great," expresses the nature of deity without limiting it to an object or personage, as does the awkward English translation, "The Great Spirit"). And so it goes for every tribal language we might look at.

What different cultures are taught to see, how they see it, and how they describe it are thus worlds apart (though not, I think, mutually exclusive). One culture looks for meaning in the visible, one looks for meaning beyond the visible, one looks for movement, one looks for objects, one looks for stasis, one looks for flowering. For one group, eternity is found at the end of a long, straight line (running from alpha to omega); for another, eternity is found within the ever-recurring reciprocations of an interactive system. One thing we can learn from this rich variety is the stunning range of ways in which humans have registered the realities and nuances of the world in which they live. Rather than being frightened by this variety, or—worse—feeling that we must choose the *right one* from among them, we need to use them to expand our capacity to understand, to train ourselves to see better, to extend our willingness to discuss religious experiences (and cultural meaning generally) from a perspective broader than the one we were equipped with by our culture's assumptions. How many sheep does religion hold? It all depends on how you look at it.

Romancing Mora

Eduardo Paz-Martinez

The warm winds of an early July afternoon whip through downtown Mora, clouding up the main street in yet another swirl of blowing dust openly disdaining the land, the buildings, and the people. It is a harsh scene, yet oddly, hardly anyone notices. Women on their way into the county courthouse do no more than take hand to hair; men stumble out of pickups to tug down on gimme caps before ambling into Theresa Marie's restaurant for long conversations and a potful of coffee that comes a cup at a time.

Along this isolated stretch of the rural northern New Mexico byway, it is not the summer's dust devils that much bother residents. Like other seasonal meteorological roars, winter snowfalls included, this sandstorm, too, comes and goes.

Suddenly a more excitable sort of environmental angst is capturing the attention of people who live in the Sangre de Cristo Mountains' charming Mora Valley: namely, a growing perception that, with each passing weekend, more and more people are pulling into town. When they look out the picture windows at Theresa Marie's, they see rental cars and Winnebagos on slow, sightseeing crawls.

Enigmatic Mora—rich in French and Spanish settler history that dates back to the late 1600s but saddled for the greater portion of this century with the reputation of being a poverty-stricken, backwoods region of the state—is being discovered anew.

For residents used to living the easy, uncomplicated lifestyle of the countryside, this is the best and worst bit of news. It is good in a business way for residents, such as Katie Almanzar, who along with her husband owns the Almanzar Motel.

"Weekends are really good," she says cheerfully. "It's people who say they passed through here last year and fell in love with the valley. They've come back. Others say they're from out of state and looking for land to buy."

Among those staying at the ten-room motel last week was a small group of visiting Germans on their way to Taos, who told Almanzar the local scenery reminded them of home.

Another who has welcomed the first signs of a tourist trade is Mora Valley rancher David Salman, who says positively: "Our major resource today is our beauty, the pristine environment. To try to deny that they don't exist is a fallacy. Tourism—and I mean more than just a van full of people—is coming."

That would seem to be true.

"You could say it's summer and people are on vacation," says native Tony Martinez, owner of the popular Cleveland Bar. "But you could also say these people are way out of their way. I can't imagine they'd come through here on their way to the Grand Canyon or Disneyland. Do you?"

Tucked in a cupped-palm valley of the august Sangre de Cristos, snow-capped Jicarilla Peak rising majestically to the west, Mora is about ninety-five miles from Santa Fe by way of Las Vegas. The land rolls in dignified geography, painted by proud piñon, stately evergreens, and busy, clear streams. Such beauty contrasts with the residents' modest contribution—basic architecture from another era, a good chunk of it abandoned: Mora and its decaying downtown structures; neighboring Cleveland and now-closed groceries of yesteryear; Holman and its adobe churches; Chacon and its weed-filled cemetery. Beauty and remnants of history for everyone.

But for residents, tourism is, for the moment, more discernible. They see the travelers and even talk to them. Development is not visible yet, although real estate agents say more outsiders are inquiring about Mora County properties. Still, drive up and down the valley and you see new redwood homes here and there, some dressed up with satellite dishes and gleaming metal fireplace piping.

Ask real estate agent Marcia Leyba, who lives in Grants but journeys to Mora from the western New Mexico city to do business as MJ Realty, and hear this: "My impression is that there is a discernible increase in outsiders. It's too early to say that they are buying everything in sight, although I hear people in Mora telling me they see more and more tourists coming by. Tourism could be a good thing for them."

But even as young and old couples from Texas and California shyly walk into Theresa Marie's for a glass of iced tea or pull into a service station for another tank of gasoline, some in Mora firmly believe these are not just tourists out to see the American West.

There are those who see these visitors as outsiders out to become neighbors. "People with big city ways and needs," is Tony Martinez's read. Newcomers eager to whip out their wallets and buy in, goes the line. Already, residents note, a sprinkling of high-windowed, Santa Fe–style homes have been built on the picturesque hillsides overlooking Highway 518, which cuts through the center of Mora and its tiny neighbors of Cleveland, Holman, and Chacon.

To some extent, Martinez is right. Names to be found these days on the Mora County property tax roles include recent buyers from Los Angeles, San Jose, and Pueblo, Colorado, as well as Amarillo, Texas. Their designation as "non-residential" property owners does not mean that the acreage is zoned for business use as much as it means the new owners do not yet live in the county.

Taken together, the signs of activity keep growing, convincing Mora's residents that their way of life is changing. More visitors are coming, more residents are coming—and the resistance that held them off for decades is finally weakening in the face of the inevitable.

Seated behind his executive desk at the Mora Valley Clinic, Antonio Medina, a descendant of one of the community's early Hispanic settlers, isn't quite ready to side with Salman. He sees any talk of growth as loss of more than just chunks of land down by the verdant banks of the pretty Mora River. Medina, like other Hispanics in the valley, worries that a rediscovery of his homeland may lead to something bigger: newcomers without a clue of the area's past; people more interested in arts colonies than in his culture.

"I like Mora the way it is," Medina says firmly. "If it's changed to something else, it will be ruined. I have a very serious problem with development that is going to exploit our natural resources for the benefit of the wealthy outsider."

So what's going on in Mora?

The exchange between Salman, a wealthy landowner who'd like to see Mora plunge into the 1990s, and Medina, who has a reputation as a defender of all things Hispanic, is legendary. The two have clashed repeatedly, always about something new and different wanting to come to the sleepy valley.

Salman, who came to Mora forty-nine years ago from Houston, sees tourism and new residents as viable vehicles for the region's needed economic growth. Medina believes tourism means fast-food eateries, chain hotels and motels, and shopping centers.

More to the point, Medina insists he does not want to see Mora become a "little Santa Fe," insisting that northern New Mexico villages "need not take an 'Old Town' image and become 'art and culture' havens and museums for non-Hispanics."

[handwritten margin note: interesting point]

In 1979, when Salman sought to help stage the tenth anniversary of Woodstock in Mora, it was Medina who led the opposition, raising a loud voice in public forums at which he characterized the proposed rock concert as "wild desecration of our hallowed lands."

Salman lost that one, and not a sound from Country Joe & the Fish was ever heard.

In the early 1980s Medina fueled protests against construction of an Allsup's convenience store. Steadfast in their belief that the twenty-four-hour store's arrival would kill off smaller family stores, Mora residents organized to fight it, spreading posters throughout the community, the mildest of which said Allsup's Must Go.

In the end, Medina lost that one. Today Allsup's is a thriving enterprise, and the stores it replaced are notches on its gun handle.

The 1990s began with both men on opposite sides of a proposed experimental fish hatchery that appears to be on its way to Mora County. Medina and his Mora Water and Land Protective Association say the project is unnecessary. The $16 million hatchery, to include construction of a four-building compound, is expected to bring twelve to fourteen jobs to Mora. The association has vowed to seek legal action on environmental concerns the moment the federal U.S. Fish and Wildlife Service breaks ground.

Salman, on the other hand, is all for the hatchery. He argues that it is a model for the sort of new industry the community should be soliciting. He sees the hatchery not only as an aid to research but also as an eventual tourist attraction.

Medina's point is really the same one he uses to say tourism is bad for Mora: erosion of natural beauty and loss of privacy. In the case of the hatchery, whose primary mission would be production of trout, he is also concerned that it would drain yet another resource he deems precious: water.

"Water is our past, our present, and our future," Medina says. "We can't be dislocated. This is a monster water project, and I am not convinced that the government has answered all our questions."

That battle is yet to be resolved, but still another telling skirmish came after publication in the *Wall Street Journal's* April 21, 1988, issue of a quote from Salman. His words were part of a front-page story about the three poorest counties in the United States, of which Mora was one. "The main thing," he said, "is that there is nothing here. There's no agriculture, and there's no industry. There are no resources, no oil, no minerals. There's nothing a family can get by on."

Medina laughs at the newspaper story, which, while saying Mora is a "region of haunting beauty," described it as "a place of vacant storefronts."

"I am not against economic development," Medina insists. "I want business growth from within ourselves, which means that whatever we go after is from the bottom up and from within. I am not one of those who see the arrival of fast-food joints as being progress. Tourism is seen here by a handful as a panacea, but it's the biggest lie. Tourism will not cure the ills of our elderly."

Mora is poor. No one disputes that. There are few jobs. Indeed, nearly seven of every ten residents employed in this part of western Mora County draw their paychecks from the government—county, state, or federal. Its annual per capita income of $8,194 ranks it thirty-second among New Mexico's thirty-three counties. The median family income of $8,608 is more than $5,000 below the national average. Unemployment is nearly 25 percent, a substantial portion of it in the sparsely populated valley in the western corner of the county. After the 1990 federal census, Mora County numbered only forty-two hundred people. Thus, it is not surprising that, according to government records, nearly as many residents (928) receive monthly food stamps as are unemployed.

Tough place; tough times, it would seem.

Statistics don't tell the whole story, however. Mora County remains an agrarian community and that, too, is a big part of its history. Once, in the late 1800s, it supplied Fort Union, the largest army post in the Southwest, with livestock and grain. Earlier this century, even after the federal government shut down the army post in the early 1890s, Mora County was the acknowledged breadbasket of a younger New Mexico—providing wheat, oats, alfalfa, corn, barley, rye, potatoes, and vegetables. Indeed, multistory stone structures that housed many of the area's mills still stand in Mora, their exteriors a portrait of weathered stone, wood, and rusted metal.

Varied reasons have been given for the industry's collapse, but central to it was a decision by the railroad companies to abandon service to Mora in the mid-1920s. ("We used to have our farmers line up for miles to get their crops aboard the trains," recalls Father Walter Cassidy.) The advent of high-tech farming—bigger spreads farming larger acreage elsewhere—coupled with modern-day trucking, also contributed to Mora's fall.

Semblances of those days can still be found, however. Visit with a handful of residents and see it at work. The house and yard may not be pretty, but out back invariably are a cow or two, some chickens, a small vegetable garden, and peach trees. This is subsistence farming, the growing and raising of food and animals for home use. It is an aspect of rural life that rarely finds inclusion in state and federal social aid programs that are more interested in how much cash you earn—or do not earn. In Mora it appears to work.

But along with the country lifestyle has come the outside microscope. Valley residents unhappily acknowledge that they have a history of being dangled at the end of negative newspaper and magazine reports.

"Drinking," says Tony Martinez. "They always write about our drinking. We don't drink any more or any less than they do in Santa Fe. Hell, I could go to Santa Fe and come back and write a real story about drinking in that town."

People drink alcohol in Mora. They admit that some of their neighbors have drinking problems. But they also laugh. They fight. They wake up early, work hard, go to bed late. They file lawsuits against family. They worry about their kids and about paying bills.

"We're really no different than any other small town anywhere else," says school board member John Romero. "But outsiders want to come here and tell us what's wrong with Mora. It's almost like a sport for people in the city."

Tourism may or may not help the area, but what it will do is bring dramatic change to a lifestyle many in Mora are not interested in losing. Things could get better in various ways, however.

A sizeable increase in population could finally bring door-to-door mail delivery. More residents and increased business activity could mean the Bank of Las Vegas would open a full-service facility instead of the branch office it currently operates in Mora. The community could get a newspaper like the *Mora County Star*, a crusading weekly that fell out of grace with several local politicians and was ultimately run out of town in the early 1980s.

The lack of a newspaper never killed off a town, but it helps substantiate resident Dan Cassidy's claim that Mora is "an insular community."

"There is a strong historical tendency to hold on to history around here," he says. "People here fear change. It's apprehension. Rumors come and go."

Additional services would in themselves boost the area's ability to entice business investment, says pro-growth advocate David Salman, who notes: "We have as much history and as beautiful scenery as Taos, but tourists hesitate because they have not been given a reason to stop."

Yet while one could quickly draft a lengthy list of things Mora does not have, it also must be said that there are many "luxuries" Mora residents have long lived without. There is no movie theater, although a video rental store does a brisk business out of a mobile home not far from Allsup's. There are no hotels. Visitors have the ten-room Almanzar Motel or the open skies. Hungry? Theresa Marie's is open during daytime hours only. Same for Hatcha's Cafe. B-Jay's ("Columbus ate here," reads its highway sign) is open whenever owner Baudy Martinez wants to open it. There is no shopping center (residents travel thirty-two miles to Las Vegas), no gift shops, and no hospital.

But some in Mora ask: Would all of these things really make the community better?

"We lived in Grants for several years, and we had everything," says Anita Lovato LaRan, who is director of Helping Hands Inc., a social service agency in town. "I mean, we had McDonald's, Baskin-Robbins, dry cleaners, movies, Holiday Inn, everything. My kids no longer watch hours and hours of television. Now they go fishing, they hike, and they play outside like kids. This is a very healthy community, and I think that's good."

So what does she think of this tourist stuff?

"I think it'll happen," she begins. "But it will be a sad time in our history. Let's be realistic, too. The state wants Mora to grow economically so that it can contribute more to tax revenues. Tourism will come, only it will not be led by people in Mora. I guess we'll fight it individually. By that I mean that if Motel 6 decides to move in next to my home, I'll fight it."

Last year Mora County contributed $755,000 in tax revenues to the state, placing it ahead of only Catron, DeBaca, and Harding counties. Taking schools, law enforcement, and administration of local government into account, the state spent more money on Mora than it got in return.

Still, Anita LaRan's exposure to tourism comes down to this: An enterprising photographer, finding her home irresistible, took his fancy camera, snapped a picture, and eventually sold it as a postcard in Santa Fe gift shops. The caption?

"He called my house 'The Red Barn,'" she remembers reading when she flipped it over. "Can you believe it? The least he could've done was stop by, knock on my door, and ask if he could use my property to make money. That, too, is tourism, I suppose."

For others, it isn't that some hamburger joint will bring its gaudy, plastic building materials to the neighborhood as much as it is a fear that new residents will dream up million-dollar homes, sending property taxes sky-high for everybody else.

"People here see Taos and Santa Fe," says Dan Cassidy, forty-year-old great-grandson of the Cassidys who built and ran the Cleveland Roller Mill. "They remember their ancestors' adobe home selling for $700,000 and how the kids were forced out when prices skyrocketed. Mora, I believe, would like to back away from that sort of growth."

Already, however, Cassidy has seen an increasing number of realty signs. In bright lettering they adorn some of Mora's older downtown buildings, ranch fences on the outskirts of town, and even a few landmarks such as the Almanzar Motel, which its owners have put on the market because of illness. Realty agent Leyba is pitching a combination general store, hotel, and warehouse that belongs to a relative and sits dead square in the middle of the small downtown skyline in Mora.

Indeed, the very fact that property owners in close-knit Mora are even willing to sell, much less advertise the idea with bright realty signs, is telling in itself.

"You know what's striking?" Cassidy asks. "Ten years ago, you'd never see a real estate sign around here. Now they're all over the place. You get the impression the whole county is for sale."

He feels someone is buying—though he, like some of his neighbors, gauges the activity by the tourist traffic. In his particular case, Cassidy sees good arguments for both sides of the tourism issue. As operator of the Cleveland Roller Mill Museum, he knows increased traffic would mean more visitors paying the admission fee to see his "roller mill in action." Yet Cassidy likes the quiet life of today's Mora and, in fact, speaks badly of time spent in Colorado and Santa Fe.

At the county tax assessor's office, Angela Romero is keeping track of newcomers who walk into her office to ask questions about various properties up for sale. Most of them, she says, ask for maps before leaving.

"I think Mora will grow," says Tony Martinez as he sits with a cup of coffee at a table near his bar's small bandstand. "I get people in my place from everywhere. And I am seeing the tourists come in more and more. But these guys don't spend that much money in Mora. Most of them come in their tourist wagons, and they carry everything on it: food, beds, and television."

Rancher Salman, who served as the area's state representative for five terms until retiring in 1979, sees Mora at the proverbial crossroads. The risk being run, he argues, is that in trying to preserve the community's seventeenth-century roots, anti-growth proponents in Mora eventually will see it become just another Western ghost town.

"Mora is already an anachronism," says Salman. "It hasn't died because people here are, by and large, elderly, unskilled, and have no place to go. A lot of it has to do with some people patronizing their own people. I think they enjoy seeing them in poverty. These same people think they can go back to the seventeenth century."

Allen A. Nysse is a former Wisconsin resident who's lived in many places and last hung his cowboy hat in Santa Fe. Last month he packed his belongings and the tools of his woodworking business and trucked it all up to Mora. With big plans in mind, he got himself an abandoned building right downtown in ex-change for a little handiwork. He's a newcomer, and to hear him talk, he feels it.

"You know, I was real anxious to leave Santa Fe after four years of rising rents," says the forty-seven-year-old Nysse, who, in his pony-tailed hair, stands out in Mora. "Everything isn't perfect here, but I think I'll stay."

He has a woman friend in town. His building is owned by an acquaintance. A large portion of the false ceiling has caved in, and the only signs of any improvement on this day are two posters of Cuban revolutionary Ernesto "Che" Guevara that Nysse has nailed on an overhang directly above his lathe.

"This is like returning to life in the 1950s," Nysse adds. "The whole world is racing, losing its values. Here it's a lot simpler."

Never mind that, try as he might, he's been unable to get the phone company to install his service. Even for that, Nysse has a ready answer: "You could say I grew tired of the fast lane and found Mañana Land. I don't need my phone by morning. I can wait."

If the myth that has long dogged the Mora Valley—that it is cold to strangers and especially cold to Anglo strangers—is accurate, Nysse has no chance. He, however, is unconvinced.

He is going places in town to speed up his assimilation. On this Saturday afternoon he is drinking beer at the Cleveland Bar. Around him, stocky Hispanic men in working clothes drink together, jousting noisily like good friends as they shoot billiards. Nysse sits by himself, conversing only with owner and bartender Tony Martinez, who tells him he should've stopped in the night before.

"Big crowd, huh?" he says to Martinez. "I walked over to The Lounge [another local bar] last night, but they were having a wedding dance there. The third place was full of old men. Sorta dead, so I went home."

Nysse is too much of a newcomer to have come to conclusions about the town. But he is nonetheless convincing when he says he has never believed the myth about coldness toward Anglos and thus feels no danger. "Most of my girlfriends have been Hispanic," he volunteers. "Maybe that'll help."

Bar owner Martinez believes the myth was created and is perpetuated by outsiders. "This county is about Mejicanos in charge, and it bothers a lot of people who do not live here," he says. "But Anglos can't say that they're mistreated. It's not that way at all. I have all sorts of customers, and aside from a few fights, which every bar has now and then, everybody gets along."

"It's a lie," adds school board member John Romero. "A damned, damned lie. That's just something that was published years ago and easy for people to repeat. The other myth is that we prefer outdoor privies out here. It's bullshit, of course."

Tuesday night at the Cleveland Bar: Tony Martinez and his wife, Connie, behind the bar. Eight Hispanics playing billiards, another three seated at the bar, one playing an out-of-tune guitar. Loud *norteño* music screaming from the jukebox, followed by a pair of tunes by the Texas Tornados in English. Rough-looking hombres; no fights this night.

Saturday afternoon at the Cleveland Bar: Young Anglo men and women on break from repair work at the Catholic church in nearby La Cueva play billiards, Hispanic cowboys play on a nearby table. Loud music. Boisterous chatter. No fights or arguments.

Father Walter Cassidy, seventy-six, has lived all his life in Mora.

"I know there are people who are absolutely isolationists," he says of some of his neighbors. "They won't talk to strangers. I call them xenophobes."

He remembers when trains rolled into Mora, when the now-gone Butler Hotel hosted gala Saturday night dances featuring the beloved Mora Jazz Babies of the 1920s, when the valley's agriculture helped feed people elsewhere in the state, and he scoffs at the myth of <u>unsociability</u>.

"My father came here and practically forgot he was Irish," the retired priest adds. "He grew up with Spanish kids and herded goats with them. He got along famously with Hispanics."

Mora County is <u>a Hispanic stronghold</u>. Hispanics hold every seat on the three-member county commission. A Hispanic serves as county manager, sheriff, treasurer, magistrate, and county clerk. This pleases the population, which, depending on whom you talk to, is anywhere from the federal Census Bureau's estimate of 85 percent Hispanic to, if you accept the local figure, 95 percent Hispanic.

Sit inside Theresa Marie's and hear a language that is a mixture of English and Spanish. ("*Ese* earthquake in California," one man is telling others at his table. "*Es muy* amazing *tan pocos* died, no?") Also obvious to a visitor is the bond, the community. With each patron entering the cafe comes a round of greetings, handshakes, and *abrazos*. The only ones left out of the circle are the tourists, who invariably stop what they're doing and look up and smile.

Still, as school board member Romero put it, there is little the community can do to replace its less-than-complimentary reputation. Romero believes bad publicity has hurt the region for years.

Just what are they saying about Mora, anyway? A call to the New Mexico Tourism Department yields this information:

"Mora is not a big community, but we're really not that familiar with it, sir. We do not have a tourist brochure on it, for example."

"Is it safe for travel?" we ask.

"You should visit Los Alamos," replies the woman pleasantly over the telephone.

"No," we say next. "Not Los Alamos. We're thinking of visiting Mora."

"Mora?" she chips in. "You're still stuck on that one? No one has ever called us to ask for tourist information on Mora, sir."

In June 1989, on the occasion of a visit to Mora by the then-governor Garrey Carruthers for Government Day in Mora County, Antonio Medina rose to give a speech he wanted the governor to hear. It concerned the area's economic future, and it came soon after the governor's special force had identified socioeconomic problems facing Mora.

Medina read from a prepared text outlining his ideas of how to usher Mora into the twenty-first century. Surprisingly, he conceded that the idea's time had come, but he told the governor and the others in attendance at the high school gymnasium that economic development would have to be a process "of the people, by the people, for the people."

"That is, economic development from the bottom up, so that those who have the greatest need benefit the most," he said at the time. "Our long-term goal is to live gracefully and die proudly," he concluded.

When he recalled the speech, Medina explained that the conclusion was a jab at the governor, who, he says, had answered a question about the future of New Mexico's poor rural towns by saying he hoped they'd all simply die gracefully.

Medina won't let Mora die, but just how hard would he fight the arrival of tourism?

"It would be the Mora Bean Dip War," he says without hesitation.

"You Don't Know Cows Like I Do"

twentieth-century new mexico ranch culture

Steve Cormier

In the twentieth century, New Mexico ranching underwent modernization and mechanization. Railroads, selective breeding of livestock, telephones, computers, pickup trucks, and improved veterinary medicines all helped change the face of ranching. Census information from 1900 to 1960 suggests that the number of ranches declined as their average size increased. For example, the Bell Ranch was broken into six pieces in 1947.[1] From approximately 440,000 acres it became approximately 145,000 (it was later increased to approximately 300,000 acres). But the Moise Livestock Company increased its holdings during the same period to two ranches totaling approximately 72,000 acres.[2] Similar increases in ranch size occurred with Frank Bond and Company and the Ilfield Brothers. Other Bell Ranch–size ranches like the Flying A and the CA Bar, both headquartered out of Roswell, were also broken up and eventually sold as smaller parcels.[3]

As ranches grew in size and dwindled in number, another basic trend emerged: the loss of homestead land due to inhospitable weather conditions. As Agnes Morely Cleveland, Fabiola Cabeza de Baca, and Mae Price Mosely have pointed out, some of the homesteaders who came west between 1902 and 1934 lasted longer than others, but eventually almost all either turned their land over to merchants as debt payment or sold outright to ranchers.[4] Many of these homesteaders returned from where they came or became ranch hands on the more successful, larger ranches. Census reports indicate that the number of ranch employees reached a high in the 1920s, probably due to homesteaders losing their land and taking ranch employment, and then declined steadily to the present level.[5]

New Mexico ranchers embraced modern methods of raising cattle as soon as these ways proved profitable. Rarely, if ever, was sentiment for the "cowboy ways" of the past allowed to interfere with profit. By 1950, for example, pickup trucks rather than horses were the norm on ranches. From the single Longhorn breed of the mid-nineteenth century, ranchers progressed to the Hereford and Durham imports of the late nineteenth century, and finally to the dozens of exotic and crossbred breeds of the present.

In the nineteenth century, the spring roundup basically consisted of "working" the calves by branding them with the owner's brand and castrating the male calves. By mid-twentieth century, "working" the calves consisted of branding, castrating, dehorning, vaccinating for various diseases, and implanting the calves with a growth hormone calculated to increase weight by as much as 10 percent. Roping of the calves and dragging them to the work crews had also generally been replaced by chutes that closed around the animals and restrained them while they were being "worked." As Diane Ackerman described ranching in 1980, "The modern cowboy carries a syringe instead of a six-shooter, wears bell-bottom jeans, dries his hair with a blowgun, and watches color TV."[6]

Ranch employees were also greatly influenced by twentieth-century trends. Who were the ranch employees? Census figures for 1900 through 1960 indicate that "stock herders, drovers, and feeders" increased in number until 1930 and then steadily declined until 1960.[7] Roughly the same percentage of men and women were employed on cattle and sheep ranches in 1960 as in 1900. In 1900, 4.2 percent of the total number of ranch hands were women.[8] This figure varies from census to census. In 1910 it was 2.4 percent; in 1920, 2.9 percent; in 1930, 1.4 percent; in 1940, 0.06 percent; in 1950, 2.5 percent; and in 1960, 3.7 percent.[9] The number of women ranch employees reflected the general employment trends during these decades. From the figures just cited, it is obvious that the Depression years of the 1930s, hard enough on the male ranch employees, were equally hard on the women.

And what of the racial makeup of ranch employees? Official census reports did not delineate racial composition until 1970. Census reports prior to that time grouped Hispanics and Anglos together as "white." "Non-white" people were understood to be either Native American or African American ("Negro"). However, the Census Bureau has recently issued racial breakdowns for the years 1900, 1910, and 1920. Researchers such as Mo Palmer have made invaluable inquiries into subsequent years. Palmer's research points to the ever greater realization that the New Mexico "cowboy" of story, myth, and history book is in fact as much a "vaquero" as a "cowboy." Palmer's research in Mora County and around Santa Rosa for the years 1900, 1910, and 1950 suggests that a majority of "agricultural workers" were Hispanic.[10] In other words, the majority of *ranch hands* were Hispanic. This should not be surprising. Although by 1890 Hispanics had lost 80 percent of the lands guaranteed to them by the Treaty of Guadalupe-Hidalgo due to fraud and lawyers fees,[11] they remained on the land and continued working for ranchers (predominantly Anglo) who purchased or otherwise acquired the available land. Even in "Little Texas" (southeast New Mexico) vaqueros found employment, predominantly on sheep ranches, much to the disgust of the incoming cattle-raising Texans,[12] who believed both Mexicans and sheep raising to be inferior.

New Mexico is often depicted as the land where three cultures—Anglo, Hispanic, and Native American—have blended harmoniously to form a unique individual: the New Mexican. Social, economic, and political progress is portrayed as ever upward, and in some cases this may be true. But a melding of cultures, especially Hispanic and Anglo, has not successfully occurred with regard to ranch culture. Disputes over land have occurred periodically throughout the twentieth century and continue to this day. From clashes in "Little Texas," to legal battles involving all three cultural groups in northern New Mexico during the 1930s,[13] to the Tijerina-led disputes of the 1960s, to the most recent troubles involving out-of-state real estate developers near Chama, Anglos and Hispanics (and sometimes Native Americans) have been defining and redefining their relationships.

It is essentially the same in ranch culture. Hispanics developed many of the ranching practices of the twentieth century, including the roundup, roping animals to doctor them, large-acreage grazing, and, of course, the use of the horse to herd their animals. A very good case could also be made for the sport of rodeo being Hispanic. And yet, very few rodeos in the first half of the century involved Hispanic participants. A review of national rodeo champions during this period reveals not one Hispanic name.[14] This is particularly ironic in light of the fact that the great New Mexican bronco rider, José Gonzalez, gave an exhibition of his skill in front of Theodore Roosevelt at the 1899 Rough Riders Reunion in Las Vegas, New Mexico.[15]

At times a great deal of friction occurred between the Anglo and Hispanic ranch cultures. Frank Brito, recalling his family history, states that in Torrence County during the 1920s, "Newcomers moved in from nearby communities. Homesteaders arriving by wagon trains from Texas and Oklahoma brought much unrest and demanded services and land from the native Spanish. Fight, bloodshed and horse-dragging settled disputes. Eugenio and I were always in the midst of these fights."[16] Ralph E. Fresquez, who also wrote about friction between the two cultures, claims that "two societies" existed in and around Roswell between the world wars.[17] Needless to say, Anglos and Hispanics were not always at odds, but a social differentiation existed (and still does). Hispanic ranch culture has its own rhythm. Amado Chavez, writing in his family history, puts it this way:

> We had many neighbors—the José Giron family, the Sernas, the Candelarias and the Lovatos. Dances were held at the ranches. They included "Valse de la Silla" and "Quadrillas." People were of a very happy nature. At New Years, the men banded together and serenaded all homes. They started at 12:00 at night. They had wonderful times. At each home the women and children welcomed them with "pastelitos" and "mula" (white mule) brewed at home. The women baked in outside ovens.[18]

Also from a family history come these comments by Teodocio Herrera:

> Life was hard but everyone helped and things were good until, in 1961, disaster struck. While everyone was in church for Good Friday services the house burned to the ground. It was a sad time in our lives but with the help of family and people from Torreon the new house was built and we started over one more time.
>
> During these years there was not much money for entertainment, but people could always drive by and hear the playing of guitars as we'd gather on our front porch to sing songs of past and present. Or, I remember how the girls used to try and get ready by kerosene lamp for the Saturday night dance. It was fun to watch them fuss and bother to make sure their only pair of bobby sox were the whitest they could be.[19]

Like Hispanics and other marginalized ethnic groups, women have not received their rightful due in ranch culture. Traditional western historians such as J. Frank Dobie, C. L. Sonnichsen, and David Dary have basically viewed women as secondary partners who helped men with ranch work but were primarily confined within the home perimeter. More balanced and thorough treatments of ranch women have been provided by Teresa Jordon, Joan Jensen, Stan Steiner, and Sharon Niederman. The point emphasized here is that ranch women in New Mexico were and are an integral part of the culture. They are not just ranch wives to be mentioned parenthetically in some historical account. The primary literature is simply too rich with accounts by women as employees or full-fledged partners to relegate them to such a minor role. If a woman is married to a man, and they have a ranch on which they raise sheep and/or cattle, this does not automatically mean that he does all the outside work and she does all the inside work. Many, many times, all of the work, wherever it occurs, is shared. This means that a woman can be as much a ranch hand as a man is, even though, quite often, she may defer to him in a traditional manner. County histories and personal reminiscences bear this out.

Writing of her life around 1904, Jesse Prado Farrington recalls that "Tommy and I joined all the nearby roundups, and I learned to 'herd a bronc.' . . . I became quite a cowhand as far as roundup, or cutting out cattle went, but I never became a roper or 'bronco buster.' "[20] The Chavez County Historical Society reports that Nettie Lusk Amonett worked cattle at an early age on the family ranch, Portia Jones ran the family ranch by herself from 1943 to 1970 after her husband's death, and Beryl Kimball and daughter Genevieve did the same with their sheep ranch from 1955 until 1970.[21]

From the *History of Torrence County* comes this account by Ruth Elliott of her years on her father's ranch:

> Dad was going to the top of the hills to see if he could see me every so often. He did that several times and didn't see me. When I got to the northeast corner there was a dirt tank of water with cattle all around it. Dad was getting aggravated. Well it took some hard riding to get all those cattle away from that tank and started toward the house. In a little while he saw me driving that long string of cattle so he knew what had happened. He had a few head of cattle. I had 100 or more.[22]

Also from the *History of Torrence County* is this account of Maud (Hawk) Medders: "Will (Maud's husband) passed away in 1965. Maud kept on ranching till a broken hip confined her to a walker, but she still goes to the mesa to check cattle with her son, Bill."[23] And from the same volume comes this account of Virginia O'Neal: "Both Virginia and Lewis were equally equipped to deal with digging post holes by hand, feeding cattle by sleds in the winter, breaking ice, breaking horses, branding cattle, growing gardens, hauling water, living on gravy and red beans and all the other things that make up routine living on a ranch."[24]

From the turn of the century until World War II, women were an integral part of rodeo, as they were in ranch life, not only in New Mexico but throughout the West. Authors James Hoy and Michael Allen suggest that women were removed from rough stock riding and roping events because of financial troubles and the desire to make rodeo look "more professional."[25] This, of course, minimizes the contributions to rodeo by such greats as Fern Sawyer of Nogal and Goldy Smith of Raton. Fern Sawyer has received credit for her ability from Teresa Jordon, but Goldy Smith, from the pre–World War I generation of women rodeo athletes, has remained unsung until now. From the recollections of E. L. "Steve" Stephens we have this anecdote about Smith:

> Went through Raton and into Colorado and delivered the cattle. Was a big wild West rodeo going on in Trinidad, Colo. We stayed there three days and taken the rodeo in. Some of us punchers entered all the bronc riding shows. We drew every day. The second day was four of us drew. Was 2 prizes. The first prize was $500. The second prize was $250. They was three boys and one girl and then we drawed who we was going to ride against, so it fell my way to ride against the girl.
>
> Her name was Goldy Smith. So we drawed to see who rode first. She rode first so she came out of the chute on a bay pony. He was a good pony. They drove a buckskin pony in the chute and I buckled my saddle on him and crawled on him and said let him out. He done everything but chin the moon. I could see his head. The girl beat me on points. She got the money, so I went over where she was and thanked her and patted her on the back.[26]

Since World War II, because of male chauvinism passed off as concern for the safety of women riders, women have been able to participate only in barrel racing on a professional level. From the 1960s, in New Mexico and throughout the nation, they have struggled to gain decent and equal prize money and to overcome their image of a "cheap contract act." This they have done, and thanks to efforts by such athletes as Peggy Jo Koll and Charmaine James Rodman, today's professional women rodeo contestants enjoy prize money comparable to that of the men.[27] Women have also formed their own rodeo association, the Girls' Rodeo Association, in which they ride bucking horses and bulls, and rope competitively. New Mexican women rodeo athletes should be just as widely recognized as are Bob Crosby (roping), Roy Cooper (roping), Harley May (bulldogging), Homer Pettigrew (bulldogger), and Troy Fort (roping).

American popular culture and media have focused considerable attention on the various expressive forms of ranch culture. Although both cowboy and vaquero culture have their traditional music, for both groups much of the old work music (story oriented) has been replaced by "Nashville" (non-work-oriented) music. With the coming of the record player, radio, movie theater, television, satellite dish, and portable cassette player, ranch employees (and those who wish they were) have been exposed to music that sings the praises of open spaces, beautiful sunsets, and idyllic ranch settings. It is not uncommon for a New Mexico ranch hand to be driving his or her pickup, checking the condition of the fences, with the radio or cassette player blaring the latest Nashville song. This music has become the "cowboy music" of the twentieth century. There is currently a revival of "cowboy" poetry at annual gatherings such as Elko, Nevada, Fort Stockton and Lubbock, Texas, and Lincoln and Ruidoso, New Mexico. Much of this poetry (and some music) reflects the working ranch culture that has never died out. The poems are both nostalgic (describing horses, cattle, etc.) and modern (describing fencing in the winter, opening gates from the pickup truck, fixing windmills, etc.).[28] The media has descended on these poetry gatherings, and several working ranch hands have found secondary careers reciting poetry, often for as much money in one night as they would make in one month as a ranch hand.

Among ranch employees, these gatherings are a welcome respite from the isolation of their work. Whether these gatherings will have the permanence of rodeo life or will go the way of the "urban cowboy" craze remains to be seen. It is evident, however, that this poetry "revival" has a great deal of authenticity to it. Probably because of this, it is not likely that the national media will cover it on a steady basis as they do, say, the opera, the symphony, "Nashville music," or pop music. Perhaps cowboy poetry will occupy a niche of profitability in the larger culture that will keep it alive among those who are not directly connected with ranching. If not, it will recede from the national scene.

Where is vaquero culture in all this? Aside from an occasional beer and cigarette commercial in Spanish, the cultural image that emerges is primarily Anglo. In film this is quite obvious. Americans have watched hundreds of movies and television shows since the first "western" movie—*The Great Train Robbery*—was made in 1903.[29] In almost all of them Hispanics have been utilized primarily as villains or sidekicks. One exception was the *Cisco Kid*, which aired on 1950s television. Zorro, the story of an upper-class Spaniard in colonial California righting the wrongs of a corrupt governor, starred an Anglo named Guy Madison. When Disney aired *The Nine Lives of Elfego Baca*, the lead was again played by an actor who was not Hispanic: Robert Loggia. When Hispanics (or Mexicans) did have prominent roles, such as the actress Katy Jurado, they often portrayed easily excitable, overly emotional people who primarily thought with their hearts rather than their brains.

Other stereotypes have similarly dominated the media. More than eighty movies have been made about Billy the Kid, a psychopathic killer who was not an important force in New Mexico politics. No laws were enacted because of his actions, no politicians seriously influenced. The repetitious telling of his story misses a far more important story about the 1870s and 1880s. During that period and the years that followed, a more significant battle was waged: racial conflict between the incoming Texans and the indigenous Hispanic ranchers, vaqueros, and farmers. That story of the conflict in "Little Texas" has yet to reach the screen, even though it had an important influence on the history of this area.

What have New Mexico ranch people thought of all this? For the most part they have recognized the phoniness of Hollywood and its habit of inaccurate portrayal. A western film festival held in Santa Fe in 1981 revealed this clash between the perspectives of local ranchers and the romanticized attitudes of actors and filmmakers.[30] Many famous film "cowboys" attended, including actors Charlton Heston, Buster Crabbe, Lee Marvin, and James Coburn. Directors King Vidor and Sam Peckinpah were there as well. One of the panel discussions was entitled "Did the West Really Exist?" Included on this panel were Heston and ranchers Cleofes Vigil and Janaloo Hill. Vigil stated, "Ranch life isn't anything like a Western movie. It's more honest. Western movies are a bunch of lies."[31] Heston defended himself and westerns by asking, "Since there is no 'truth' about the West, what is the responsibility of the filmmaker to tell the 'truth'?"[32] Vigil then replied to Heston, "I don't believe in lies."[33] Earlier, Heston had said that ranch life was too mundane to portray on the screen. "Besides," said Heston, "cows are boring." To this, panelist and Shakespeare, New Mexico, rancher Janaloo Hill replied, "Mr. Heston, I guess you don't know cows like I do."[34]

In a very real sense, however, Charlton Heston has a point. Cows are not prime material for an action-packed adventure film. Nor is fencing, tending wells, doctoring sick animals, speaking Spanish, and not looking like John Wayne, Charlton Heston, or Kevin Costner. What is prime material for movies is what sells. What sells is white guys righting wrongs and never tending cattle or fixing fences or windmills. What sells in the city is overpriced clothing that has no practical use. What sells to the general populace is looking like a cowboy or vaquero but not having to do the onerous drudgery that is the lot of the real ranch employee. In short, real ranch culture does not sell.

In the face of media-generated inaccuracies, it is worth noting the essential positive qualities of New Mexico ranch culture. These qualities include: the loyalty of the people to one another; the beauty of the land; the supplying of essential food to the consumer; and, finally, the positive sense of community that ranching people exhibit in the face of great odds, whether it be difficulties due to nature, animals, the government, or their fellow humans.

Endnotes

1. See David Remley, *The Bell Ranch* (Albuquerque: University of New Mexico Press, 1992), introduction, p. 3.

2. Author's conversation with the foreman of the Moise Livestock Co., 1987.

3. Elvis E. Fleming and Minor S. Huffman, eds., *Roundup on the Pecos* (Roswell, N.M.: Chaves County Historical Society, 1978), pp. 39, 241.

4. Agnes Morely Cleveland, *No Life for a Lady* (Lincoln: University of Nebraska Press, 1977), pp. 331–33; Fabiola Cabeza de Baca, *We Fed Them Cactus* (Albuquerque: University of New Mexico Press, 1954), pp. 149–53; Mae Price Mosely, *Little Texas Beginnings* (Roswell, N.M.: Hall-Poorbaugh Press, 1973), pp. 48–49.

5. U.S. Census Reports, Agriculture, 1920, 1930, 1940, 1950, 1960.

6. Diane Ackerman, *Twilight of the Tenderfoot: A Western Memoir* (Ithaca, N.Y.: William Morrow, 1980), p. 39.

7. U.S. Census, Occupations.

8. U.S. Census, Occupations, Female, 1900, table 41, p. 341.

9. Ibid., 1910, table VII, p. 493; 1920, table 1, p. 979; 1930, table 16, p. 1078; 1940, table 13, p. 319; 1950, table 74, pp. 31–103; 1960, table 120, pp. 33–219.

10. Individual Enumeration Records, Precinct 8, Guadalupe County, 1900, 1910, and 1950. Microfilm. New Mexico State Historic Preservation Survey for Mora County. Researched by Mo Palmer. Manuscript in possession of author.

11. Victor Westphall, *The Public Domain in New Mexico, 1854–1891* (Albuquerque: University of New Mexico Press, 1965), p. 49.

12. Mosely, *Little Texas Beginnings*, p. 19.

13. See David H. Dinwoodie, "Indians, Hispanos, and Land Reform: A New Deal Struggle in New Mexico," *Western Historical Quarterly* 17, no. 3 (1986): 291–323.

14. Robert D. Hanesworth, *Daddy of 'Em All: The Story of the Cheyenne Frontier Days* (Cheyenne, Wyo.: Flintlock Publishing Co., 1967), pp. 162–66; Max Kegley, *Rodeo, the Sport of the Cow Country* (New York: Hastings House, 1942), passim.

15. Cabeza de Baca, *We Fed Them Cactus*, p. 129.

16. "Frank Brito Family," in *History of Torrence County* (Estancia, N.M.: Torrence County Historical Society, 1979), p. 108.

17. Fleming and Huffman, *Roundup on the Pecos*, pp. 212–16.

18. "Amado Chavez Family," in *History of Torrence County*, pp. 120–21.

19. "Teodocio Herrera," in ibid., p. 181.

20. Jesse de Prado Farrington, "Rocking Horse to Cow Pony," *New Mexico Historical Review* 26 (1956): 43.

21. Fleming and Huffman, *Roundup on the Pecos*, pp. 108, 271, 438.

22. "Ruth Elliott," in *History of Torrence County*, p. 149.

23. "Maud (Hawk) Medders," in ibid., p. 223.

24. "Lewis O'Neal Family," in ibid., p. 234.

25. At the Western Historical Association meeting in Austin in 1992 Prof. Hoy delivered a paper entitled "Marge Roberts: National Cowgirl Hall of Fame." Prof. Allen's paper was entitled "Mabel Strickland: National Cowboy Hall of Fame."

26. E. L. "Steve" Stephens, "West of the Pecos," *New Mexico Historical Review* 35, no. 2 (1960): 98.

27. Author's conversations with Peggy Jo Koll, 1989 and 1992.

28. See Hal Cannon, ed., *Cowboy Poetry: A Gathering* (Salt Lake City: G. M. Smith, 1985), passim.

29. Ironically, *The Great Train Robbery* was filmed in New Jersey.

30. Stan Steiner, "Real Horses and Mythic Riders," *American West* 18, no. 5 (1981): 55–59.

31. Ibid., p. 55.

32. Ibid.

33. Ibid.

34. Ibid., pp. 55–56.

Native America

For Native Americans the Southwest is the "middle world" and the "place of emergence." These sacred tenets have united peoples whose experience otherwise is diverse and myriad. Today we are fortunate that powerful and inspired voices speak from the vantage point of the Navajo, Apache, Pueblo, Pima, Papago (Tohono O'odham), and other southwestern tribes. In Part III we include some of the foremost voices who are articulating the collective knowledge of their people in a distinctly "non-Western" manner, locating the Southwest not on a map, but on a temporal plane that evokes cosmic and spiritual meaning. Their vision is just as "true to North" as is the compass's needle. These writers counsel us that if we are to "heal the split" produced by a ravaging of the natural environment, we must consider the essential ties humans have to the natural world. We are fortunate that Native Americans have not forgotten this fundamental idea and now offer it to the larger society as a philosophy and a practice. The views expressed by Native Americans about Native America also delineate the dilemmas that present generations face as they endeavor to continue traditional practices in a world of urban blight, poverty, casino gaming on reservations, high-tech manufacturing, and consumer society.

Although the necessity of living in two or more worlds—for example, maintaining one's traditional customs while participating in "mainstream society"—can be deeply troubling, the authors in this section point out that it can also be an experience that adds depth and insight to one's vision of humanity. One worldview need not replace or invalidate another. The Navajo physicist, trained in the "Western" scientific manner, can continue to be a religious leader who recounts the tribal origin myth with utmost respect and sincerity.

3 AM

Joy Harjo

in the albuquerque airport
trying to find a flight
to old oraibi, third mesa
TWA
is the only desk open
bright lights outline new york,
chicago
and the attendant doesn't know
that third mesa
is a part of the center
of the world
and who are we
just two indians
at three in the morning
trying to find a way back

and then I remember
that time simon
took a yellow cab
out to ácoma from albuquerque
a twenty-five-dollar ride
to the center of himself

3 AM is not too late
to find the way back

Raisin Eyes

Luci Tapahonso

I saw my friend Ella
with a tall cowboy at the store
the other day in Shiprock.

Later, I asked her,
Who's that guy anyway?

Oh, Luci, she said (I knew what was coming),
it's terrible. He lives with me
and my money and in my car.
But just for a while.
He's in AIRCA and rodeos a lot.
And I still work.

This rodeo business is getting to me, you know,
and I'm going to leave him.
Because I think all this I'm doing now
will pay off better somewhere else,
but I just stay with him and it's hard
because
he just smiles that way, you know,
and then I end up paying entry fees
and putting shiny Tony Lamas on lay-away again.

It's not hard.
But he doesn't know when
I'll leave him and I'll drive across the flat desert
from Red Valley in blue morning light
straight to Shiprock so easily.

And anyway, my car is already used
To humming a mourning song with Gary Stewart,
Complaining again of aching and breaking,
Down-and-out love affairs.

Damn.
These Navajo cowboys with raisin eyes
And pointed boots are just bad news,
But it's so hard to remember that all the time,
She said with a little laugh.

Remembering Tewa Pueblo Houses and Spaces

Rina Swentzell

Santa Clara Pueblo was a wonderful place to grow up. I was a child there in the 1940s and remember the incredible sense of well-being and containment—both socially and physically. From the plaza or *bupingeh* (literally, the middle-heart place) of the pueblo, we could see the far mountains encircle our lives and place. Those mountains not only defined the far boundaries of our world but also were where the primary drama of our lives—the growing of clouds and the bringing of that movement and water—was initiated. We continually watched those mountains to see the clouds form out of them and to know on which of their valleys or summits the sun would rise or set. Those mountains, or world boundaries, were far away and were the province of the men and boys who went to visit the shrines there, and who would bring back the spirit and energies of the deer, bear, ram and evergreen plants to blend with ours in the dances and ceremonies of the middle-heart place.

The spaces between those mountains and the pueblo were shared by everyone (men and women, boys and girls). They included the low hills and small canyons where coyotes, rabbits and squirrels lived and where roots, herbs and other ground plants were found. There also were the fields and the large flowing water (the Posongeh or Rio Grande) which snaked along the base of the Black Mesa. The Black Mesa included the cave that went down into the center of the earth and was the home of the Tsavejo or the masked whippers. There were dark areas, such as the cave, and light areas, such as the top of the low hills, from which we could see the far mountains of the four directions and a large part of the north-south valley within which lay the Posongeh and the pueblo.

As the pueblo, or human space, was encircled by high mountains, low hills and flat fields, the center point (*nansipu*), from which the people emerged out of the underworld, was also girdled by different spaces within the pueblo. The nansipu, marked by an inconspicuous stone, was located within the middle-heart place, or the plaza. The plaza was bounded by house structures, which in turn were encircled by the corrals or places where horses, pigs and chickens lived. Beyond that, or sometimes overlapping, were the trash mounds. The trash mounds flowed into the fields, and from there the energy moved into the hills and mountains where it entered those far shrines, moved through the under-world levels or existences and re-emerged through the nansipu.

The stories of the old people told us that we came to live on this fourth level of existence with the help of plants, birds and other animals. Once we emerged out of the underworld, we continued to need those other living beings. In order to find the center point, or the nansipu, the water spider and the rainbow were consulted. Water Spider spread its legs to the north, west, south and east and determined the middle of this world. Then, to make sure that Water Spider was right, Rainbow spread its arch of many colors to the north, west, south and east and confirmed Water Spider's center point. There, the people placed a stone, and around that stone was defined the middle-heart place. Next, the living and sleeping structures were built in terraced forms, like moun-tains, with stepped tiers which enclosed and protected the plaza, or the valley of the human place.

The house and kiva structures also emulated the low hills and mountains in their connectedness to the earth. The adobe structures flowed out of the earth, and it was often difficult to see where the ground stopped and where the structures began. The house structures were, moreover, connected to each other, enclosing an outdoor space from which we could directly connect with the sky and focus on the moving clouds. Connectedness was primary. The symbolic flowed into the physical world as at the nansipu where the po-wa-ha (the breath of the cosmos) flowed out of the underworld into this world.

The kiva structure was totally symbolic. Its rooftop was like the pueblo plaza space from where we could connect with the sky, while the rooftop open-ing took us into the kiva structure which was like going back into the earth via the nansipu in the plaza. Within the feminine dark interior, the plaza space configuration was repeated with the human activity area around a nansipu, the earth floor under and the woven-basket roof above, representing the sky. The connecting ladder made of tall spruce or pine trees stood in the middle near the nansipu. Everything was organized to remind us constantly of the primary connections with the earth, sky, other life forms and the cosmic movement. These primary connections were continually reiterated.

The materials used for construction were also symbolically important. In the Rio Grande area, most of the building was with adobe-mud mixed with either ashes or dried plant material. In the Tewa language, the word for "us" is *nung*, and the word for the "earth" or "dirt" is also *nung*. As we are synonymous with and born of the earth, so are we made of the same stuff as our houses.

As children, we tasted houses because of their varying textures and tastes. Not only could houses be tasted, they were also blessed, healed and fed periodically. Before the actual construction of a house, offerings were placed at its four corners. Later, during the house building, prayers would be said, and more offerings were placed within the walls and ceiling beams to bless and protect the completed whole. Thereafter, the structure was blessed and fed cornmeal during specific ceremonies. Houses were also given the ultimate respect of dying. During my childhood, when I walked back and forth between the pueblo and the Bureau of Indian Affairs' school, which was about one-half mile away, I would meander among the pueblo structures tasting them. One day, I noticed a crack forming in the wall of a particularly good-tasting house. I watched the crack grow over several weeks until I became concerned about the house falling. I asked my great-grandmother why the people who lived in that house were doing nothing about fixing the crack. She shook her finger at me and said that it was not my business to be concerned about whether the house fell down or not: "It has been a good house, it has been taken care of, fed, blessed and healed many times during its life, and now it is time for it to go back into the earth." Shortly afterward, the house collapsed and, in appropriate time, the same materials were reused to build a new structure in the same place. It was not always easy to tell if walls were going up or falling apart.

Not long after that house fell down, my great-grandmother and I stood and watched the house that we lived in slowly, and most elegantly, crumble into a pile. I had watched, again, a crack working its way down the wall as I washed my face in the washbowl. It was a few minutes before I had the presence of mind to grab my great-grandmother's hand and pull her out the door before the house collapsed.

Building for permanence was not a priority and as a result, the structures were interactive. We built them, tasted them, talked with them, climbed on them, lived with them and watched them die. They, in turn, would either be kind and warm or torment us with "not good" energies which they might embrace. Many different kinds of energies flowed through the structures because they shared in the energies of the people who lived and died within them, or sometimes, they joined the "bad winds" which blew through them. Periodically, cleansing and healing them was, therefore, very important.

Also important was that everybody—men, women and children—was involved in the building process. Building was not a specialized activity to be done only by men. Women and children shared equally in all but the heaviest part of the work. Maintenance was more often the responsibility of women and children. I remember the two weeks every August before our Santa Clara feast day as an exhilarating time, because everybody would be plastering houses and outdoor ovens and generally re-creating the entire pueblo house. Being knee deep in mud, carrying buckets of it or patting the heavy, gelatinous mixture into the wooden adobe-brick forms were very ordinary activities of our everyday lives.

Through all the spaces that we created, our everyday lives flowed easily. The use of outdoor areas for cooking, eating and visiting was still common during my childhood years in Santa Clara. Communal activities such as husking corn, drying fruit and baking bread happened anywhere from the corral areas where the animals were kept, to the main plaza area. The walls and structures defined those other very important outdoor community activity areas. The focus, then, was not only on what happened indoors—within structures—but also outdoors, where the community came together most often.

Indoors, the rooms were multi-functional. The kitchen was used for cooking, eating and receiving people. Sleeping areas also doubled as living and storage rooms. Rooms for food storage were an important part of the structures because farming was still an integral life activity. Again, there was little specialization of indoor areas or creation of spaces for decorative or image-promoting reasons. All areas were functional.

That straightforward approach applied both indoors and outdoors. Landscaping, or the beautification of outdoor spaces, was a foreign concept. The natural environment was primary, and the human structures were made to fit into the hills and around boulders or trees. In that setting, planting pretty flowers that need watering was ridiculous. Decoration for decoration's sake was unnecessary. Sometimes, murals were painted on interior walls, but they were symbolically significant; they were explicit reminders of the meaningful connections in the world.

It was not until I was well into my adult years that I began to realize that the process of building and the interaction with the buildings and the materials that we used were very much an extension of our worldview as Pueblo people. It was at that time that an insatiable urge to see the ruins of the Old Ones (the Anasazi) came upon me. I was beside myself when I "discovered" shrines in mountains far from home, openings into the earth in the bedrock at Chaco Canyon, nansipus within kivas within plazas in Sand Canyon, south-facing cliff dwellings in Mesa Verde, unbonded walls throughout the Southwest and hand-prints of the builders (women, men and children) on sandstone cliffs over falling walls in Hovenweep.

I began also to understand the value of our lifestyle, beliefs and architecture for ourselves as well as for other people who have moved away from an intimate relationship with the land, clouds and all other life forms. I now appreciate the emphasis on the whole in that architecture. The entire community was the house, and the parts (house units) were important for their role as connectors to the other parts and to the earth. I see that the respect for the natural environment that was inherent in the style and process of building was special—and is crucial for the survival of the world. I value tremendously the unselfconscious-ness and absence of aesthetic pretension, which led to doing everything straight-forwardly yet which still considered the context and the connections so that practical and symbolic function were never lost. Most important, I treasure the sense of sacredness which pervaded that old Pueblo world. All of life, including walls, rocks and people, was part of an exquisite, flowing unity.

And Then I Went to School
memories of a pueblo childhood

Joe Suina

I lived with my grandmother when I was five through nine years of age. It was the early fifties when electricity had not yet entered our Pueblo homes. The village day school and health clinic were first to have it, and to the unsuspecting Cochiti, this was the approach of a new era in their uncomplicated lives.

Transportation was simple. Two good horses and a sturdy wagon met the daily needs of a villager. Only five, maybe six individuals possessed an automobile in the Pueblo of four hundred. A flatbed truck fixed with side rails and a canvas top made the usual Saturday morning trip to Santa Fe. It was always loaded beyond capacity with people and their wares headed for town for a few staples. The straining old truck with its escort of a dozen barking dogs made a noisy exit, northbound from the village.

A Sense of Closeness

During those years, Grandmother and I lived beside the plaza in a one-room house. Inside, we had a traditional fireplace, a makeshift cabinet for our few tin cups and bowls, and a wooden crate carried our two buckets of all-purpose water. At the innermost part of the room were two rolls of bedding—thick quilts, sheepskin, and assorted—which we used as comfortable sitting couches by day and unrolled for sleeping by night. A wooden pole the length of one side of the room was suspended about ten inches from the vigas and draped with a modest collection of colorful shawls, blankets, and sashes, making this part of the room most interesting. In one corner sat a bulky metal trunk for our ceremonial wear and a few valuables. A dresser which was traded for her well-known pottery held the few articles of clothing we owned and the "goody bag"—an old flour sack Grandma always kept filled with brown candy, store-bought cookies, and Fig Newtons. These were saturated with a sharp odor of mothballs. Nevertheless, they made a fine snack with coffee before we turned in for the night. Tucked securely beneath my blankets, I listened to one of her stories about how it was when she was a little girl. These accounts appeared so old-fashioned compared to the way we lived. Sometimes she softly sang a song from a ceremony. In this way, I went off to sleep each night.

Earlier in the evening we would make our way to a relative's house if someone had not already come to visit us. There, I'd play with the children while the adults caught up on all the latest news. Ten-cent comic books were finding their way into the Pueblo homes. Exchanging "old" comics for "new" ones was a serious matter that involved adults as well. Adults favored mystery and romance stories. For us children these were the first links to the world beyond the Pueblo. We enjoyed looking at them and role-playing our favorite hero rounding up the villains. Grandmother once made me a cape to leap tall buildings with. It seems everyone preferred being a cowboy rather than an Indian since cowboys were always victorious. Sometimes stories were related to both children and adults at these get-togethers. They were highlighted by refreshments of coffee and sweet bread or fruit pies baked in the outdoor oven. Winter months would most likely include roasted piñon nuts and dried deer meat for all to share. These evening gatherings and the sense of closeness diminished as radios and televisions increased over the following years. It was never to be the same again.

The winter months are among my fondest memories. A warm fire crackled and danced brightly in the fireplace, and the aroma of delicious stew filled our one-room house. The thick adobe was wrapped around the two of us protectingly during the long freezing nights. To me, the house was just right. Grandmother's affection completed the warmth and security I will always remember.

Being the only child at Grandmother's, I had lots of attention and plenty of reasons to feel good about myself. As a pre-schooler, I already had chores of chopping firewood and hauling in fresh water each day. After "heavy work" I would run to her and flex what I was convinced were my gigantic biceps. Grandmother would state that at the rate I was going I would soon attain the status of a man like the adult males in the village. Her shower of praise made me feel like the Mr. Indian Universe of all time. At age five, I suppose I was as close to that concept of myself as anyone.

In spite of her many years, Grandmother was highly active in the village ceremonial setting. She was a member of an important women's society and attended every traditional function, taking me along to many of them. I'd wear one of my colorful shirts she made by hand for just such occasions. Grandmother taught me appropriate behavior at these events. Through modeling she showed me how to pray properly. Barefooted, I greeted the sun each morning with a handful of cornmeal. At night I'd look to the stars in wonderment and let a prayer slip through my lips. On meeting someone, Grandmother would say, "Smile and greet. Grunt if you must, but don't pretend they're not there." On food and material things, she would say, "There is enough for everyone to share and it all comes from above, my child." I learned to appreciate cooperation in nature and with my fellow men early in life. I felt very much a part of the world and our way of life. I knew I had a place in it, and I felt good about it.

And Then I Went to School

At age six, like the rest of the Cochiti six-year-olds that year, I had to begin my schooling. It was a new and bewildering experience—one I will not forget. The strange surroundings, new ideas about time and expectations, and the foreign tongue were at times overwhelming to us beginners. It took some effort to return the second day and many times thereafter.

To begin with, unlike my grandmother, the teacher did not have pretty brown skin and a colorful dress. She wasn't plump and friendly. Her clothes were of one color and drab. Her pale and skinny form made me worry that she was very ill. In the village, being more pale than usual was a sure sign of an oncoming fever or some such disorder. I thought that explained why she didn't have time just for me and the disappointed looks and orders she seemed always to direct my way. I didn't think she was so smart since she couldn't understand my language. Surely that was why we had to "leave our 'Indian' at home." But then I didn't feel so bright either. All I could say in her language was, "Yes, teacher," "My name is Joseph Henry," and "When is lunch?" The teacher's odor took some getting used to also. In fact, many times it made me sick right before lunch. Later I learned from the girls this smell was something she wore called perfume.

An Artificial Classroom

The class, too, had its odd characteristics. It was terribly huge and smelled of medicine like the village clinic I feared so much. The walls and ceiling were artificial and uncaring. They were too far from me and I felt naked. Those fluorescent light tubes made an eerie drone and blinked suspiciously over me, quite a contrast to the fire and sunlight my eyes were accustomed to. I thought maybe the lighting did not seem right because it was man-made, and it wasn't natural. Our confinement to rows of desks was another unnatural demand made on our active little bodies. We had to sit at these hard things for what seemed like forever before relief (recess) came midway through the morning and after-noon. Running carefree in the village and fields was but a sweet memory of days gone by. We all went home for lunch since we lived a short walk from school. It took coaxing, and sometimes bribing, to get me to return and complete the remainder of the school day.

School was a painful experience during those early years. The English language and the new set of values caused me much anxiety and embarrassment. I couldn't comprehend everything that was happening, but I could understand very well when I messed up or wasn't doing so well. Negative messages were communicated too effectively and I became more and more unsure of myself. How I wished I could understand other things in school just as well.

The conflict was not only in school performance but in many other areas of my life as well. For example, many of us students had a problem with head lice due to the "unsanitary conditions in our homes." Consequently, we received a harsh shampooing which was rough on both the scalp and the ego. Cleanliness was crucial, and a washing of this sort indicated to the class that one came from a home setting which was not healthy. I recall one such treatment and afterwards being humiliated before my peers with a statement that I had "She'na" (lice) so tough that I must have been born with them. Needless to say, my Super Indian self-image was no longer intact.

"Leave Your Indian at Home"

My language, too, was questioned right from the beginning of my school career. "Leave your Indian at home!" was like a school trademark. Speaking it accidentally or otherwise was punishable by a dirty look or a whack with a ruler. This reprimand was for speaking the language of my people which meant so much to me. It was the language of my grandmother, and I spoke it well. With it, I sang beautiful songs and prayed from my heart. At that young and tender age, it was most difficult for me to comprehend why I had to part with my language. And yet at home I was encouraged to attend school so that I might have a better life in the future. I knew I had a good village life already, but this awareness dwindled each day I was in school.

As the weeks turned to months, I learned English more and more. It may appear that comprehension would be easier. It got easier to understand, all right. I understood that everything I had, and was a part of, was not nearly as good as the white man's. School was determined to undo me in everything from my sheepskin bedding to the dances and ceremonies which I had learned to have faith in and cherish. One day I dozed off in class after a sacred all-night cere-mony. I was startled awake by a sharp jerk on my ear, and informed coldly, "That ought to teach you to attend 'those things' again." Later, all alone, I cried. I couldn't understand why or what I was caught up in. I was receiving two very different messages; both were intended for my welfare.

Values in lifestyle were dictated in various ways. The Dick and Jane reading series in the primary grades presented me pictures of a home with a pitched roof, straight walls, and sidewalks. I could not identify with these from my Pueblo world. However, it was clear I didn't have these things, and what I did have did not measure up. At night long after Grandmother went to sleep, I would lie awake staring at our crooked adobe walls casting uneven shadows from the light of the fireplace. The walls were no longer just right for me. My life was no longer just right. I was ashamed of being who I was, and I wanted to change right then and there. Somehow it became very important to have straight walls, clean hair and teeth, and a spotted dog to chase after. I even became critical of, and hateful toward, my bony fleabag of a dog. I loved the familiar and cozy environment at Grandmother's house, but now I imagined it could be a heck of a lot better if only I had a white man's house with a bed, a nice couch, and a clock. In schoolbooks, all the child characters ever did was run at leisure after the dog or kite. They were always happy. As for me, all I seemed to do at home was go for buckets of water and cut up sticks for a lousy fire. Didn't the teacher say drinking coffee would stunt my growth? Why couldn't I have a nice tall glass of milk so I could have strong bones and white teeth like those kids in the books? Did my grandmother really care about my well-being?

Torn Away

I had to leave my beloved village of Cochiti for my education beyond six. I left to attend a Bureau of Indian Affairs (BIA) boarding school thirty miles from home. Shined shoes and pressed shirt and pants were the order of the day. I managed to adjust to this just as I had to most of the things the school shoved at me or took away from me. Adjusting to leaving home and the village was tough enough. It seemed the older I got, the further I got from the ways I was so much a part of. Since my parents did not own an automobile, I saw them only once a month when they came in the community truck. They never failed to come supplied with "eats" for me. I enjoyed the outdoor oven bread, dried meat, and tamales they usually brought. It took awhile to get accustomed to the diet of the school. Being in town with strange tribes under one roof was frightening and often very lonely. I longed for my grandmother and my younger brothers and sisters. I longed for my house. I longed to take part in a Buffalo Dance. I longed to be free.

I came home for the four-day Thanksgiving break. At first, home did not feel right anymore. It was much too small and stuffy. The lack of running water and facilities was too inconvenient. Everything got dusty so quickly, and hardly anyone spoke English. It occurred to me then that I was beginning to take on the white man's ways that belittled my own. However, it didn't take long to "get back with it." Once I reestablished my relationships with family, relatives, and friends, I knew I was where I came from. I knew where I belonged.

Leaving for the boarding school the following Sunday evening was one of the saddest events in my entire life. Although I had enjoyed myself immensely the last few days, I realized then that life would never be the same again. I could not turn back the time just as I could not do away with school and the ways of the white man. They were here to stay and would creep more and more into my life. The effort to make sense of both worlds together was painful, and I had no choice but to do so. The schools, television, automobiles, and many other outside ways and values had chipped away at the simple cooperative life I began to grow in. The people of Cochiti were changing. The winter evening gatherings, the exchanging of stories, and even the performing of certain ceremonies were already only a memory that someone commented about now and then. Still, the two worlds were very different and the demands of both were ever present. The white man's was flashy, less personal, but very comfortable. The Cochiti were both attracted and pushed toward these new ways which they had little to say about. There was no choice left but to compete with the white man on his terms for survival. To do that I knew I had to give up part of my life.

Determined not to cry, I left my home that dreadfully lonely night. As I made my way back to school my right hand clutched tightly the mound of corn meal grandmother had placed there and my left hand brushed away a tear.

Ode to the Land

the diné perspective

Luci Tapahonso

When a Diné child is born, part of the birth ritual includes the burying of the umbilical cord outside the family home. This ensures that throughout life, she or he will always return home, that the child will always care for his or her parents and that the child will not wander aimlessly as an adult. Since the Diné emerged from Mother Earth, Nahasdzáán in northwest New Mexico, burying the baby's cord signifies the importance of Nahasdzáán in the child's life, as well as her spiritual role in Diné history. It symbolizes the child's metaphorical and symbolic link to the earth. There are other rituals that emphasize this important concept.

We are taught that our land, Diné Tah or Navajo Country, was specifically created for us. There are many stories, songs and prayers that focus on various aspects of this knowledge. The informal and sometime highly ritualized instruction is integrated into daily life from early childhood. The role of Nahasdzáán is easily understood in most stories, yet is intensely complex in symbolic and sacred terms.

Stories associated with landscape are plentiful and are often told as traveling stories, bedtime or mealtime stories or as part of explaining various characteristics of certain people or places. To be a part of such stories confers a kind of respect, affection and joy in the participants' presence. People of all ages never tire of "hané," the telling and sharing of stories. It is in this spirit that the following stories associated with the specific places in Diné country are presented.

Dzilná'o oditii (Huerfano Mesa)

Dzilná'o oditii is the center mountain of Diné Tah, the doorway to the six sacred places. Many centuries ago, Changing Woman, the most beloved of deities, was raised atop this mesa by First Woman and First Man. She later reared her sons, the Twin Warriors, here. The Holy People lived at Dzilná'o oditii and here the foundations of Diné thinking, knowledge and way of life were established. The presence of these Holy People is powerful on Dzilná'o oditii; the logs from the *hooghans* (hogans) remain, the cistern where Changing Woman bathed her babies remains and the footprints of the giant whom the Twins eventually slew are embedded atop the mesa.

This is considered the "doorway" to the past and to the future. As they created Dzilná'o oditii, the Holy People clothed her in precious fabrics as a symbol of soft goods. Thus, clothes of shiny, soft fabrics are especially valued among the Diné. "We dress as she does," we say. For special events, men and women, as well as the children, dress in velvet blouses and shirts, their silver and turquoise jewelry shines like clear water in a mountain stream. The dark, lush fabric lends an understated elegance to the men's black hats and the smooth, dark hair of the young girls and women. The long-tiered skirts flow soft and shiny. During annual fairs, parades, weddings, school programs and various events, the Diné put on their finest clothes. This is the attire considered to be the real "Navajo look." In doing this, we honor Changing Woman. In doing this, we dress as they have taught us. In doing this, we embody Dzilná'o oditii—the most sacred of places.

Rainbow over Chaco Canyon

In the old stories, the Diné say the Holy People traveled on sunbeams and a rainbow beam. Today, when a rainbow appears after a cleansing rain, it tells us the Holy Ones have returned. They remember and visit their children, those called the "Old Ones," the Anasazi at Chaco Canyon.

When they created this world, Blanca Peak, the sacred mountain in the east, was decorated with a rainbow beam and adorned with white shell and morning light. In the north, Mount Hesperus was fastened to the earth with a rainbow beam and adorned with black jet to represent peace and harmony. Each night, Mount Hesperus urges us to rest. She is our renewal, our rejuvenation. She exists because of the rainbow beam. We exist because of the rainbow beam.

When the Holy People return, they marvel at the growth of new spring plants, revel in the laughter of children splashing in fresh rain puddles and, like us, they inhale deeply the sweet, clean air. A rainbow in the clear sky over Navajo land sparkles with particles of dew, pollen and the blessings of the Holy Ones.

Shiprock (Tsé Bit'a'í)

In one story about Tsé Bit'a'í, huge flying monsters once lived atop the Shiprock pinnacle and they would swoop down, snatching human prey to feed to their babies who remained in the nest. The people lived in fear. Finally, one of the Twin Warriors slew the birds, making it safe for the Diné to live here.

From the west, looking out from the Carriso Mountains, stands Little Shiprock. Shiprock looms in the background. My father was born almost 100 years ago, west of Little Shiprock, at Mitten Rock. This panorama reminds me of his childhood, our parents' first home, and the many relatives who live in the area around Oak Springs and Red Valley.

The vast, beautiful distance is filled with stories of people traveling on horseback across the distance, sometimes in wagons when children were taken to school, and sometimes in backs of pickup trucks filled with laundry and groceries. Always it fills one with a longing for drives that wind around sandstone formations, in and out of valleys, and the car filled with the silence of sleeping passengers, or with music—the radio playing or someone singing old Navajo songs. These drives are for telling stories—old stories of long ago, or maybe about something that happened yesterday. When one has grown up traveling miles and miles to school, work or for groceries, the hours spent driving become a time to share, to laugh, to teach and to simply be together.

I return often to my parents' home on the east side of Shiprock and, in the mornings, I walk through the furrowed fields with Chahbah, the family dog, and in the distance stands Shiprock. It is clothed in a soft, purple glow, majestic against the turquoise sky and surrounded by the dark blue mountain range in the west. As children, we woke to this sight each morning. Shiprock seemed to merge with the edges of our father's fields and so we thought it was part of our land. Each evening, the sunset's brilliant hues turn the huge rock into yellow, orange, red, pink, then purple before darkness moves in and it stands velvet black in the night.

In the darkness, it is easy to imagine huge monster birds perched atop the rock. It is natural to whisper thanks to the Twin Warriors and to Changing Woman for having raised them to be courageous and fearless.

Mount Taylor (Tsoodzit)

More than 100 years ago, as the Diné were returning from imprisonment at Fort Sumner, they wept at the first sight of Mount Taylor. "Now we'll surely make it home," they cried. They were weary from the long journey, but seeing Tsoodzit, the sacred mountain in the south, revived them physically and spiritually. They were strengthened because Tsoodzit represents adolescence—the strongest time of life. Tsoodzit helps us envision our goals and reminds us of our inner strength. Tsoodzit teaches us to believe in all ways of learning.

A stone knife was used to fasten Tsoodzit to the earth, then Tsoodzit was dressed in turquoise to represent the importance of positive thinking. It is the home of several Holy People, including Turquoise Girl and Turquoise Boy. Thus we wear turquoise in their honor, as well as to honor the males in our families.

Today, we tell the story over and over of our forebearers' return from Hweeldi and of all they endured and of the strength Tsoodzit gave them as they approached home.

Narbona Pass

When one travels through this pass, it is easy to imagine the huge sheer cliffs moving together to crush intruders as it was said to have done long ago. When the Twin Warriors went to visit their father, the Sun, they encountered many obstacles. With the help of Spider Woman, they were able to find a strong, unbreakable log to hold the huge rocks apart as they entered and passed through. Since then, the rocks have remained in place, the powerful danger dissipated by the Twin Warriors and the Holy People. The Twins continued on their journey and were eventually reunited with their father, who helped them rid the Earth of several deadly monsters who roamed about freely.

Centuries later, Narbona, an influential Diné leader, was killed in this pass by the United States Cavalry. Narbona had sought peace between the Diné and the U.S. forces, and had brought horses and sheep as part of the ongoing treaty negotiations. Because one of the Diné horses was mistakenly thought to have been stolen, Narbona was shot in the back four times. Six other Diné were also slain. Ironically, Narbona Pass was named "Washington Pass" after Col. John Washington, who had ordered the shooting. It was changed recently to honor Narbona.

Today, as people ski, picnic, hunt and hike in the area they are appreciative of the overwhelming beauty, yet are aware of the historical significance Narbona Pass represents. They tell and retell the stories of the huge rocks and, in doing so, pay homage to the spirits of Narbona and the Twin Warriors.

Diné Tah/Petroglyphs at Diné Tah

At the beginning of Diné time, the Holy People dwelled in Diné Tah. They created the world from this powerful place. But they also hunted, cooked, slept, sang and raised children much as we do today. They constructed the first hooghans—the round-topped female one for everyday living and the cere-monial, forked-top hooghan. There was an abundance of game and plant life at Diné Tah. Fortified structures of mud and stone also were constructed to provide protection from enemy tribes. This is where the foundations of Diné life were established. Indeed, the patterns they set were intricate and complex, yet easy to incorporate into modern life.

Diné Tah is said to embody the beginning of Diné knowledge: our history, language, ceremonies and beliefs. Before they left to live within other sacred mountains, they instructed that drawings be made as a legacy for the present-day Diné. They ensured that the medicine people would have a source of ancient knowledge and it is further evidence of their concern for us.

There are symbols of renderings of ancient ritual masks and symbolic images of various Holy People. There are portrayals of corn, deer and antelope, all life sustaining elements. They range from the earliest of times and end at the time of Spanish and American contact in the mid-16th century.

Sadly, many of the drawings are marred by vandalism today. Nevertheless, as the Diné travel here to pray and sing, the quiet solitude and the powerful presence of the Holy Ones cannot be lessened by modern intrusions. The most sacred of places is made powerful by the history, stories, songs and prayers it contains. As we see this place, it is an experience of awe and gratitude. It is as if the Holy People are physically comforting us, encouraging us, smiling at us, strengthening us. That Diné Tah seems an empty, barren place suits us—we are among the most fortunate people in the world because of it.

"We're Not Extinct"

David Pego

The American Indians who call Texas home have widely different perspectives. Many live in cities, retaining their heritage but blending into the community. Others, such as the Tonkawa tribe from Central Texas, live in reservation-like communities in Oklahoma. And on the three Texas reservations, families struggle to build better lives.

It is hard for some of the 250 descendants of early Central Texans in Tonkawa, Oklahoma, not to hold a grudge about the way their land was taken away.

"I'm a Christian and I should be forgiving," says Vivian Cornell. "But I can't help it. I feel hurt. You would, too, if you were in my shoes."

Cornell, whose feet on this day are shod in colorfully beaded moccasins for a tribal dance, is one of the oldest members of what remains of the once-powerful Tonkawa tribe. At 71, she has heard stories firsthand of the tribe's glory days through the early 1800s, when bands of Tonkawa roamed freely across what is now Central Texas, living off a bountiful land.

Today she and the other Tonkawa live in modest frame and brick homes in a small tribal community near the northern Oklahoma town of Tonkawa, just off Interstate 35. There is little for the families to do other than visit neighbors, shoot baskets at a rusting hoop or watch others chase the American dream on television.

The tribe is virtually unknown to most Central Texans in the 1990s. They may run across the Tonkawa name in a history book or be told that a local site once could have been a Tonkawa encampment, but there are few permanent reminders of the tribe that populated the area for centuries. Artifacts and remains believed to be of Tonkawa origin recently were uncovered near Georgetown. A planned display of that find may help more people learn about the tribe that nearly disappeared after being driven from Texas.

The Tonkawa were among thousands of Indians forced to move into Oklahoma, then called Indian Territory in the late 1800s. After several resettlements, the Tonkawa survivors were given their current land in 1884. Unlike federally administered reservations in other states, Indian property in Oklahoma is owned by individual tribal members and not called a reservation.

In Central and Southeastern Texas, the Tonkawa were classic hunters and gatherers, according to tribal historians, archaeologists and anthropologists. They followed herds of game and made use of whatever grains or other foods they could find. They lived mainly in rounded brush arbors, but some were in the shape of tepees. Some experts believe they also camped under creek-side rock ledges such as the one at McKinney Falls State Park in Austin.

University of Texas archaeologist Thomas Hester says uncovering the ancient history of the Tonkawa and other native Texas tribes is difficult detective work. Information is still being collected from studying Spanish military documents and by closer examination of artifacts, which include a new find at the Sun City Georgetown development. The picture of how the Tonkawa once lived is changing.

Hester says evidence obtained about nine years ago suggests that the Tonkawa came into Texas from Oklahoma during the early 1600s. But he admits it is difficult to tell the difference between various Texas tribes, which often shared utensil production techniques and frequently intermarried.

"The material culture of these tribes is virtually indistinguishable," Hester says.

Tonkawa tribal historian Don Patterson has interviewed elders among his tribe and has read printed accounts by early historians. He bristles at any suggestion that the Tonkawa did not originate in Texas.

"We were in Texas from the Creation until the early 1800s," Patterson says. "There was a book called 'The Indians of Texas.' It was written by an expert on Texas Indians. The author closed a chapter by saying we were extinct. I sent him a letter and said, 'We're not extinct. We have a village up here.' We never heard from anyone about it."

"I'm the expert," stresses Patterson. "It's like asking if Jane Goodall is the expert or the chimpanzee. The chimpanzee is going to know more about himself than Jane Goodall ever will know."

W. W. Newcomb Jr., a retired professor and former director of the Texas Memorial Museum at UT, wrote the 1961 book that Patterson was talking about—*The Indians of Texas from Prehistoric to Modern Times*. He says today that a lot of the earlier assumptions about the Tonkawa and other Texas tribes "were in part guesswork."

"Slowly and surely, we're getting a more accurate picture," Newcomb says.

Still, that picture is coming without any contact with the Tonkawa. Neither Hester nor Newcomb ever have talked to tribal members.

"The modern Tonkawa have no more knowledge of their past than anybody else," Hester says. "Sometimes, they have folktales or stories about the past. But it's like everyone else's folktales. You can't take them to be 100 percent accurate."

Return to Texas?

Members of the tribe have mixed feelings about whether they would like to return to Texas someday to live, although 20 years ago they went to the federal Indian Land Claims Commission to try to gain back some of their land. Those efforts failed.

"If it's ours I'd like some of it back," says 63-year-old Bernice Sands.

Her friend, Barbara Allen, wonders what the tribe would do with the land. "Most of the people around here have no desire to be back in Texas," she says. "We've been down there two or three times. Some of them [Texans] still think we're extinct."

The Tonkawa people are far from extinct, but they are not exactly flourishing in their new home, either. Their community is called Fort Oakland and is a hand-me-down from the Nez Percé tribe, which found a way to return in the late 1800s to their own homelands in what is now Idaho.

More than half of the Tonkawa adults are jobless. Tribal President Richard Cornell, the 37-year-old son of Vivian Cornell, said the tribe is negotiating with several companies to bring manufacturing to the community, but so far nothing has worked. The latest effort has been a series of negotiations with a boat manufacturing company.

A bingo operation has not been seriously considered by the tribe because of the sparsely populated area around the village and because so many other Indian communities in the state already have bingo games.

This year federal budget writers have targeted Indian programs for cuts of nearly 20 percent, despite promises of "eternal training" and assistance outlined in various treaties.

"We're really feeling the pinch in education," says Cornell, although he adds that cuts could affect many programs. "We don't know the bottom line yet."

Ribbons Replace Scalps

Nonetheless, the Tonkawa are proud of advances that have been made since they were forced out of Central Texas. Even younger adults recall days when the tribe had no indoor toilets and everyone had to bathe in small, hand-filled tubs. Just a few decades ago, some families were relying on coal-oil lamps for lighting and hung meat to dry because of a lack of refrigeration.

Today, there are satellite TV dishes outside several of the homes that dot the Fort Oakland community. It is amazing progress for a tribe that was down to only 72 people in 1900.

"We were almost wiped out," Cornell says.

Although the tribe survived, almost all of their culture has been extinguished.

"It's probably 99 and 44/100ths gone," says Marilyn Cornell, 50, who is the tribal president's sister.

She says the Tonkawa have revived the Scalp Dance ceremony, in which women dance around a drum and celebrate the victory of the men by raising scalps of the enemy to the heavens. These days, ribbons are used instead of scalps. Other adaptations also are made. Because Marilyn cannot afford buckskin for dance moccasins she fashions them out of a thick velour cloth.

"They look like the real thing from a distance," she says, smiling and winking quickly.

The tribe used to have strong traditions involving almost every aspect of life. For example, says Allen Cornell, who is Richard's brother, no one would eat after dark because it was believed that you would get sick if you did. Also, people who left food out on the table would place a knife gently over the top of it to keep evil spirits away. Only a few practice such traditions today.

Fewer still remember any of the Tonkawa language. The last remnants of it were literally buried in the late 1960s along with the last fluent speaker. Tribal members then were so grieved at the loss that they cast the last remaining audio tapes of people singing in their old language into the casket, and the language was lost under the red-tinged Oklahoma soil.

Indian Artifacts at Sun City

The tribe is doing what little it can to restore its traditions. Patterson makes occasional trips to Austin to study more about the tribe in early Texas historical accounts at UT libraries. He also visited Central Texas recently to meet with officials of the Del Webb Corp.'s Sun City Georgetown.

When housing construction began in the huge retirement development last year, bulldozers uncovered caves with Indian remains and artifacts. The bones, arrowheads, stone tools and pottery fragments were collected and the Tonkawa tribe was contacted. The remains have been given to the Tonkawa, and the artifacts are being prepared for display at Sun City's visitors' center.

The Tonkawa hope to attend the Nov. 2 Austin Independent School District Powwow and American Indian Heritage Festival, which officials at several education organizations believe may be the nation's largest public school event not related to sports. Organizers of the powwow had invited Tonkawa representatives to attend last year and had offered them financial assistance to make the visit, but a snag developed.

"We didn't have one single reliable car on the entire reservation that could have made the trip," Richard Cornell recalls.

A handful of Austin residents made their biggest impact on the Tonkawa community last December after a tribal official informally asked the city for help. "The kids were going to have a skimpy Christmas," said Melissa Cornell, Allen's wife and coordinator of the tribe's substance abuse programs.

A truckload of toys, T-shirts, turkeys and holiday goodies donated by Austin area residents was sent to the Tonkawa. The effort was organized by David Rockwood, who works in marketing for the Chuy's restaurant chain.

"It was our best Christmas ever," Melissa Cornell remembers.

The tribe remains hopeful that the future holds more memorable days. Members are trying as best they can to come to terms with all they have lost.

"It's OK," says Vivian Cornell. "We've learned to live the white man's way."

And someday, she says, she is hoping for a miracle. When the Tonkawa were moved to Oklahoma a second time after returning to Texas during the Civil War, some of the tribe bolted and escaped as the others were crossing the Red River. Vivian Cornell says she has no idea whether those lost Tonkawa fled into Mexico or found a quiet corner of Texas in which to live.

"Someday I'd like to go to Texas and be reunited with them," she says. "Now wouldn't that be something?"

PART IV

Hispano-Mestizo America

In purely chronological terms, the Spanish/Mexican legacy represents the second major cultural element that defines the Southwest. Meinig describes the region as a zone of interaction and interrelatedness among Native Americans, Hispanics, and Anglos. A homeland for Mexican Americans, the Southwest encompasses what historians have labeled the Spanish/Mexican Borderlands. Two decades before the Mexican American civil rights movement of the 1960s, Carey McWilliams recognized the roots of the mestizo experience in the Southwest. McWilliams asserted that "the Spanish-speaking have an identification with the Southwest which can never be broken. They are not interlopers or immigrants but an indigenous people."[1] At present, nearly two-thirds of the Mexican Americans reside in the five southwestern states: Texas, New Mexico, Arizona, Colorado, and California, an area Spanish speakers consider their traditional region of settlement. The experience of this group is also of long standing in the region and is best expressed in the Spanish word *querencia*, that is, an enduring love and respect for land, home, and community.

New Mexico's Spanish-speaking group, the Hispanos, have shared their struggle for survival with their Pueblo neighbors. In no other part of the Southwest do Indian and Hispanic peoples seem so much alike, living as they do in close proximity, eating similar foods, residing in parallel village systems, revering shared sacred sites and landscapes; yet, paradoxically, nowhere else do they hold so tightly to their identities as distinct peoples.

Endnote

1. Carey McWilliams, *North from Mexico: The Spanish-Speaking People of the Southwest* (1948; reprint, New York: Greenwood Press, 1968), p. 9.

Milo Maizes

Fabiola Cabeza de Baca

The rain ceased after three days of good drenching and the land took on a new aspect. In a week, the grass seemed to have grown inches and the cattle were happily grazing and putting on slick covers on their bodies. Ours was a happy household!

The ground became dry enough for the boys to resume their daily labors and Papá at breakfast was making plans with El Cuate and the boys for the day's work.

"We shall start fencing on the Pajarito today," he said to the boys. "Cuate, you and Luis will go with me to survey the land, while Pedro and Nereo haul the wire and posts. It will be several days before we will be ready for them, but you can start digging the post holes."

I was delighted, for I would ride out and explore new country. Contrary to Spanish custom, Papá always allowed me to go wherever he or Luis went. The men were always kind and I ruled the rancho like a queen during my summer vacations. There was so much unwritten history of the Llano, and as I rode out in the pastures, ruins of houses and chapels made me wish they could speak so that they might tell of the life of the inhabitants who had dwelt within. But they were silent and I had to create in my mind imaginary characters living in these lonely ranchos. Yet they may not have been lonely; there may have been much gaiety and real living with nothing to disturb their tranquillity.

The country not only held in secret the lives of the Spanish colonists, but of the Indians who thousands of years before had inhabited the land. There were the petroglyphs depicting human figures, animals and other signs. What did they mean? In my mind, I would decipher the figures to give directions towards where the enemy were encamped or where there was a spring of clear water for the nomads—or were they nomads? I would often picture villages of happy primitive people living abundantly from the soil with no destructive civilization to mar their joyful lives. I lived in the past as I roamed the range and studied the petroglyphs. These may have been relatively recent, for in the rocks were deep grooves where the women ground the maize into meal.

My brother and I hunted for arrowheads and other artifacts and these we found in profusion. Luis has a fine collection of arrowheads, scrapers, awls, points, axes and grindstones, and all these were found in our pastures or within a radius of fifty miles.

While the men were fencing, I was free to wander into secluded canyons and caves and to acquaint myself with the wonders of a country new to me. Yet those before us certainly had known it well but had left few records for posterity.

We had to fence our lands, for the country was being settled, and where once the boundaries over which our cattle grazed had been the earth's horizon, now we were being pushed in and in, until it became necessary to build fences.

In the pre-Hispanic era, the Llano Indians walked—with the Spaniards came horses and the life of the Indians changed. Then came Ciboleros using *carretas* pulled by oxen to go into the Llano for their meat supply, and later wagons with horses began to wind their way over the Llano's rough roads.

The railroad came through Las Vegas in 1879, and the Santa Fe Trail, with its caravans of ox wagons, passed into history. The Plains Indians were on reservations and life became tame for the New Mexicans who had traveled over the trail. Las Vegas became an important railroad center, but it also continued to be the market for sheep, cattle, wool and hides from the Llano country.

Over the Vega Hill, where Señor Mariano daily played host to travelers, came hundreds of wagons to trade in the Meadow City, yet many of the sheep and cattle from the Llano were driven to Liberal, Kansas, where the Rock Island Railroad had its terminal. From Liberal the stock was shipped to Kansas City, St. Joseph and Chicago.

In 1900 the Rock Island was being built across the Llano country, and by 1901 it had reached Santa Rosa, where it connected with the El Paso and Southwestern to El Paso, Texas.

The land of the Comanches and the Ciboleros underwent great changes in the years 1900 and 1901. The Rock Island gave contracts for the building of its lines. Camps dotted the Llano country from Kansas into New Mexico. These camps were a bedlam of foreigners, where many tongues were spoken. There were Italians, Austrians, Greeks, Slavs, Chinese, Negroes, Mexicans and, of course, Americans.

Men were killed by rocks from blasting, and it is rumored that many a man lies buried in the fills of the roadbeds.

On the Pajarito ranch of Don Nicasio Cabeza de Baca, my late uncle, one of these camps was located. There was a commissary in each camp, but there were many articles which were not carried in their stock. My uncle took advantage of the opportunity and set up a store in which he carried clothing and food.

The Italian workers had great confidence in him and when payday came, they turned over their money to him. He took it into Las Vegas for deposit in the bank, and a great deal of it he sent to the families of the workers. My aunt, Doña Isabel Stephens, Don Nicasio's wife, tells that when the money started rolling in, she feared a holdup, since there were many bad men among the workers. Until Don Nicasio was ready for the one-hundred-mile trip to Las Vegas, she kept the money in her baby's carriage under the mattress. They did not have a safe and she felt that no one would think of disturbing the baby if someone came to rob them.

There were two really bad characters in the camp, and these were a Filipino and a Mexican. One morning, as Don Nicasio started on his monthly journey to Las Vegas, he saw two men standing on either side of the road, a mile or so from the camp. It was still dark, but he recognized them as the Filipino and the Mexican of bad repute. Don Nicasio always carried a gun by his side, and before the desperados had a chance to point their guns, he had his in his hand. He ordered them to move on. Don Nicasio was not alone in his carriage, a niece was riding with him to Las Vegas. Perhaps the criminals did not recognize in the darkness that the person was a woman, for they quickly disappeared.

Many incidents happened in the year that the camp was located on the de Baca ranch, but considering the many hundreds of laborers and no officers of the law, it was quite peaceful.

A young man from St. Louis, Missouri, who came from a wealthy and influential family, strayed into the camp as a laborer. He was refined and highly educated and why he was there, no one knew. One day, while working, the foreman of the crew became angry at him because he did not work as fast as the other laborers. The foreman used a horsewhip on him. The boy swore that he would have revenge. That night he decided to avenge his wrong, and knowing where the foreman was lodged, he approached the tent. It happened that, for one reason or another, the foreman had changed tents and the boy shot the wrong man, an Italian worker. The boy hid in some caves in the nearby hills and there his buddies supplied him with food and water. There was a search for him, but he remained safe in his hiding place until the first flatcars rolled over the tracks. One evening, one of his buddies came to pick up the boy's baggage at the de Baca home, where he always kept it. No one ever heard about the mysterious boy again. Mrs. de Baca says that the boy's luggage was of the most expensive type of its day and often, when the boy came to the house to get clothing, she noticed that his clothes were such as only the wealthy could afford.

The workers lived in tents and the camp manager with his family lived in a dugout which he built for their abode. The Italian workers were very economical and usually saved all of their wages. They lived on bread, rabbits and tea made from snake brush (*Gutierreza teunis*). They used milk in their tea for extra nourishment. Ruins of the mud ovens which the Italians built for baking bread can still be seen on the old de Baca homestead.

The land on the Llano is not for the tenderfoot, and an incident which happened at the camp proves it: A young easterner came as office secretary and on the first night of his arrival, a thunderstorm, such as can be experienced only on the Llano, struck the area. Lightning and thunder, followed by a cloudburst, kept him awake in his tent all night. In the morning, as he was rolling up his bed, two rattlesnakes were coiled under it. He took the next stagecoach for other terrain.

At the time the railroad was in process of construction, the Mesa Redonda (Round Mesa) Brothers, notorious bandits, were making stops at the camps all along the way, robbing and pillaging. On one occasion, two of them stopped at the de Baca store, where they bought lunch goods. No one could have picked them out as lawbreakers, for they had pleasing personalities. They wore elegant clothes and their fingers shone with diamonds. They must have been bold to make their appearance in broad daylight where they planned to make a holdup. They were heavily armed. That evening they held up a Mr. Buckley, who had charge of the camp commissary, and got away with more than three thousand dollars. To the de Bacas they were friendly and left them unmolested, although there they could have found more money than in the railroad commissary.

These bandits lived on Mesa Redonda, just over the bluffs of the Staked Plains. The flat top of the mesa is extensive, comprising ten thousand acres or perhaps more. There the bandits kept stolen cattle, horses and other loot. It is very rugged with only one or two accessible places and these the brothers kept carefully guarded. They lived there from 1901 until 1907, when the homesteaders began to populate the country. On top of the mesa, there are several natural lakes and *aguajes*, water holes, which made it very convenient for the robbers to live unmolested.

After the coming of the railroad, many towns sprang up along the way over the Ceja and across the Llano. Tucumcari, today one of New Mexico's larger cities, came into being because of the railroad. Santa Rosa was, because of its location, the logical point for the railroad shops—and they were built there. But, unfortunately, the hard water of the Pecos River at this point was not usable for the desired purpose and Tucumcari profited from Santa Rosa's misfortune.

Santa Rosa and Tucumcari grew into towns and many small towns benefited by the coming of the Nesters, at least for the duration of the influx of the homesteaders. Montoya, named after the Pablo Montoya Grant and situated within its boundaries, was an important trading center for some twenty years. The few cattle and sheep owners, the homesteaders and railroad section hands living on the Ceja, traded in Montoya. There was a large general store, several smaller ones, a drug store, two hotels, a three-room public school, a newspaper, a land office, a country doctor, one or two Protestant churches, and the one Roman Catholic chapel—which still exists and is a *visita* of the Tucumcari parish. Montoya was a busy place while the money of the homesteaders lasted and until the droughts put the stockmen out of business. Today, Montoya is a ghost town and survives only because of U.S. Highway 66 and the few railroad section hands who make up its population.

Cuervo, another railroad station, is the trading center for the ranchers from Garita, Cuervo Creek and others who are running sheep and cattle in the surrounding country.

The people of the vast Conchas country—which lies northeast of Cuervo Creek—formerly traded in Las Vegas. After the coming of the railroad over the Llano they turned to Cuervo and Santa Rosa for the shipping of their wool, sheep and cattle.

The decision of the courts about land grants, the coming of the homesteaders, the railroad over the Llano and the building of highways caused a transition in the history of the Ceja and the Llano. Amarillo and Tucumcari grew into cities and Las Vegas remained static, contented with one main highway and the crossing of the Santa Fe railroad through its boundaries. Many of its inhabitants little know that once it was the largest trading center in the vast state of New Mexico.

With the coming of the railroad over the Llano, immigration started. Caravans of covered wagons dotted the country over the buffalo and Comanche trails. Another people came to settle where once the New Mexicans of Spanish extraction had lived, where they had found the promised land for their flocks and herds. Gone were the sheep and only a few cattle ranches remained.

Papá was unhappy as he saw the shacks of the newcomers rise on the acres which had been his pastures.

Papá was in good humor when we started out one day, but as we reached the place where they were going to start surveying, his mood changed, for just a quarter of a mile from his boundary line, a wooden cabin had gone up overnight and then Papá was infuriated.

Angrily, he alighted from the wagon and turned to El Cuate, saying:

"If those 'Milo Maizes' have put their house on my land, they shall rue the day they came here. They will ruin the land for grazing and they will starve to death; this is not farming land."

"Calm down, Papá," I said. "Wait until you find your boundaries and then get angry. These people have a right to file on the land. You have always owned land, thousands of acres; they are entitled to their half section."

"No one has a right to ruin pasture land and those idiots in Washington, who require that they break eighty acres for farming, are to blame for these poor fools destroying the land. It is a crime for these misguided people to try to make a living in a country that does not have enough rain for growing crops," Papá answered.

I felt sorry for the homesteaders. Young as I was, I realized that they could not make the land provide them with even a meager living. I had grown up with a ranch background, where sheep and cattle furnished our livelihood, and I knew the hard times Papá and Grandfather had endured in order to survive. Then, we had control of the land, and only that had saved us from destruction. I knew that, along with the "Nesters," we were due for a transition. They could not exist from farming and we could not increase our herds in the land that was left for grazing. Papá had been resourceful and had acquired all the patented land available, school sections and what he could file for a homestead, but this was not enough. We had to think of droughts and when they occurred we had no lands toward which the cattle could be moved. On the Llano, unless it is very unusual, droughts are not general; there are always spots where it rains when others are dry. In one's pastures there are rainy and dry spots, and the pioneer sheep and cattlemen knew them.

In 1901, after the coming of the railroad, the Rock Island line promoted colonization into the land it traversed over the Cap Rock. Chartered immigrant cars brought a big colony of Iowa farmers. In the cars came draft horses, farming implements, dairy cows and household furnishings. These people were good farmers, but the Llano country was not farming land. The horses did not become accustomed to the country and neither did the dairy cattle. The Iowans built good substantial homes, but their endurance soon gave out and in order to prove up on the land, they commuted for $1.25 per acre. In three or four years, all but a handful moved to other states or went back to their homeland. Papá liked these Iowans and counted them among his best friends. He bought a great many acres from them upon their departure.

When the Enlarged Homestead Act was passed, families from Texas, Oklahoma, Arkansas and other Southern states began to look towards New Mexico as the land of promise. These families had been sharecroppers or tenant farmers in their own states and to own the land was their most cherished dream. By saving and skimping, they accumulated two or three hundred dollars in cash. With a wagon, a team of horses, chickens, possibly a milk cow and their household goods, they joined other caravans and the march started toward the Utopia of their dreams.

Lent in El Paso, Texas

Alicia Gaspar de Alba

blows forty days
of dust-devils

lentil soup
capirotada

and the daily litany
of wind across the city.

Afternoons, the cottonwoods
tumble like sagebrush

the ocotillos creak
like crucifixes

and women walk
with their buttocks

tucked in tight
under their skirts.

All along the border
the river speaks

in wild tongues
the voices of the penitent

ululate in jail cells
and confessionals

and women weep
for their murdered sons.

At night the litany stills
on the branches and the grass

rises again, dazed
after the whipping

but stronger and more alive.
In El Paso the wind of Lent

blows forty faithful days
without contrition.

Sunday Mass

María Herrera-Sobek

Sunday
was a time for misa
my wispy hand in yours
we walked the cobblestones.

"Oh dear, we are too early
the Anglo mass is on."

We wait our turn
The Mexican store
offers us quick shelter
from the onslaught
of our thoughts:
caramelos
colaciones
chocolates.

Sweet nothings
for our battered souls
It's ten o'clock
your forehead
sprinkled with
summer heat
begins to rain.

It's time to enter
the Mexican mass begins.

A house divided
by the colors of the rainbow
White Brown Black
Do not disturb the universe.
The blue-eyed God
wants it so.

Sombras de la Jicarita

Gabriel Meléndez

La Jicarita Peak, twelve thousand feet in the air; *xumatl*, the sky bowl of our indomitable spirit.
La cumbre de la Jicarita, doce mil pies sobre el nivel de mar; xumatl, el jumate celeste de nuestro espíritu indomable.

I

Most certainly, we have never thought to discard the litany of ancestral souls that accompanies the birth of each person born at the foot of La Jicarita Peak, nor can we neglect the accompanying clamor of a multitude of voices that impregnates the very air we breathe and is with us at each moment of the day and of the night. Our ancestors are the unseen visitors that sit at our kitchen tables when we speak of the past; they are the ancestral countenance that we believe we've recognized on the faces of strangers that we pass on the street. Now they are the elongated shadows that move in the old abandoned patios and the unearthed bones that walk the earth and do not know eternal rest or peace.

II

In late summer, rain clouds thicken quickly on the ridgeline of the sierra and the distant rumble of their thunder echoes endlessly in the mountain canyons and in the tall stands of spruce until, like the water in the river, the sound ebbs its way out to the open llanos to the east. As the Valley fills with a gray light, the animals feel the air tingle across their spines: yellow house cats jump suddenly from the windowsills lined with coffee cans potted in geraniums; village dogs creep under the porch steps or find the last dark corner of the storeroom to hide from the storm; young mares and stallions race along the pasture lands to the river bank, their nostrils flaring, their manes flying in the air, the mirrored image of the fields caught in the obsidian light of their frightened eyes. Fire dances everywhere on the mountain and lightning cracks the skies. The mountain's fire flashes like a knife blade through the crisp air above the deep green of the scrub oak.

This kind of lightning has broken the backs of prize bulls grazing in the high pastures, leaving their carcasses bowed and bloated in the middle of boggy meadows; it has split open the massive trunks of conifer trees and left the forest smoldering from blackened wounds in the earth; it has caught unfortunate stockmen crossing barbed wire fences on their way to shelter and left them dangling there like fish on a trout line. The rising waters of the downpours that follow, rushing down the mountain, have swept away young calves, have cut apple orchards and beanfields in two; have washed away bridges lifting them like tiny wooden boats on the swell of their crested muddy waters, and have snuffed out the life's breath of infant children caught with their parents midstream in old model-T Fords. The memory of such mishaps is held in the gaze of the old people of the Valley, like the yellowed news clippings of defunct newspapers pressed into the pages of family Bibles.

The old people have known the delicate dance of the Earth's elements: wind, fire and water. They've seen the changing masks of life and death, and death and life, on the face of each new day's horizon. When the storms appear and the fury of the mountain sounds, the old women step out in the rushing wind, their long gray hair filled with electricity, and they cut at the clouds with long kitchen knives and cast salt to the four directions of the wind and they chant the song of lives upon lives of endless memory: "Santa Bárbara *doncella, líbranos del rayo de la centella.*" Then the flashing light and the windblown shadows of the clouds dance about the fields and above the rusted tin roofs of the village and through the cottonwoods along the river, flashing off windowpanes recessed deep in timeless adobe walls. Many people swear to have seen the shadows of the dead in this half light, moving through the open doorways of the old abandoned houses, walking silently behind the tongued flames of oil lamps into the inner rooms where they are lost from sight. Are they dancing in the dark? Are they praying at their altars in the dim glow of candles? Are they covering the mirrors with black cloths to draw away the lightning? Are they the half-clothed bony skeletons of lovers locked in loving embraces, awaiting their turn at life again?

III

Oh, I think it was about one-thirty, just after the noon hour, and as I got up to put away the dishes, the washcloth fell from my hand and I thought to myself, surely someone is going to visit me. Well, ten minutes hadn't gone by when I heard a knock, first at the window and then later at the screen door. I looked out but I saw nothing. I suppose the neighbor here is nailing a board or something around by his house, I thought, and I even called out, "Hey, friend, what the devil are you up to?" and since I didn't hear anyone answer me, I sat down again and picked up a book I have here about Vicente Silva's gang of bandits and then, again, after only a short time I heard a knock, but this time it was very loud and I heard what sounded like rocks rolling off the tin roof and, by God, just then the screen door opened wide and I felt a cold chill in the air and that's when I saw her. There was no doubt about it. It was my comadre Petra, just as she had been in life, though not old as she had become in recent years. It was Petra as she was when we were young and her eyes were full of fire. And I heard her call out in a very low and serene voice as if she were very far away, "Ay, dear one, the joy of my youth." Because, you know, my comadre Petra loved me very deeply. Now I'm sure she came that afternoon to take her leave because she had never forgotten me. They say that she cried as if her heart was about to burst when I was first sent to the war in France. When I came back and they had already married her to the now deceased Don Benito Sánchez, what could be done? But she often thought of me and never forgot the times we had as lovers. Oh yes, I knew her as a man knows a woman way before Don Benito and as the song goes, "Oh what times those were my friend, Señor Simón." We shared nights when we didn't sleep and we romped in bed like wolves in heat until the first light of day scratched the sky. It must be as they say, my friend, the blood is known to boil, the blood is known to boil. The next day after Petra's visit, my cousin Evaristo Trujillo came to tell me that Petra had died over in Las Golondrinas that previous afternoon and that she had been in her agony for a long time. Evaristo took it upon himself to let me know because having attended to her in the last hours, he had heard her call out, "Ay, Manuel, my dear one, the joy of my youth!" Oh yes my friend, that's exactly how these things are.

MexAmerica

Joel Garreau

Richard Milhous Nixon always liked Coronado Island, and no wonder. It would take an incomprehensible hardening of the soul not to feel a surge of gratitude toward the Pacific Ocean for creating the beaches, waves, and breezes that give the island what is possibly the finest year-round climate in North America.

But perhaps more important to him, the island, just an hour south of San Clemente, is full of the former president's kind of people. Many of San Diego's financial heavies live on Coronado Island. Half-million-dollar condominiums are taken for granted along this beach. The houses there are the kind, like Nixon's old Casa Pacifica, that, when put up for sale, are offered through special agencies that would never think of advertising in a mere newspaper.

And Coronado Island's political views are consistent with the cash value of its ocean views. Not far from here, a successful candidate for office once proclaimed, less than half-jokingly, that he'd joined the Orange County John Birch Society in order to capture the middle-of-the-road vote.

Contributing to the sense of righteousness on the island is the plethora of retired admirals who live there. Coronado Island is the sunsetward-most piece of bread in a sandwich, the meat being San Diego Harbor, and the eastern layer being the mainland and the city of San Diego. The marvelous harbor that Coronado Island protects from the western waves is the home of the Seventh Fleet. There's more retired Navy brass in the San Diego area than anywhere else on earth.

For them, one of the nice things about living on Coronado Island, if they can afford it, is the great view of the ships you can get from the San Diego–Coronado Bridge. Row upon row of mammoth hulls are tied up to the mainland: destroyers, frigates, tankers, freighters, troopships, aircraft carriers. Lost in a thicket of radar, the ships fade into their field of gray paint, incongruous in the land of fierce sun and bright colors.

The reason the view of the fleet is so good is that the San Diego–Coronado Bridge is so high. Because the bridge was engineered to ensure that all future floating war behemoths, no matter how conceivably large, could glide under the span on their way to make Asia safe for democracy, the approaches have to start lifting off almost a mile inland. If they did not get a running jump on the harbor, which is not all that wide, the roadways could not achieve the proper altitude while maintaining the sweeping French curves of the classic California freeway—curves that resemble a flight path more than a roadway.

There's little way to overemphasize the importance of preserving the geometry of these boring, banked curves. The pace of the Southern California autobahn is exact. On these fast, crowded roads, one changes lanes with precision, courage, and nonchalance, or one spends an inordinate amount of time in fear. Surprises are not welcome or expected. The freeway is especially not a good place for a rich, conservative Anglo to confront, on his way home, a twenty-foot-tall brown man with a book in one hand and one very big hammer in the other.

Victor Orozco Ochoa knows that well. As the mural coordinator of Chicano Park for ten years, he smiles as he thinks of the unsuspecting Republican whose car, climbing the bridge to Coronado under cruise control, is about to bring its driver face to face with the stunning giant, only one of dozens of huge, vibrant images painted on the concrete pylons supporting the on-ramps. Orozco Ochoa gets a kick out of the way Barrio Logan, the community that lives under the approaches to the San Diego–Coronado Bridge, and that created the murals of Chicano Park, startles Anglos from time to time.

It's not as if the Anglos don't have it coming.

They started the whole thing back in the sixties. That's when the city fathers of San Diego decided that a bridge to speed the affluent to their Coronado homes from downtown was a good idea, and that ripping out a long swath of a down-at-the-heels part of the city in the process was an even better one.

The hitch was that what the Anglos saw as a blighted area given over to junkyards, sandblasting, and arc-welding shops, Mexican-Americans who lived there saw as their homes and their jobs. More than that, it was their "barrio," and a barrio is not the same thing as a ghetto. It means neighborhood, but often is translated as community, and a community is not something you flee, much less casually tear down.

But the voice of the Mexican-American community was not loud then, and even if it had been, the Anglos at that time were not disposed to listen, so the bridge to Coronado began to take shape. All the people of the barrio had to show for it was what they thought was the following understanding: after the construction was finished, the neighborhood kids would be allowed to play in the shadow of the bridge, on the land that had been cleared for the tall support towers.

It's never been made completely clear what led the city to try to build on that land a parking lot for the much-hated police, rather than a playground. But there's no doubt it was a spectacularly inept move, with a predictable outcome. There was an uprising. The fragmented, acquiescent community of Logan Heights suddenly found an issue around which it could coalesce. In defiance of the city, hundreds of Mexican-Americans attacked the construction-scarred land with shovels, picks, wheelbarrows, and hand labor, making the land a park hospitable for people, not cop cars, and vowing violence if anybody tried to stop them.

And so was born Chicano Park, which today, almost a decade later, is a quiet, grassy, pleasant spot, with basketball hoops, a small open stage shaped like an Aztec temple, and a forest of these strange urban "trees," the size of sequoias, made out of T-shaped concrete, supporting five "vines" of multilevel, twisting, curling freeways high above your head leading from Interstate 5.

It's weird, standing in this park on a sunny Sunday afternoon surrounded by these Stonehenge-like monuments, gazing up at tiny cars whizzing past with tiny passengers in them. It's clear there are physically two worlds in operation here. One, in the park, is on foot, relaxed, girl-watching, having quiet conversation. The other is fifty feet straight up—directly over the heads of playing children—screaming past, encased in Detroit iron, with its thoughts definitely elsewhere, probably not even aware the road has left the ground.

It's surreal even without the mammoth murals, which from ground to highway completely obliterate the grayness of the concrete in eye-socking acrylics the color of sun-brightened stained glass.

And these murals are dizzying. On one side of a column, there is a thirty-foot-tall Virgin of Guadalupe, the brown-skinned Madonna who, 450 years ago, only a few years after the Spanish started their New World conquest, appeared to an illiterate Mexican Indian with the revolutionary message that the poor were her people, whom she would protect. Her image is inextricably, and purposefully, bound to the flip side of the pillar, on which is a stylized rendition of the pagan earth goddess Tonantzin, whose veneration the Virgin superseded.

Serpents rear their heads on these murals and scream in a style reminiscent of the horse in Picasso's *Guernica*. The snake was venerated by the Central American Indians, to the horror of the first padres, who saw it as a symbol of evil. But to the Indians, the earth was holy, and the snake was the being always closest to it, and as a result, he was a symbol of wisdom.

A thoughtful mural dedicated to a gunned-down farm laborer depicts, in Dali-like fashion, stoop-laborers chained to the cornucopias of vegetable crates they fill.

On another column Cuauhtémoc, the last emperor of the Aztec, and an eagle both fall. The artist has played complicated tricks with perspective and light to make his point about the ancestor of today's Chicanos.

And all the while, the cars roar overhead, on the way to Coronado Island.

The murals of Chicano Park are in a strange space, existing, as they do, in two such different worlds. On the one hand, though fastidious art magazines rave about them, Anglos, flashing by on the interstates, usually experience them unexpectedly, and in the blink of an eye.

On the other hand, they are statements made by hundreds of ordinary people, immigrants or children of immigrants, many of whom have not yet learned to speak English, but who, painting in groups, express themselves vividly, and with complexity of image, variety of style, and great technical ability, on the concrete of a civil works project even the Toltec would have considered to be of grand scale.

In a way, this strange space exists all over the North American Southwest, for the Southwest is now what all of Anglo North America will soon be—a place where the largest minority will be Spanish-speaking. It's a place being inexorably redefined—in terms of language, custom, economics, television, music, food, politics, advertising, employment, architecture, fashions, and even the pace of life—by the ever-growing numbers of Hispanics in its midst. It is becoming MexAmerica.

"A binational, bicultural, bilingual regional complex or entity is emerging in the borderlands," wrote the late Carey McWilliams, historian and editor of *The Nation*. "Nothing quite like this zone of interlocking economic, social and cultural interests can be found along any other border of comparable length in the world."

MexAmerica is most evident along the 1,933-mile border that the United

States shares with Mexico, but it is highly visible as well in such diverse non-border cities as Los Angeles, Phoenix, Albuquerque, Santa Fe, Pueblo, San Antonio, Austin, and Houston.

Los Angeles is not only the second-largest metropolitan area in the United States; it's the second-largest Mexican city in the world, after Mexico City, with at least 1.5 million American citizens of Mexican heritage, and an estimated half-million more illegal immigrants. In San Antonio, the tenth-largest city in the United States, there are already fewer Anglos than there are Tejanos, as some Texans of Mexican descent like to call themselves.

Within the borders of MexAmerica, the approximately eight million Mexican-American United States citizens—not counting illegals—vastly out-number blacks, Asians, and all other minorities, reaching statewide levels as high as 36 percent. Some estimates have been published saying that as early as 1985, the Spanish-surnamed population of the United States—including people from the Caribbean, and Central and South America, but predominantly Mexi-cans and Mexican-Americans—is expected to outnumber the thirty million blacks in the United States.

Over one hundred million federal dollars are spent in the United States each year on bilingual education. Much of the money is spread throughout the Southwest, teaching Spanish to Anglos, and English to Mexican-Americans, with the goal of making students fluent in both. The face of the future can be seen in the kindergartens of Los Angeles, where the majority of the kids claim Spanish as their first language. Busing to enforce racial integration is hampered in portions of L.A. because there simply are not enough Anglos to go around.

In Houston, a Parisian restaurant advertised its crepes as "French en-chiladas." In San Antonio, cigarette billboards urge you to *Saberro* [savor] *Salem*. In a suburb of Phoenix, street signs read Avenida del Yaqui and Calle Sahuan. In Los Angeles, Coors is advertised as *cerveza* as often as it's advertised as beer.

Western Union is diligent in supplying services in Spanish, if for no other reason than that billions of dollars in money orders are sent to relatives in Mexico by workers in the United States every year. Even Datsun advertises in Spanish, following the lead of the Bank of America.

The growing Mexican influence is evident in food, fashion, and music. Dos Equis and Carta Blanca are offered as premium imported beers in California clone bars. The standard alternative to a roadside steakhouse in the Southwest is a Mexican restaurant, exactly the role Italian restaurants play in the Foundry. Tacos and burritos are as common as lasagna and ravioli elsewhere, although Mexicans view the spreading of hot sauce over everything as an American—and especially Texan—habit as barbarous as the suggestion that pizza was invented in Rome.

White, cotton Mexican dresses with meticulous, colorful embroidery are gaining favor among Anglo women during the long, hot southwestern summers. Anglo men becoming bored with oversized Texas cowboy hats are discovering that there are dozens of styles of Mexican broad-brimmed hats—each of them specific to a Mexican state—which are at least as rakish as anything Dallas can produce.

Austin as a country-and-western-music center that produced the likes of Willie Nelson and Waylon Jennings is also becoming a cultural crossroads in which not only do U.S. and Mexican tunes influence each other, but an even greater musical gap is bridged—that between Hispanics from northern Mexico and Hispanics from the Islands.

"Norteño" music is as characteristic of northeastern Mexico and south Texas as Dixieland is of New Orleans. This Norteño music, which is sung in Spanish, is itself a cultural fusion over a century old, borrowing the beat and instruments of Germans who settled in Texas after their country was wrung by revolution in 1848. The lead instrument is a diatonic accordion (played by the musician's manipulating rows of buttons, a far more difficult task than dealing with an instrument that comes with a pianolike keyboard). Its rhythm is a catchy, but boxy, Germanic "oompha." This Norteño music is so foreign to syncopated Latino beats that Texan-Mexican kids, at a disco in Austin, when confronted by reggae or a cha-cha-like tune, sit it out, saying, "You can't dance to it." But that may be changing, because many of the Mexican polka bands of south Texas are listening to the new waves of Hispanic beats coming out of New York, Los Angeles, and the Caribbean, and are trying to adapt it to their style.

In the same spirit, Anglos like Ry Cooder are now cutting albums with Norteño sidemen, and Mexican-Americans like Freddy Fender and Johnny Rodriguez are making it big on Anglo hit charts.

In MexAmerica, languages are converging, so that an Anglo may be asked to *préstame su credit card*. But also, a Mexican-American is confronted by a used-car dealer whose sign says: COMPRO Y VENDO CARROS. Buy and sell cars is what it means, but "carros" is not a Spanish word. Like the commonly heard "truck-os" and "hamburgesa," it's an adaptation of English. The question "Where do you work?" can even come out "*¿Dónde puncheas?*" That lifts not only an English word, but a labor concept that certainly did not originate in rural Mexico. The question, in effect, is "Where do you punch (your time clock)?"

Increasingly, Spanish can be seen in U.S. print. Emergency warning cards on Texas International Airlines, legal advertisements in Houston, and dialing instructions on telephone booths throughout Southern California are printed in both languages. So are popular magazines, such as *Nuestro—the magazine for Latinos.*

It's come to the point where a weary official of the Mexican American Cultural Center in San Antonio told me he'd just come from an organizational meeting for a new weekly at which a ferocious argument had been waged over which of *three* languages the paper should be printed in.

One possibility was English. The second was traditional Mexican Spanish, which holds in high esteem a richly colored, quasi-poetic, Cervantesque style of writing. But the most controversial choice was, for lack of a better word, Mex-American. This language, built on Spanish, not only relies on adaptations of English words for much of its vocabulary, but, most important, has a fast-paced, direct, United States style that says what it has to in a hurry. "Those Mexicans!" said the Hispanic official with a sigh. "They want to make a minor point, and they build up to it, and build up to it, and build up to it, and it can bore your ass off."

Jerry Warren is the editor of the *San Diego Union*, a once undistinguished if not terrible paper that is recruiting a lot of fresh talent and is beginning to make a name for itself. The *Union* has begun to do pioneering work in the coverage of politics and corruption in northern Mexico and how it affects the United States side of the border. But the reporters were frustrated by the lack of effect their English-language articles were having until Warren decided to have one particularly controversial report translated, reprinted, and trucked twenty miles south to Tijuana, where a free and feisty press is less than a sacred tradition. The appearance of biculturalism and binationalism in the form of American-style muckraking in Spanish had an explosive effect.

Ironically, Warren the border-blurrer is the same man who, in 1969, as deputy press secretary to Nixon, had to stand up and explain to doubtful reporters why Operation Intercept was a good idea. Operation Intercept was an attempt to seal hermetically the United States–Mexican border against drug smuggling. It succeeded most markedly in displaying a complete lack of understanding of the geography of MexAmerica on the part of the authorities who thought it up. Operation Intercept coincided with a dramatic rise in the sale of four-wheel-drive vehicles along the border. Local teen-agers, who knew the desert areas of the borderlands as well as they knew their own backyards, soon realized that one quick smuggling run through the vast desert, bypassing the newly toughened road checkpoints, could pay for a brand-new truck outright.

Thus, what had once been a tight-knit, controllable drug-distribution network was transformed overnight into a wild, every-man-for-himself collection of individualistic and hitherto law-abiding entrepreneurs. The new arrangement exists to this day.

Spanish is also becoming the language of the U.S. airwaves. The Southwest used to have only a handful of Spanish-language radio stations. Now there are thirty-seven in Texas, twenty-three in California, six in Arizona, and four in New Mexico. There is virtually no major city in the entire United States without at least one Spanish station. Even television is changing. Broadcast and cable television bring full-time Spanish programming as far north as San Francisco, just as it brings English television as far south as Mexico City. MexAmericans who don't want to watch Walter Cronkite can catch Jacobo Zabludovsky, who's known as the Uncle Walter of Mexico.

Sometimes the cultural cross-fertilization can get very confusing, such as when an American is watching Mexican television and a show that looks naggingly familiar reveals itself to be a knock-off of the popular U.S. movie series *Benji*, named after the star, which is a dog. The plot on Spanish television is exactly the same. Only the language, the scenery, and the dog (an Airedale, not a lovable mutt) are different.

Politics are changing: Democrats in control of the 1979 California legislature put $800,000 in the state budget to encourage participation by illegal aliens in the 1980 U.S. Census. The census totals determine how many congressional seats a state gets, how many presidential electors it gets, and how $50 billion worth of federal programs, ranging from school and housing aid to community-improvement projects and affirmative-action goals, are divided up. And nowhere does the law say that census totals should distinguish between residents with passports and residents without.

Organized labor is changing. The International Ladies' Garment Workers Union, which once was violently against illegal immigration as an unlimited source of cheap labor, has shifted its stance in California and is now actively and successfully recruiting undocumented workers. It realized that it would have to represent illegal aliens if it was going to continue representing garment workers. Other unions, such as farmers', retail clerks', and the textile workers', have followed suit.

Even religion is changing. Among those in the Southwest who do go to church, the majority are Catholic, and two-thirds of these are Mexican-American. This, too, is altering balances. After long being ignored by the U.S. hierarchy, Mexican-Americans in the decade of the 1970s saw an average of one new Hispanic bishop named per year, an amazing statistic for such a historically glacial institution.

Father Virgil Elizondo of San Antonio, who has studied the role of Catholicism in the Mexican-American culture, suggests that there are some devotional practices that non-Hispanic Catholics take as dogma that may have more to do with the juridical minds of Irish priests than they do with the faith. Compulsory Mass on Sunday is one example he uses. In English, he points out, the Third Commandment is "Remember, thou keep holy the Lord's day." In Spanish, the commandment is much different. It's "Sanctify your feast days." There are thousands of Mexican-American Catholics who feel they are complying with God's will, thus stated, without necessarily checking in with the parish priest every seven days.

Similarly, researchers had some of their assumptions rearranged for them when they started investigating the success Protestant denominations have had in recruiting Mexican-Americans. (It shouldn't have surprised me, but it did, the first time I saw the sign in Los Angeles that read SALÓN DE LOS TESTIGOS DE JEHOVA—Jehovah's Witnesses.) On asking a brand-new Baptist why she left the Catholic Church, the researcher was told, "Oh, I haven't left the Catholic Church. I go to it, too. I'm a Baptist-Catholic." Father Elizondo, taking note of people who describe themselves as Methodist-Catholic and Presbyterian-Catholic, remarked, "They'd heard of biculturalism and bilingualism, but they didn't know what to put on their computer cards when they hit bireligionism."

The Anglo influence south of the border, meanwhile, is as casual and pervasive as the pay telephone in Rosarito, Baja California Norte, south of Tijuana, which will not accept pesos. Only dimes. Or the stop signs that have the 7-Up symbol on them. Or LA RECETA DE CORONEL SANDERS. Visit the "Coronel"?

Anglos with a stereotype of persons of Mexican ancestry as pickers of fruit and drawers of water like to forget history. Americans who mutter darkly about "alien hordes" ignore the fact that, like the French of Québec, the Spanish-speaking people of the Southwest were here first. MexAmerica bulges hundreds of miles north of the border into New Mexico, Colorado, and California, because, for example, a flourishing Spanish civilization existed at Santa Fe before the Pilgrims landed at Plymouth Rock. The Santa Fe Trail was important to Missouri frontiersmen in the early 1800s, because it opened up trade to a city then already two hundred years old. Place-names, from San Antonio to Los Angeles, bespeak the ancient Spanish presence. The northern borders of California, Nevada, and Utah are at the 42nd parallel, because that's where the

Spanish empire of Alta (Upper) California (as opposed to Baja [Lower] California) ended.

The conquistadors and the padres saw this region whole, without imaginary lines creating divisions between the state of Sonora and the state of Arizona. The desert was the same, the cactuses were the same, the climate was the same, and the people were the same. And the descendants of the conquistadors are still here. Hispanics in New Mexico still refer to themselves as Spanish, rather than Mexican-Americans, partially out of snobbery, but also out of a sense of historical accuracy. In Santa Fe, because of intermarriage, the lineage is thoroughly European. Mexican-Americans, by contrast, claim a far more indigenous North American ancestry. Their forefathers may have been European, but their maternal ancestors were Aztec and members of the other highly developed nations of Central America that flourished before the white man came.

The Anglo world is the latest invader of these parts, not the Indian, Mexican, and Spanish. It's the borders that have moved, not the founding cultures. There are great numbers of Hispanics in the Southwest who can't be told by ignorant Anglos to go back where they came from. They *are* where they came from.

Mexican Children Get Hard Lesson

new laws cut them from n.m. schools

Steve Fainaru

As dawn breaks over the rocky plains of Columbus, New Mexico, hundreds of children cross from Mexico into this sleepy border town. Toting backpacks and lunchboxes, the children pile into buses and make their way north for another day of school in the United States.

For nearly half a century, the local school district has been educating children this way—regardless of their nationality. But the cross-border tradition has come under attack from new federal immigration laws designed to prohibit "aliens" from receiving publicly funded education.

The results have been dramatic in this lonely corner of the Southwest, where changing attitudes on immigration have come into conflict with the cozy relationship between Columbus, population 800, and Palomas, Mexico: border communities that share the same Rotary Club, holiday celebrations, and even a few phone lines.

Between 40 and 50 Mexican children already have been "disenrolled" and sent back across the border under the new laws, according to the Deming (N.M.) School District. The children include high school students who were close to graduation, grade-schoolers, and even an 11-year-old special education student.

"It's a tragedy, like we've been hit by a killer earthquake," said Phoebe

Watson, the 86-year-old former principal of Columbus Elementary School, who started the cross-border education program in the 1950s. "People who thought they were going to get an education have been told that they can't, and that's one of the worst things that you can imagine. Every child in the world deserves an education."

"It seems so unjust," said Dora Luz Nieto, 16, who had been on track to graduate this year from Deming High School, about 30 miles north of Columbus, but now is working as a clerk in a Palomas store while attending night school. "I'd worked so hard and I was making my plans to apply to university and then suddenly I couldn't go anymore."

But supporters of the new laws said they reflect the reality that U.S. tax-payers are no longer willing to provide services for non-citizens. "I don't think there's anybody who opposes educating children, but why should the taxpayers of New Mexico pay for the children of Mexico?" said Gordon Maxwell, a former California Highway Patrol officer who retired to Columbus five years ago.

"Where is the cutoff point?" he said. "Are we going to take responsibility for teaching the children of Central America? Are we going to teach the children of South America? Are we going to teach all the children in Africa?"

Others argue that the new laws fail to take into consideration the special relationships that knit together hundreds of communities on both sides of the border. Although Columbus is the only U.S. city to openly educate Mexican children, the practice is believed to be common in towns all along the Texas, Arizona, and California portions of the 2,000-mile frontier.

Certainly, the lives of Columbus and Palomas are intertwined. Columbus's farmers take advantage of Palomas's abundant and cheap labor. The town's many retirees cross the border for inexpensive health care and prescription drugs. Meanwhile, Palomas is so poor it lacks a paved road, a drainage system, and, until recently, a high school. Many Palomas residents cross over to Columbus—legally and illegally—to seek jobs and education. Palomas schools have drafty, cramped rooms with no computers and too few schoolbooks, heaters, and teachers.

Watson said the practice of accepting children from across the border began when about a dozen children showed up at her school one morning. "I didn't plan to do this; the kids were there and I let them come in," she said. "I never asked whether they were Mexican or American. They were children and they needed an education. Then the next year their brothers and sisters showed up. Then came the cousins."

Before long, more than 400 children per year were crossing the border to attend four district schools from kindergarten through the 12th grade. The cost to state taxpayers rose to over $1 million per year. The district, concerned that the students were traveling to school by cramming themselves into unsafe vans, began to send school buses directly to the border over a decade ago.

For years, few complained about the arrangement. In New Mexico, the government pays for public education by evenly redistributing tax revenue, so the cost to the individual taxpayer was minuscule.

Education officials said a state statute obliged them to provide free education to any child "present" in the state. In addition, the issue of nationality had become muddled: Most of the children already were U.S. citizens, because their mothers had traveled to the United States to give birth.

The issue began to come to a head three years ago over the issue of overcrowding. MaryKay Gibbs, a member of the Deming school board who opposed the cross-border program, said: "I know that a lot of them are American citizens, but I owe it to the people of the district to take care of them first, and a lot of questions come out of that: Is there enough room? Is there enough funding there?"

Carlos Ogden, the mayor of Columbus, disagreed. "It just doesn't seem right, to say 'You're from there. You can't go to school over here.'"

The two sides settled on a compromise by allowing some 400 students residing in Mexico to continue to attend Deming schools, as long as the district cut off new enrollment to all non-district residents.

Then the federal government stepped in. Unbeknownst to the district, the Illegal Immigration Reform and Responsibility Act of 1996 contained a section prohibiting "any alien from receiving an F-1 student visa if the alien was coming to attend a public elementary school, grades kindergarten through 8, or a publicly funded adult education program."

High school students were allowed to attend for one year, as long as they paid the cost of their education. In the Deming school district, tuition was set at $4,100, far beyond the means of most Palomas residents: subsistence laborers who earn the Mexican minimum wage of about $3.50 per day.

"My personal opinion is that this is one of those cases where people who were forming the federal legislation didn't look into the specifics of who would be affected," said Carlos Viramontes, the Deming superintendent, whose district will lose as much as $900,000 in state funding because of the new laws. "What we had here was a model of how education should work along the border."

Alejandro Anaya, a Palomas physician, had three children attending Columbus elementary. His 11-year-old son, Alex, who received special education because of vision and hearing problems, and his 8-year-old daughter, America, were forced to return to Palomas because they were not born in the United States. His 6-year-old daughter, Cindy, who was born in Deming because his wife needed an emergency Caesarian operation, was allowed to stay.

Last year, Anaya sat down with Alex and America. "It was a difficult moment, let me tell you," he recalled. "My children asked me, 'Why us? Are they discriminating against us?'"

"I had to tell them, 'No, it's only because you weren't born over there.'"

PART V

Borderlands America

The experience of the Southwest is best described as the overlay of cultures and of the influence of the various peoples that have resided here. The essays in this section, to one degree or another, share the idea that geographically and historically the Southwest is a palimpsest which, like an ancient map, shows evidence of having been drawn and redrawn many times. In the Southwest one is able to discern where the marks left by one civilization seep through the layers of the past and reveal themselves, alive and present. Trace over these lines and they tell of migrations, conquests, rebellion, settlements, trails, and boom-and-bust enterprises. Like the map that has been drawn and redrawn, the topography of the Southwest reveals that, for much of its history, the region has been a borderland, a crossroads of experience.

One feature of this history has remained constant: the region has always existed on the extremities of power and empires but has never been the locus of that power. Old maps and documents reveal that it was once the Aztlán of Aztec mythology, the Seven Cities of Cíbola of the Spanish Empire, Mexico's buffer against American expansion, and America's frontier. Today it remains a region of intense transition, sharing a two-thousand-mile international border with Mexico. Nowhere else in the world does the First World grate so dramatically against the Third World, and nowhere else are the consequences of such contact so evident.

Today, we all live on or at some border, be it geographic, cultural, economic, racial, technological, or temporal. In this context, the experience of the Southwest as a place of shifting and yet, paradoxically, interlocking Anglo,

Hispanic, and Indian political and socioeconomic zones provides us with count-less examples by which to measure the effects of social segmentation, economic dislocation, and cultural alienation.

To live in the Borderlands means you

Gloria Anzaldúa

are neither *hispana india negra española*
ni gabacha, eres mestiza, mulata, half-breed
caught in the crossfire between camps
while carrying all five races on your back
not knowing which side to turn to, run from;

To live in the Borderlands means knowing
    that the *india* in you, betrayed for 500 years,
    is no longer speaking to you,
    that the *mexicanas* call you *rajetas*,
    that denying the Anglo inside you
    is as bad as having denied the Indian or Black;

Cuando vives en la frontera
    people walk through you, the wind steals your voice,
    you're a *burra, buey,* scapegoat,
    forerunner of a new race,
    half and half—both woman and man, neither—
    a new gender;

To live in the Borderlands means to
    put *chile* in the borscht,
    eat whole wheat *tortillas*,
    speak Tex-Mex with a Brooklyn accent;
    be stopped by *la migra* at the border checkpoints;

Living in the Borderlands means you fight hard to
    resist the gold elixir beckoning from the bottle,
    the pull of the gun barrel,
    the rope crushing the hollow of your throat;

In the Borderlands
    you are the battleground
    where enemies are kin to each other;
    you are at home, a stranger,
    the border disputes have been settled
    the volley of shots have shattered the truce
    you are wounded, lost in action
    dead, fighting back;

To live in the Borderlands means
    the mill with the razor white teeth wants to shred off
    your olive-red skin, crush out the kernel, your heart
    pound you pinch you roll you out
    smelling like white bread but dead;

To survive the Borderlands
    you must live *sin fronteras*
    be a crossroads.

gabacha—a Chicano term for a white woman
rajetas—literally, "split," that is, having betrayed your word
burra—donkey
buey—ox
sin fronteras—without borders

Baroque Principles of Organization in Contemporary Mexican American Arizona

James S. Griffith

This essay deals with one of the cultural components of the region—
Mexican American culture. It focuses on a much broader issue: the aesthetic
ideas that seem to underlie and inform much of what is produced by that culture.
I have often been struck by what I perceive as strong cultural continuities over
time in the Pimería Alta.

Three centuries after Father Eusebio Francisco Kino introduced wheat and
beef into the region, those foods remain the staples of our traditional diet. Over
200 years after Tucson was founded as a Spanish cavalry presidio, or fort, Tuc-
sonans are concerned lest the federal government lessen its commitment to
Davis-Monthan Air Force Base. Mining and over-promotion of natural resources
have likewise been important economic activities in southern Arizona for more
than two centuries. And, as I shall try to show in this essay, the ideas of how
elements are assembled into a whole which is dramatically expressed in the architectural decoration of the eighteenth-century mission church of San Xavier del
Bac still live as active principles within the local Mexican American community.

San Xavier del Bac

The eighteenth-century mission church of San Xavier del Bac stands some
twelve miles south of Tucson, Arizona, on the San Xavier District of the Tohono

O'odham Reservation.[1] Finished in 1797, it is the most nearly complete Spanish colonial baroque architectural ensemble in the continental United States.

Begun around 1778 under the direction of Father Juan Bautista Velderrain, O.F.M., the church was completed by his successor, Father Juan Bautista Llorenz, O.F.M., after Velderrain's death.[2] The church is remarkable for its state of preservation: almost every statue and mural painting that it contained at the time of its dedication is still in place, albeit in slightly deteriorated condition. Since February 1992, an international team of expert conservators from Italy and Turkey have been working to stabilize and clean the murals and statues. The project was finished in 1997, the 200th anniversary of the church's completion.[3]

Like so many Mexican churches of its period, San Xavier del Bac is a cruciform building with a dome over the crossing and two bell towers flanking the facade. In the case of San Xavier, one of the bell towers remains unfinished, as do other details inside and out. The exterior of the church is covered with lime plaster; this whitish color is interrupted by the light brown of the elaborately carved plaster portal. This portal is organized in three stories, each level consisting of one or more sets of columns flanking a central opening or sculptural arrangement. There are two columns on each side of the lower two stories and one column on each side of the upper level. The columns themselves are of the type called *estípites,* popular in most of colonial New Spain during the eighteenth century. These estípites are elaborate combinations of shapes and appear intended not so much to hold up the next level of architecture as to add structure, complexity, and motion to the facade.

Between the pairs of estípites on either side of the two lower levels of the facade are niches containing saints' statues. The third level is taken up with low relief sculpture including an emblem of the Franciscan order, the monograms of Jesus and the Virgin Mary, wheat stalks and grape vines, and the two lions which normally support the Spanish coat of arms.

The whole portal was at one time painted in brilliant colors. It is rich in texture, detail, and imagery. Looking at it, one gets the impression of a fascination with complexity, almost for its own sake. Here nothing is simple. Lintels move in and out as they progress from side to side. Complex lines and low relief sculpture serve to catch constantly changing shadows as the sun moves across the sky. Sharp angles cause the eye of the observer to shoot off into space. The whole ensemble clamors for attention, now as a whole, now as a mass of independent details.

The interior of the church is filled with even more intense color and motion. Angels flutter over the main altar and on the three brick and plaster *retablos* (altarpieces) that soar to roof level. These retablos are organized in much the same way as the portal, with multiple levels supported by estípite columns, and saints' images between the estípites. The retablo over the main altar is covered with gold and silver leaf, while all the retablos are painted in rich, brilliant colors.

The rest of the church interior is given over to murals. Scenes from the life of Christ and the Virgin are painted in both side chapels and along the nave. Many of the murals have painted frames around them; a few appear to be suspended by painted ribbons from painted scrollwork. Some of the plaster is painted to resemble ceramic tiles, other parts to resemble veined marble. Doors are painted on blank walls to balance actual doors opposite them. The entire interior exudes richness, drama, motion, and a certain ambiguity or sense of illusion. These characteristics tie San Xavier del Bac solidly into the baroque style of eighteenth-century colonial Mexico, relating it to hundreds of its contemporary churches miles to the south.

Baroque Architecture in New Spain

Because it was built on the extreme northwestern frontier of New Spain, San Xavier is relatively small in size and conservative in some of its details. However, it is just as solidly within the eighteenth-century Mexican baroque style as are such larger, richer, better-known examples as Santa Prisca y San Sebastián in Taxco, Guerrero,[4] or San Francisco Xavier (now the Museo Nacional del Virreinato) in Tepotzotlán, Mexico.[5] The best way to understand San Xavier is as an example of its style—the eighteenth-century baroque architecture of New Spain.

The outstanding characteristic of the Mexican baroque style of architecture is that it is basically a style of applied decoration. While the manipulation of space is an important, if not vital, aspect of much European baroque architecture, most Mexican baroque buildings are simple blocks with a greater or lesser degree of plastic, decorative detail added to them. In the case of churches, the decoration (and it is often overwhelming in its impact) is usually added on to a building much like San Xavier: cruciform, with a dome at the crossing or over the main altar and one or two towers flanking the portal.

Much excellent research and writing has been done on Mexican baroque architectural decoration. Typologies and even chronologies have been suggested, the most effective of which are based on the shape of the columns that play such an important role in the portals and in the retablos that provide the focus of so much of the baroque decorative impulse. A convincing sequence moves from the tubular column shaft through the twisted *salamónica* that was dear to the seventeenth century to the broken form of the estípite (as seen on the facade of San Xavier) and beyond to no columns at all but merely a series of vertical decorative zones separating rows of images in niches. This last is referred to by some Mexican art historians as the *anastilético*, or "style-less" style.

However, as Weismann has pointed out in *Art and Time in Mexico*,[6] all these styles persisted together in various parts of Mexico right on through to the end of the eighteenth century. For this reason, the sequence, useful though it is as an ordering device, does not really help date the building one is looking at, outside of Mexico City and a few other centers of fashion.

Another way to look at the entire movement of the Mexican baroque in the eighteenth century is to try to isolate the aesthetic rules and preferences that underlie the style—the general principles on which it seems to be assembled. While such a general approach is not likely to be helpful in establishing a chronology, it should serve as a useful descriptive tool for comparative purposes.

One characteristic of the Mexican baroque seems to be a sense of dramatic contrast. This contrast may be between plain and decorated surfaces, as is the case on San Xavier's facade, where the plain bases of the towers flank the elaborately textured portal, or in its interior walls, where large stretches of white walls relieve the intensity of the murals and retablos. It may involve colors, as again at San Xavier where the white of the plain plaster is played off against the brown of the portal. It may be between light and dark, as has been eloquently described by Kubler in his treatment of New Mexico's colonial churches, with their transverse clerestory windows which allow a shaft of light to illuminate the altar at the end of a relatively dark nave.[7] A more common light/dark contrast is between brightly lit and deeply shadowed exterior surfaces and involves the use of deeply cut relief to catch the shadows.

Motion seems to be another characteristic related to the baroque style. Paintings often depict action—sometimes violent action. Statues gesticulate and frequently seem to be on the verge of movement. Architectural lines, like the vestigial broken pediment on San Xavier's portal, do not form closed, restful patterns but rather propel the eye of the observer off into space. Indeed, when a framing line such as a lintel is carried from one point to another, it usually moves along a complex path consisting of both vertical and horizontal zigzags and undulations.

The most important aesthetic principle behind the organization of the Mexican baroque decoration is the importance of richness—richness of materials, so that the retablos glow with gold leaf. Richness of colors, as in the use of dark red and dark green along with the gold on San Xavier's retablos. Richness of texture, as in San Xavier's facade, which is covered with vines and other devices (which also create a sense of motion and provide shadow-catching projections). And a final kind of richness: a richness of content and meaning. What I mean by this is that baroque ensembles such as the one at San Xavier are themselves composed of a vast number of small, complete, independent details, each one of which possesses meaning of its own and each one of which brings that meaning to the total assemblage.

Sometimes the meanings may be complex and the motives for the inclusion of details may be difficult to isolate. For instance, over the central window of San Xavier's facade is carved a scallop shell. This motif is echoed inside the church, over the main retablo, as well as in niches in the nave and transepts and elsewhere in the church. In his analysis of San Xavier's retablo *mayor*, or "main retablo," Goss states that the scallop shell is associated with the pilgrimage cult of Saint James the Greater, Santiago de Compostela.[8] As Santiago Matamoros (Saint James the Moor-Killer), Saint James was the patron of the militant expansion of Spanish Catholicism, and the establishment of San Xavier del Bac as a mission to the O'odham was certainly a part of that expansion. However, Goss also notes that for the peoples of the Mediterranean in classical times, the scallop was associated with the goddess Venus and symbolized the female reproductive organs. By extension, it was also a symbol of birth and regeneration. In a Christian connotation the regeneration can be taken to mean baptism. In early Roman times it became a symbol of resurrection during funeral rites—a meaning it carried over into early Christian art. Many of the pre-Christian meanings of the scallop were revived by the artists of the Renaissance. Finally, the shape of the scallop shell provides a complex, curving, occasionally angular outline, along with a ribbed surface that catches and holds shadows.

Which of these sets of meaning and characteristics explains the presence of the scallop motif at San Xavier? My suggestion would be: a shifting combination of most or all of them, possibly combined with others with which I am not familiar. And one must not neglect the possible importance of precedent—of a design simply being carried over from one building to another without much consideration of its specific meaning.

This very ambiguity and complexity of meaning strikes me as yet another characteristic of the baroque style. Things are not always what they seem to be. I have already mentioned that in San Xavier there are painted doors on the walls opposite real doors, paintings that imitate the effect of glazed ceramic tiles, and painted surfaces that resemble veined marble. This flirtation between reality and unreality is carried a step further by the realistic treatment of the sculptures. Flesh tones are carefully made to imitate real flesh. Draperies that appear to flow like cloth are actually carved from plaster or wood. This sense of ambiguity that comes from illusion as well as from possibly multiple meanings seems to be part of experiencing the baroque art and architecture of New Spain.

One final point should be made concerning the interior of San Xavier del Bac: its arrangement is by no means static. Older photographs prove that a few of the saints have been shifted from one niche to another. But the truly dynamic aspect of the interior operates on a seasonal cycle. In November the patronal statue of Saint Francis Xavier is taken down from its niche in the retablo mayor and placed in a small, portable shelter the size of a telephone booth. This latter is covered with fine-meshed gauze, to which are attached paper flowers. Here the saint stays until December 3, his day in the Roman Catholic calendar, and here he is visited by long files of devotees.

Later on in December, the church is decorated for Christmas. The angels flanking the triumphal arch are given special white gowns, and banners are placed in their hands. Commercial tinsel swags are hung across the nave of the church. A *nacimiento*, or "Christmas crib," made by a local O'odham carver is erected on an altar in the east transept. Other seasons bring other changes, apparently in perfect keeping with the overall aesthetic mood of the church interior.

The underlying aesthetic impulses behind the baroque style of eighteenth-century Mexico, then, appear to be as follows: dramatic contrast, especially between light and dark and plain and decorated surfaces; motion, represented in painting and sculpture and implied in the use of complex curved and broken lines; richness of materials, details, and meaning; and a certain sense of ambiguity. These organizational principles or rules affect the appearance of San Xavier del Bac just as surely as they affect the appearance of countless other churches, great and small, throughout New Spain.

It may well be that their influence extends even farther. Over the course of several years of investigating and documenting the contemporary traditional arts of southern Arizona's Mexican American population, I have come to the conclusion that much of this art follows the principles I have just described for the eighteenth-century baroque of New Spain.

Three Contemporary Mexican American Folk-Art Displays
in Southern Arizona

In an attempt to demonstrate this thesis, I shall describe three folk-art ensembles which I documented in southern Arizona in the 1980s. Two are permanent, if changing; one was ephemeral. They are a front yard shrine in South Tucson, a grave marker in the Casa Grande Cemetery, and a low rider display at the Pima County Fairgrounds just east of Tucson.

Front yard shrines are an important feature of the landscape of those parts of Tucson occupied by Mexican Americans and by Yaqui Indians, who have adopted (and adapted) much of traditional Mexican culture. Some of these shrines are fairly simple freestanding *nichos* (niches) containing one or more Catholic holy images. Others, however, can become very complex indeed. For instance, one shrine in a front yard near the Yaqui chapel of San Martín de Porres on South Tucson's 39th Street is constructed in the form of a wishing well. (This phrase was used in describing the shrine by its maker, a Yaqui man who wishes to remain anonymous.) The base of the well (which is in fact a solid platform and not a well at all) is made of cement which has been scored to resemble bricks. The scored bricks are painted alternately green and white. On this base sits a white plaster shell or nicho containing a brilliantly painted statue of the Virgin. The nicho is edged with bits of red, black, and blue plastic tile. A cross surmounts a small projection on top of the nicho, with similar projections flanking it.

The nicho is shaded by a pitched, gabled roof, held up by four green wooden posts. The front edges of the posts are bevelled to create an undulating outline. The fronts of the posts are overlaid with black and white cruciform plastic tiles. The roofline is painted green and white. In the center of the gable stands a white wooden cross, overlaid with colored plastic tiles and bearing a red plastic heart in its center. Immediately below the cross on the gable end is an automobile decal featuring Our Lady of Guadalupe and crossed Mexican and American flags. The boards of the gable itself are painted white and have their ends rounded and adorned with small tiles. The shrine is decorated with tiny, flashing Christmas-tree lights; a string of larger, colored lights has been hung on the eaves of the house directly behind it.

Traditional Mexican American cemeteries often abound with grave markers which have been made or assembled by the families of the deceased.[9] One such marker is in the public cemetery at Casa Grande, in Pinal County, Arizona. When I visited the grave in 1984, it was surrounded by a raised cement curb.

Within this curb, lying flat at its west end, was a commercially sand-blasted marker bearing the name and dates of the deceased (a woman) and an image of Our Lady of Guadalupe. Behind this commercial headstone, the head of the curb was backed by a low wall with a nicho at its center. Inside the nicho was a statue of the Virgin flanked by statues of angels and a small vase of artificial flowers and by statues of Saint Anthony and Saint Martin of Porres. On the rear wall of the nicho, behind the central Virgin, was an architectural setting consisting of two columns flanked by vertical volutes. A depiction of the Last Supper was painted on the low vertical wall below the nicho. Flanking the nicho were a statue of the Sacred Heart of Jesus, another Virgin, a small holy-water stoup, bunches of plastic flowers, a candle, a ceramic planter in the form of a cactus, and another small ceramic planter containing a cactus.

This assemblage is by no means static. The description above is based on slides taken in 1984. A slide dated 1982 slows a different arrangement of objects and reveals that most if not all of the statues had been repainted in the intervening period. When I revisited the grave in 1987, the following changes had taken place.

The headstone had been raised to a slant and propped against the low wall below the nicho, covering the Last Supper painting. Inside the nicho, which had been stripped of its columns and volutes, were a picture and statue of the Holy Child of Atocha, a rosary and a palm leaf cross, statues of Saint Anthony and Saint Martin de Porres, three angels (one wooden, one ceramic, and one a ceramic candle holder), a small glass votive candle container, two pots of artificial flowers, and a stuffed toy mouse wearing a sailor suit. Outside the nicho and flanking it were eight arrangements of artificial flowers (one made of seashells) and a ceramic statue of the Holy Child of Prague.

I attended a Low Rider Happening at the Pima County Fair Grounds in 1982. One low rider car display was particularly striking. The car was painted a medium green with heavy metallic flake and some yellow inserts. Painted on the trunk was a scene of a car wash, with several (allegedly identifiable) cars and motorcycles in front. The left side of the car was jacked up off the ground and a mirror had been placed under the car to reveal that most of the metal underside had been chromed or freshly painted. Cheech and Chong appeared in the reflection, painted on the bottom of the gas tank. They were brandishing huge marijuana joints. On the edge of the open, left-hand door was painted a frog in a zoot suit. Miss Piggy languished seductively on the door of the glove compartment.

The interior of the car was upholstered in deep yellow pile. The steering wheel was small, made of chain link, and chromed. A built-in TV set occupied the space between the swivel-mounted bucket seats. Inside the hood, much of the engine was chrome-plated. The underside of the hood was upholstered in the same yellow pile used for the car interior. Beside the car, next to the display panel giving the names of the owner and the various artists who had worked on the project, stood a pedal-operated toy truck, painted and upholstered to match the low rider. It was occupied by a stuffed toy bear.

It should be clear what I am suggesting. The shrine, grave assemblage, and low rider display are all organized along lines which seem strikingly similar to the principles I have suggested for the organization of eighteenth-century Mexican baroque churches such as San Xavier del Bac. Let's run down the list once more. Motion—the implied motion of the car with one corner tilted up, the flashing colored lights, and the undulating supports of the shrine. Contrast—present on all three examples, which have both plain and decorated surfaces. Ambiguity—most evident, perhaps, in the shrine with its references to wishing wells, but present in the other examples too.

But the parallel with the Mexican baroque of the eighteenth century should be most obvious in the area of richness. Richness and elegance of material, with downright opulence in the case of the low rider display. Richness of color in all three examples. And most particularly richness of detail and of various kinds of meaning. The multiple meanings of "wishing well" and "niche with holy statue." The multiplicity of sacred images—Our Lady of Guadalupe; other Virgins, angels, and saints; the Last Supper; and the Sacred Heart of Jesus—brought together on the Casa Grande grave marker, along with such purely secular images as cactus planters. The presence at the grave site of a number of candles, each of which may well represent a distinct prayer on the part of an individual. The images of the car wash, Cheech and Chong, the zoot-suited frog, and Miss Piggy combined in the low rider display, apparently without the need for a thematically unifying device.

Each of these images, all of which come together in each instance to produce a remarkable impact, is a totally independent entity which has its own meaning and existence outside of the ensemble. Miss Piggy enhances the low rider display, but she has nothing to do with low riders in general. It is the same with the repertoire of sacred figures. Each has its own life and identity, but once in the ensemble, they add to the totality of that ensemble. In just the same way, the flowers, scallop shells, angels, and saints bring their own identity and meaning to the totality of the retablo mayor at San Xavier del Bac. They, too, in a sense, are just visiting.

These organizational features are not the only similarities between eighteenth-century baroque architectural decoration and contemporary Mexican American folk art in southern Arizona. One shrine in a Tucson yard is a miniature replica of an eighteenth-century-style baroque church,[10] another incorporates the salamónicas, or "twisted columns," which were so popular in seventeenth- and eighteenth-century Mexico. Countless wrought-iron crosses in southern Arizona graveyards echo the curvilinear decoration that may be seen on the eighteenth-century cross topping San Xavier's central dome.[11] These and other details are predictable results of living in proximity to a baroque church which was built by carriers of an earlier version of one's own cultural tradition. They have reentered the folk repertoire, or possibly have never left it, as discrete motifs. In the language of art history, they and their like can be labeled "neobaroque."

The same label can be used for those styles of Anglo-American mainstream architecture that employ Spanish colonial details. Mission revival and baroque revival buildings have existed in Arizona for almost a hundred years. They seem to represent an attempt on the part of mainstream architects and builders to dramatize Spain's presence in this part of the United States. I have discussed this aspect of the neobaroque in more detail elsewhere.[12]

The three ensembles I have been discussing, however, seem to be a little different. They do not involve images taken from the baroque repertoire but rather seem to be organized along the same principles that the architects, planners, and artists of eighteenth-century New Spain used for their ensembles.[13] What is more, these principles seem to apply to the organization of other aspects of contemporary Mexican American life.

Two Socio-Religious Events

I attended a Yaqui wedding held in the mid-1980s just south of Tucson on the Pascua Yaqui Reservation. Even though the families involved were Yaqui, the events of the wedding ceremony were no different from the traditional Mexican weddings of the region. At the beginning of the ceremony, a group of hired singers and musicians played while the formally attired principals and their retinue marched down the aisle in procession. (The musical group was the one which usually played at Sunday Masses in that particular chapel and consisted of Yaquis, Mexican Americans, and an Anglo. The instrumentation included a violin, two guitars, a *guitarrón*, and a *vihuela*.)

Mass started and continued up until the exchange of wedding vows. After that, several special elements were introduced into the ceremony, each one preceded by a statement from the officiating priest identifying the action and explaining its symbolism. These elements included the blessing and exchange of rings, symbolizing the fidelity of the couple to each other; the blessing and placing of the *lazo*, an out-sized Rosary with two loops that were placed over the heads of the couple to symbolize their union within the Catholic religion; and the blessing and exchange of coins, symbolizing the couple's prayers for earthly security. Each of these discrete acts involved assistance from others in the wedding party; thus, each act created or strengthened ties between the newly wed couple and other individuals.[14]

At the end of the Mass, the bride, accompanied by her husband, placed her bouquet (which had previously been blessed) before an image of the Virgin. The wedding party then filed out of the church, posed for photographs, and signed the necessary documents before proceeding to a private home where a reception and several specifically Yaqui ceremonies took place.

The musicians played several times during the ceremony. Sometimes they were instructed to play specific songs that reinforced the meaning of the moment or added new layers of meaning, drawing on a combination of traditional Mexican and popular Anglo repertoires. Thus they played the mainstream "Wedding March" as the wedding party entered the church, a special song about wedding rings during the exchange of rings, a hymn to the Virgin during the dedication of the flowers at the end of the ceremony, and "La Marcha Zacatecas" as a recessional.

The other socio-religious event is a pre-Mass procession as it was planned and executed for the annual Tumacacori Fiesta in Tumacacori National Monument in the late 1980s. Tumacacori National Historic Monument is a small tract of land situated between Tucson and Nogales, Arizona, just east of Interstate 19. The Monument's most prominent feature and the reason for its existence is an unfinished nineteenth-century mission church. Tumacacori National Historic Monument's purpose is to preserve that church (along with two nearby ruins) and tell the story of Spanish mission activities in this part of northwestern New Spain.

Each year on the first Sunday in December, the Monument hosts the Tumacacori Fiesta. The event features traditional food, music, crafts, and dance from bearers of Mexican American, Tohono O'odham, and Yaqui cultural traditions. Inasmuch as a Catholic church is the central feature of the Monument, the fiesta always includes Mass at the old mission, often celebrated by the Bishop of Tucson or the Archbishop of Hermosillo, Sonora, Mexico. Before and after Mass there is a procession involving the clergy, the mariachis or other musicians who play for the Mass, various Indian religious musical and dance groups, and the Knights of Columbus.

In this particular instance, the Mexican American leader of el Grupo Cristo Rey, the musical group engaged to play at Mass, was helping with ideas for the organization of the procession. First would go the Yaqui Matachinis, a group of men and boys who perform contradances as an act of devotion to Our Lady of Guadalupe. In Yaqui tradition, they always lead a religious procession, blessing the ground with their music and dance. They (and their musicians playing violins and guitars) would be followed by Yaqui pascolas and a deer dancer, with their musicians which include violinists, a harper, and a flute and drum player. They in turn were to be followed by a group of young Tohono O'odham costumed for the traditional O'odham *chelkona* dance and carrying replicas of birds and clouds over their heads. Their singers, accompanied by a basket drum and rattles, would follow them. A Tohono O'odham pascola dancer, accompanied by his violin and a guitarist, came next. He was to be followed by the clergy and then by the Grupo Cristo Rey. The processional path would be lined by Knights of Columbus, saluting the Bishop with their swords and then bringing up the rear after the musicians had passed.

Each group, except the Knights, would be playing its own music, performing its own dances, and "doing its own thing," without reference to the others. The resulting procession (for things went pretty much as planned) was a sort of audible version of a baroque altarpiece—richly textured, filled with movement, and consisting of a large number of disparate elements, each complete and independent in and of itself, each endowed with its own layers of meaning. Like a high baroque altarpiece, the end result was rather overwhelming.

After Mass, an Anglo American woman approached the leader and told him that the mariachi of which he was a member sounded beautiful, but that it was a pity that "those other groups" were playing at the same time. The leader replied hastily and emphatically to the effect that the point of the whole procession—"our custom," as he put it, was to have everyone playing, singing, and dancing simultaneously.

Conclusions

I feel strongly that connections exist between the aesthetic or organizational principles underlying the twentieth-century objects and events which I have described and those which resulted in the baroque architectural assemblages of eighteenth-century New Spain. While the concept of surviving or revived knowledge serves perfectly well to explain the objects which I have described briefly as neobaroque, I believe that the materials and events I have detailed in this essay must be explained in a different way. To treat these modes of organization as direct survivals from the eighteenth-century baroque art style would require clear evidence of survival and transmission—evidence which may not be available. It seems much more likely that both they and the style of architectural decoration we call baroque are results of a sense of how things should go together that has been a basic part of Mexican culture since at least the eighteenth century.

It may have been in place much longer than that. I have seen sixteenth-century churchyard crosses in central Mexico that seem to be expressing many of the same organizational preferences. The outdoor cross at Atzacoalco in Mexico's Distrito Federal, for instance, is covered with the symbols of the Passion of Christ, carved in low relief. The crown of thorns is draped over the neck of the cross itself, and the image of Christ's face from Saint Veronica's Veil is rendered in high relief at the crossing.[15] Both of these features tend to anthropomorphize the cross or at least render its status as an object or as a being rather ambiguous. Further ambiguity is provided by gouts of blood which gush from nail holes in the cross.[16] At San Felipe de los Alzates in Michoacán, the Christian crown of thorns in the center of the cross surrounds a flat obsidian disc. This is thought by some scholars to be a survival of the reported Aztec custom of inlaying precious stones into idols in order to give them life.[17]

Such crosses as these, with their densely packed relief sculpture and ambiguous identity as artifact or being, are not alone in suggesting that the organizational preferences usually identified with the baroque style were in place in Mexican art a few decades after the Conquest. Over and over on sixteenth-century architecture there are densely packed portals, arches, and wall paintings which attest to the same set of organizational principles.[18]

And before the century of contact? Superficially it would seem that the masterpiece of Aztec sculpture known as the Great Coatlicue, currently on display in the Museo Nacional de Antropología e Historia in Mexico City, may have resulted from the application of similar principles. In fact, it may turn out that this deeply rooted aspect of Mexican culture, if indeed that is what it is, results from an all-too-familiar convergence between European and Mesoamerican cultural elements.[19] But that is far beyond the scope of this exploratory essay.

What I hope to have accomplished in the above pages is twofold. I have tried to point out, echoing such scholars as Irving Leonard,[20] that the organizational impulse of the baroque goes far beyond the details of a specific art style in a certain time and place—eighteenth-century Mexico. At the same time I have indicated ways in which it seems that the same aesthetic value system that produced the magnificent eighteenth-century churches that have so impressed generations of art historians and others appears to be still at work in what was once the northwest corner of New Spain.

Endnotes

An earlier version of this essay was read at the annual meeting of the American Folklore Society in Albuquerque, New Mexico, in October 1987. Descriptions of the three folk-art assemblages appear in James S. Griffith, *Southern Arizona Folk Arts* (Tucson: University of Arizona Press, 1988).

1. The name is bilingual, as was the custom for naming missions in the Pimería Alta. "San Xavier" indicates a dedication to Saint Francis Xavier, while "Bac" (or Wa:k, as it is written in contemporary O'odham orthography) was and remains the native name for the village.

2. Bernard L. Fontana, "Biography of a Desert Church: The Story of Mission San Xavier del Bac," *Smoke Signal* 3 (1961) gives the best available historical treatment of San Xavier del Bac.

3. Richard Ahlborn, *The Saints of San Xavier* (Tucson: Southwest Missions Research Center, 1974), gives a photograph and description of each statue in the church. No comparable work exists as yet for the murals.

4. Manuel Toussaint, *Colonial Art in Mexico*, trans. and ed. Elizabeth Wilder Weismann (Austin: University of Texas Press, 1967), pp. 295–98.

5. Ibid., pp. 298–302.

6. Elizabeth Wilder Weismann, *Art and Time in Mexico from the Conquest to the Revolution* (New York: Harper and Row, 1985), p. 445.

7. George Kubler, *Religious Architecture of New Mexico* (Chicago: Rio Grande Press, 1962).

8. My discussion of the various layers of meaning of the scallop shell is taken from Robert C. Goss, *The San Xavier Altarpiece* (Tucson: University of Arizona Press, 1974), pp. 57–76.

9. James S. Griffith, *Beliefs and Holy Places: A Spiritual Geography of the Pimería Alta* (Tucson: University of Arizona Press, 1992), pp. 115–22.

10. A photograph of this shrine appears in Griffith, *Southern Arizona Folk Arts*, p. 143.

11. A photograph of this cross appears in Marc Simmons and Frank Turley, *Southwestern Colonial Ironwork: The Spanish Blacksmithing Tradition from Texas to California* (Santa Fe: Museum of New Mexico Press, 1980), p. 166.

12. Griffith, *Beliefs and Holy Places*, pp. 147–71.

13. It has been suggested to me by more than one person that the materials I have been discussing can be described by the term *kitsch*. This may be true, but "kitsch" is a value judgment from the standpoint of late twentieth-century American high culture, and therefore neither describes nor analyzes the objects on their own terms. See also Griffith, *Southern Arizona Folk Arts*, p. 9.

14. The individuals acting in these support roles usually become *compadres* and *comadres* of the bride and groom, thus entering into a (theoretically) lifelong relationship of mutual support.

15. John Delany, *Dictionary of Saints* (New York: Doubleday, 1980), pp. 569–70.

16. Elizabeth Wilder Weismann, *Mexico in Sculpture, 1521–1821* (Cambridge: Harvard University Press, 1950), p. 11.

17. Ibid., p. 13.

18. Weismann, *Art and Time in Mexico from the Conquest to the Revolution*, provides a good place to start an examination of the sixteenth century in Mexico.

19. Ramón Pina Chan, "Aztec Art and Archaeology," in *The National Museum of Anthropology, Mexico*, ed. Pedro Ramírez Vásquez, pp. 92, 96 (New York: Harry N. Abrams, 1968).

20. Irving A. Leonard, *Baroque Times in Old Mexico* (Ann Arbor: Ann Arbor Paperbacks, 1966).

Interview

jesús martínez and ricardo murillo

Denis Lynn Daly Heyck

The stories of these two immigrants, who initially entered the United States illegally from El Salvador, represent odysseys in some ways as remarkable as that of Cabeza de Vaca himself centuries ago. Martínez traveled on foot from El Salvador to Texas, was deported, returned, and eventually made his way to Florida. Murillo, after close encounters with unscrupulous coyotes and Mexican police, ended up in Florida (and in jail), but via the indirect route of California and Idaho.

Jesús Martínez

Everybody calls me Don Chuy, but my name is Jesús Martínez, and the Murillo family are my *amigos*. I came here from El Salvador in 1982. I came by myself, and as I had no money, I had to walk all the way from the Department of Aguachapán, El Salvador, to the United States. The main reason was because of the disruptions caused by the war in my country. There was violence every-where, factories and businesses were closing down, everything was just collaps-ing. The only hope was to go north.

I worked awhile in Mexico, in the Federal District, in a small village very near the capital. Then I went to Monterrey. There I worked doing odd jobs for a señor who was a farmer. I felt right at home working for him because I had been a farmer back in El Salvador. From Monterrey, I went to Laredo. I worked with another señor, a truck farmer, and he got me a space with seven other men to cross over. We got in the *panga*—it's like a big plastic boat—and someone had a pole and we made it across. No police or anything because these guys knew everything about the best day, hour, and minute to cross. And I didn't have to pay a centavo. The man I was working for paid for me. He was a good man.

Of course, I didn't have a centavo either. I was now on the other side with no funds, so I started working on a nearby ranch, the Rancho Loma Larga, to make enough money to go on a little further. The *tejano* I worked for was another very good man. I took care of his horses and cows and I rode a beautiful white horse. I thought, what freedom! Riding all day long in the countryside, *puro campo*. The ranch was huge; it had three parts, like three separate ranches really. The *caporal*, or overseer, asked me please to stay, that I was a good worker, and besides, what was I going to do if I went somewhere else. But I always had the idea of moving on to see what was ahead and if I could get a better job. The tejano was very good to me. I didn't pay for anything, not rent, not food, nothing, but I didn't make much either. The other guys I was working with kept on saying, "Come on, come on, let's go to Houston."

So I got all enthused and went to Houston, and I loved it. *¡Ooooo, qué va!* Wow! I liked it so much that I stayed five years. I worked in many jobs—roofing, putting on shingles, tarring roofs, painting, putting in Sheetrock, doing gardening, planting and mulching. I also worked in a plastics factory.

I have to confess that the real reason that I didn't remain at any of these jobs for very long was that at that time I had a terrible vice, alcohol. I guess it was because I was lonely and far from home. Alcohol was my ruin. In Houston, I had good jobs and I earned good money, but my vice wouldn't let me be. Every weekend, Friday, Saturday, and Sunday, I would be drinking. Monday I would wake up still drunk and be unable to go to work. In the company, you could miss once and they would give you another chance. If you were a very good worker, you could miss twice, but the third time, no way. You were out. And that's what kept happening to me. Then I would sign up for another job, get drunk, and lose that one, too. Once, I got a great job *indoors*, in an office building downtown, with good pay, but my habit—I didn't know how to control it, and it ended up controlling me.

After Houston, I came to Florida. The reason I came here was that I needed a *mica*, a green card. They were charging $500 in Houston, but I heard that they charged less in Florida. A señor came to where I was working in Houston and won me and some Mexican friends over; he sold us the cards for $300 each. I came to Florida with the contractor himself. We paid for the ride,

$150 each, in a van; we were seven people. Once we began to work here in the fields, they paid us little by little. We made between $50 and $75 per week. I worked in Wahneta for one season. The following season, I came here to the Winter Haven area, and this is where I've been ever since, like a member of the Murillo family. I plan to stay, if God wills. I am not working now, but when I'm working I pick oranges—that's what the work is here, *pura naranja.*

The truth is that I have been very lucky. It was not easy to leave El Salvador in '82, because of the war, but I escaped on foot. *En el camino no tuve piedra*—there was no stone in the road. And I had no problems with the migra until Houston. The first time they caught me I was with some Mexican friends and they took us to the border in a big van. We were all locked up in there, and I was afraid. I didn't know where they were taking me, and I had vivid memories of what happened to people in El Salvador. I saw the Mexicans as brothers because we were in the same situation. At first I was panicked by the migra, but by the third time I wasn't afraid any more. I finally learned to tell them that I was a *salvadoreño.* Then they didn't pick me up any more. Instead, they gave me a little paper and told me to present it to the migra. It was so small that I lost it, but it doesn't matter now, anyway, because we have our cards.

Ricardo Murillo

My story is a little different from Don Chuy's, though I, too, left El Salvador in '82. My brother, José Dimas, and I left in the predawn darkness on January 15, leaving everyone and everything behind. I worked in the army headquarters called El Paraíso—Paradise—in the northern zone of the country. I was not a soldier, but an employee, a bricklayer, one who builds houses. I worked making repairs on the officers' casino and other things at the *cuartel*, or headquarters. I loved this work.

The reason I left it was because each day we had to travel quite a distance to get to and from work, and it kept getting more and more dangerous every day. We never knew if we would make it home alive from one day to the next. Every day we encountered danger in the streets, either with the *guerrilleros*—the rebels—or the government soldiers. It was too tense and dangerous to keep on working. If the guerrilleros had found out that I was working in the headquarters, they would've taken me out and killed me then and there. They didn't want anyone to collaborate in any way with the military. The guerrilleros just see you and they kill you on the spot, that's that. No questions asked. The worst thing was if they found out that you worked in some way for the government; that was the biggest crime.

Sometimes, my brother and I got in trouble. There were many tense moments when we had to decide what to say and what not to say, and hope that we would not contradict each other. On one occasion some friends of ours tried to defend themselves by saying that they worked for the government, and they showed their government ID cards. What they hadn't realized was that the guerrilleros were disguised as soldiers. Right before our eyes they murdered our friends. You never knew who were the soldiers and who were the guerrilleros. They went around dressed alike. You didn't know whether to show your ID or not in order to defend yourself. You couldn't trust anyone. That's when José Dimas and I decided to leave the country. I told my wife and my mother, "I think that God wills it. The road will be difficult, but with the help of God we will continue. We will be long in returning home, but we will be alive." And then we set out. We hardened our hearts, because it is almost unbearable to leave your parents, your wife, your children. But there are moments of truth in our life when we have to make painful decisions.

We went as tourists. We got our passports and tourist visas in El Salvador to enter Guatemala and Mexico. It was all legal to Mexico. We worked in Guadalajara for several months and made good friends there. We worked very hard there in jobs that I had never done before in El Salvador. Some days we loaded trucks with stones, big stones, and the higher the load in the truck, the higher we had to lift, and then throw, the heavy stones. Those first months, we weren't tired from that heavy work, but we were exhausted from worrying about our families who we had left behind. We wrote them letters every day, but had no idea if they were getting through or not.

We also helped gather cane tips, because these make good fodder for the animals. We earned two hundred pesos a day, not enough to eat on. Impossible! On other occasions, I was able to work in construction, but one had to accept what was available in order to survive. Sometimes we became so despondent that we would ask ourselves what we thought we were doing, and what was the point of going on. But we had to keep on to achieve our goal and to keep it foremost in our mind, and that was to get to the United States. To Idaho, really, because my cousin was working there, and it was he who had been sending us money ever since we left El Salvador. On our own, we didn't even earn enough money for food, much less to be able to leave Mexico. Everything costs money, and we had to pay the *coyote* $700 each to cross us from Tijuana to Los Angeles.

Finally, my cousin called us in Guadalajara and said that it was now time for us to travel. The reason we had waited was because it was cold up there in the north.

We had arrived in Guadalajara on January 20, and *estaba el mero frío*, it was freezing cold in Idaho then. So we waited until March 3 to leave Guadalajara, and then we were in Los Angeles by March 5.

Crossing was dangerous business. A friend—well, he said he was our friend, but he was not—who we had met in Guadalajara, said that he would cross us for $1,000 total. We trusted him, and since we had known him in Guadalajara, we gave him $500 and said that we would give him the other $500 when we reached Los Angeles. Then this "friend" locked us in a room, there in Tijuana, and he himself turned us in to the Mexican federal police. However, since we had spent some time in Guadalajara and had the experience of talking like Mexicans, this helped us out. The police thought that we were Central Americans and they were going to kick us out. However, they couldn't do it because we knew the colors of the flag, who was governor so-and-so, and we showed them how much we knew about Mexican history, and we did so with a Mexican accent and vocabulary. We had bought a birth certificate that said that we were children of so-and-so, and that we were from such-and-such part of Mexico. *En México todo lo compraba con dinero*—in Mexico you could buy any-thing. They finally got tired of the whole thing, charged us five thousand pesos each, which was robbery, but we had no choice. And the señora in charge of the rooms where we were staying became worried for us and said, "I'll get someone to take you across right now, I mean right now, *pero rápido pa'l otro lado*, quickly to the other side, *antes que nos vayamos a volver a morder*, before they return for another bite [bribe]."

I think that the coyotes and the Mexican government work together be-cause the police agent knew the entire area and he knew that we were carrying money that my cousin had sent us. I was, by then, in debt to my cousin for a total of $3,000; I didn't think I would ever make enough money to pay him back. But that señora, I remember her name was Josefina, said that she would get a coyote for us right away and she did. But he came up and he said, *"No más tengo cupo para uno"*—I only have room for one of you. But we were two. And then my brother said to me, *"Mano, te vas tú. De otro lado me mandas a traer"*—Brother, you go, and after you cross, send for me. He convinced me and I left. But then, when it was time to go, I couldn't go through with it. I told the coyote, *"Yo no me voy. Si hay para los dos, me voy, si no, no"*—I'm not going. If there's room for two, fine; if not, I'm not going. He said, "Okay, okay, okay," and returned to pick up my brother, who he had left in a *locked* room. We picked him up and that night, about eight o'clock, we crossed through a hole in the fence and a cable which runs right along the border.

The coyote said, "When I say run, run; when I say stop, stop and hide." When we crossed to the other side, there were migra all over the place shining the blinding lights, shouting at us, helicopters overhead. We ran and hid in the woods, and then we walked all night, *puro caminar,* through the woods, not along the highway. There were about twenty-eight of us and two coyotes, one in front and one in back. Our only objective was to arrive, just to arrive. Dead on our feet we arrived about 6 A.M. in San Diego. At 9 A.M. a car came and put six of us in the trunk. Six people! I couldn't believe my eyes! And it was a small trunk. Well, that's how we got from San Diego to Los Angeles. It took about three hours; we couldn't move and we could hardly breathe. We arrived stiff and sore, exhausted, and nearly starving, but we arrived. *Uno sufre mucho en la vida*—one suffers a great deal in this life—but, even so, we were luckier than most.

We carried $200, well hidden, because if they see you taking money out of someplace, then it's adiós and to the hospital with you. But I had to hide our money or else we would have nothing, so I unstuck the heel of my shoe and hid it there. We stayed in Los Angeles for three days waiting for my cousin to send us our plane tickets. They just gave us one meal a day, at 6 P.M. We had to stay locked up; we couldn't go outside. We were in one of those little sheds where people store their tools; they had put a sofa in it. There were ten people waiting for someone to pick them up and pay for them. Everybody had their goal to arrive at a certain destination, and *nos iban regando a distintas partes*—we were sprinkled around to different places.

Finally, my cousin sent our tickets, and we went to the airport in Salt Lake City, in Utah. He came by car from Idaho to pick us up; it was not far from the border with Utah. We stayed there until October, working in the fields, irrigating, planting, harvesting sugar beets, wheat, beans, everything. My cousin worked on a mink farm in Idaho. He left El Salvador in '79, and moved to Idaho because when he arrived at the border there was a man there who was offering passage for Mexicans to harvest in Idaho. So he ended up in Idaho, and he liked it because he was able to get year-round work, very stable, and the boss gave him many benefits. His salary covered an apartment in good condition for only $100 a month. He had his Social Security that he had bought in Los Angeles; it was not legal, but his boss didn't mind.

Meanwhile, I was still worrying about how I was going to pay back that $3,000 in one lifetime! And the *patrón,* the boss, gave us the money! After the growing season was over, we were trying to decide what to do and there was this Pentecostal family that was going to Florida. They took us there for $600. You see, it was difficult to find a ride because nobody wanted to get in trouble with the law. The family took us, but they never let us go into a restaurant to eat. They would just bring us sodas or little snacks, which we paid for. Three days like that, without being able to get out except to go to the bathroom.

We arrived in Wahneta because that's where the Pentecostal family lived. We didn't know a soul, but this nice señor showed up and said, "If you have money, I will find you a place." We had money because the season had finished and we had worked in Idaho. This man got us a trailer, bought us the gas, everything. Then the next problem, how to get work? And, how to get a ride to work? But, God is everywhere, and a señor came up and offered to pick me up and bring me home and said that he would ask his boss if I could have a job. This man is a friend; his name is Jaime.

That was our odyssey, but it only lasted a year, 1982. We arrived here in Wahneta at Halloween. But there have been many years of struggle since then. I worked first in oranges; *era naranjero*—I was an orange picker. I wanted to do other jobs that I was qualified for, such as being a mason, but the problem was our immigration papers. We still didn't have them. The next year we got them: June 27, 1983. But first, we were picked up by the migra when we went to North Carolina to work. They took us to Miami where we were detained for two months. There were 1,500 prisoners there, from twenty-eight countries, all detained for being illegals. There were two guys there, lawyers, who took a kind of census of how many were from each country and so on. One was from Colombia and the other was from Panama. And whenever we got word that someone was going to be released, these two collected funds from all of us and gave it to the people who were being released so they would leave with some money. When I left they collected $60 for me. The Colombian was there for contraband; not for being a criminal, but for carrying marijuana. He had loaded a boat with fifty tons of marijuana, can you imagine? He did five years in prison and was free on bond paying $75,000 *por la pura fianza*—just for bail! When his time was up in jail, they sent him to Miami, where we were because he was also an illegal immigrant. So, he had served his time for his offense, but he had not yet finished his time as an illegal. He's been there a long time.

Life in prison, well, it's not difficult. Of course, *no deja de ser prisión;* it's still prison, because one has no freedom, but conditions were very good. Health was very important there; each individual had to take care of his personal hygiene. If you didn't, then they would make you, because every morning, early, you had to bathe, brush your teeth, comb your hair, and then have breakfast at seven o'clock. Then you had recreation, games, weights, whatever you liked, to entertain yourself. At eleven they locked us up again, and then at twelve we formed a line to go eat. Then we were free until four, and at five we had to line up again to eat. They let us have free time until eight, when they locked us up again. They changed your bedding every day. It was very clean. José Dimas and I were there together but we were locked in a very large room with others, about two hundred people in this one room. They had big fans for ventilation and two policemen on duty at the time so that no one would rob you.

The guards were good; there they respect the prisoner. Sincerely, I'm not going to complain about them, because the truth is that they really respected you there. Those of us who were religious could go and listen to talks by evangelicals or by a Catholic priest who came on Sundays. Saturdays, from two to four in the afternoon, they had dances, if you liked dancing. They would bring a band; the women prisoners were there nearby and they danced with us. We all had the same bright uniform; we were all bright orange.

Here, in this country, one can live in peace. If I have to choose which country I love more, of course, I have to say my country. But there I could not be free. It was like being tied up and afraid all the time. Here at least I am free, I can go to the movies or anywhere I want. But there you can't do that even at three in the afternoon much less at seven in the evening, because of the violence. Sometimes there is a curfew, but there is always violence, and your life is worth nothing in the dark. It was too much. But with God's help, I made it here.

After we got out of Miami, we came to Wahneta, without a penny, nothing. The reason we came back here was that at least we had met some people who had been good to us. My brother by then had a girlfriend, and she came to pick us up when they let us out, and she brought us back. She didn't have money for gas, but we had the $60 they had given us. Once we were back here, since some people knew us, they gave us credit while we worked to get ourselves established again. If you don't have money, you can't do anything.

Meanwhile, my wife, Rosa, was still in El Salvador. This was 1983. She arrived here November 8, 1984, two years after José Dimas and myself. We were all along sending our families a little money to maintain themselves on. When we left Miami, finally we got our permissions. It was a receipt to show in order to be able to work legally, like a voucher. You could also leave the country with it, but you could not get back in. There are newer ones now where you can return as well. I would love, if God wills, to return to visit when this orange season is over. I have applied for permission for my parents to come here, but I haven't heard anything yet. I paid a lawyer for this; if I am lucky it will turn out. My papá works in the fields; my mamá no longer works, but before, she worked in the home. That's the hard part for me, to know that they are getting older, and maybe God will take them away before I can see them again. And to know that I would not be able to go to them if they were in trouble or dying because I could not come back to my family here. But one has to trust in God.

My children need a future for their tomorrow and my wife also, and the schools there were often not even open because of the violence. Maybe you studied for nearly a whole year, but you couldn't complete it; then your whole year is lost. We decided that we needed to do everything possible for our children. I told my wife that we must make the effort for them. My papá knew the day that my wife and kids left to join me that I would never return, and he was right. But I told him that we are looking to our kids' future, and I do not regret it. Our son here, Hugo Alexander Murillo, is an excellent student. He has won himself a scholarship to high school, and look at this plaque they awarded him for outstanding scholarship. He speaks very good Spanish and English. He's working hard in order to learn, and in Michigan, where we spend part of the year, they are giving him classes in French and Japanese, too, in the seventh grade. When the season is over here, we go north, around Traverse City, where we pick strawberries, cherries, pears, and apples. The change of schools is not hard for the children. They use the same books both places, and they have friends they look forward to seeing in Michigan and in Florida.

We have much to be grateful for. This house is new; it was built for us by Habitat for Humanity. One day a señora came and told me that they would like to help me, that they had $700 from a Methodist church in Michigan, and that they would start in two days if that was okay with me. They're through now. The carpenters were very good, but I did the finishing touches myself in the evenings after work.

Legal Alien

Pat Mora

Bi-lingual, Bi-cultural,
able to slip from "How's life?"
to *"Me'stan volviendo loca,"* *
able to sit in a paneled office
drafting memos in smooth English,
able to order in fluent Spanish
at a Mexican restaurant,
American but hyphenated,
viewed by Anglos as perhaps exotic,
perhaps inferior, definitely different,
viewed by Mexicans as alien,
(their eyes say, "You may speak
Spanish but you're not like me")
an American to Mexicans
a Mexican to Americans
a handy token
sliding back and forth
between the fringes of both worlds
by smiling
by masking the discomfort
by being pre-judged
Bi-laterally.

*They are driving me crazy.

Raising Hell as Well as Wheat

papago indians burying the borderline

Gary Paul Nabhan

Entre las tribus indígenas más curiosas de nuestro país, sobresalen los Pápagos. Son 800 nada más y ocupan zonas desérticas de Sonora. Los Pápagos no se consideran ni norteamericanos ni mexicanos pero sí legítimos dueños de Sonora y Arizona.

—*El Imparcial*, the Hermosillo newspaper

Isidro Saraficio is sitting in a dry irrigation ditch, under the shade of a Mexican elderberry tree, gazing out over a wheatfield wavering in the noonday heat. It's a fine stand of wheat for a desert field grown with just the rain that ran down the arroyos this winter. Isidro diverts floodwaters from a holding pond to the field through hand-dug ditches, letting gravity rather than machines do the work. Now that the grain is ripe, his friends have come to the *ranchería* to help with the harvest. After working since dawn, they lie resting, some snoring or farting in their sleep, while digesting the lunch of beans, *carne asada*, chile, tortillas, and beer. The cool shade of the elderberry soothes them for a few minutes more before they return to the wheat patch, armed with sickles, to hand-harvest the grain.

The quiet of noon is suddenly ruptured. Like a giant raptor, a Border Patrol plane breaks into sight and roars down across the land a few hundred feet over the field, causing quail and doves to flush out of the wheat. The patrolling plane zips westward, straight above the fence line and firebreak that stretches as a scar all the way to the far horizon. Sitting up as if awakening from a bad dream, Isidro's friends realize that the nightmare sound they heard is part of his everyday world. The field lies within a mile of the U.S.–Mexico border.

Isidro planted the wheat not only for pinole and popovers, but also as a political protest. He was born here on the ranch in Sonora, Mexico, when the elderberry above him first came into bloom thirty-four years ago. Yet his family has never had a deed to this place, which they have probably farmed for hundreds of years. Isidro has planted wheat on land that another man "legally" owns. The field has been worked to show that the homestead has not been deserted. Isidro "borrowed" a tractor from a U.S. high school and illegally drove it across the border to plow the field while it was still sufficiently wet to plant. Now, six months later, his Arizona friends come through the fence as "reverse wetbacks" without visas or permits, neither reporting to customs nor paying any respects to the international line. In short, Isidro is raising hell as well as wheat. He is raising his sickle to question the existence of a boundary that his people have never acknowledged.

Isidro is a Papago Indian, sharing this borderland dilemma with 10,000–15,000 of his people who refer to themselves as the Tohono O'odham. When seventeenth-century Catholic missionaries made their first *entradas* into the Sonoran Desert, they found Papago settlements in many of the places they remain today. As northern Mexico and the U.S. Southwest became Spanish colonies, the Papago adopted many Hispanic customs and technologies. To most outsiders, a place such as Isidro's looks less American Indian than Mexican.

In 1853, a political decision made thousands of miles away divided the Papago country between the United States and Mexico. Under the Gadsden Purchase, more than 5,000 square miles of Papago homeland became part of the United States. Although the majority of Papago were now nominally under the jurisdiction of Washington, they continued to associate more with the Indians and mixed-descent mestizos south of the border than with other U.S. citizens. As late as 1900, there were still enclaves of Papago miles north of the international border who thought of themselves as Mexican.

Yet, as more economic opportunities became available for Papago workers in the United States, population shifts occurred. Families that had remained in their desert rancherías on both sides of the border now migrated to U.S. towns and artificial agricultural oases which the Anglos had created with dams and wells. Today, three-quarters of the Papago people live on three reservations established for them, and fewer than a tenth of them remain in Mexico.

Isidro's family was one of the minority that chose to stay in Sonora. Isidro's father did send the boy across the border to a Catholic boarding school to learn to read and write, but the family remained at the ranch in Plenty Coyotes village, just south of the U.S. Papago Indian Reservation on the border. Then Isidro's mother died and he came home from school to live alone with his father for eight years, helping the old man with farming, ranching, and blacksmithing. When the elderly Saraficio died several years ago, Isidro and a brother inherited the family homestead.

Isidro quickly realized that although the inheritance was strong in his heart, it was weak in the courts of Mexico. The people of Plenty Coyotes are part of those called "two-village Papago," for they spend part of the year in their fields, and part at a well village miles away. When the official Mexican surveyors came through the borderland deserts years ago, they found what they presumed to be abandoned fields, and reported them as "open land." While the Papago families who had worked these lands for centuries were just a few miles away, the land was deeded to new owners, one a wealthy rancher who spends most of his time in U.S. cities. This landlord, Juan Stone, now owns 172,000 acres of land that traditionally belongs to the Papago.

Isidro began to inquire among the authorities about how an absentee landowner could retain so much land under the land reform laws. While he was still under thirty, the Sonoran Papago elected him as their representative in order to challenge the Mexican government's neglect of Papago interests. After more than a dozen journeys to Mexico City to plead the Papago case, Isidro bitterly realized that the bureaucracy does not budge easily. The Papago in Sonora could not be given government assistance in land and water resources improvement unless they legally owned the land. And when Isidro argued that they had prior claim to the land, some officials questioned whether any Papago lived in Mexico historically—hadn't they filtered down from the "other side"?

Infuriated, Isidro left his position as representative of the Papago in Mexico to study the historic sources which documented the early O'odham distribution in the Sonoran Desert. Working in the Catholic mission archives in Arizona, Isidro set out to prove his people's rights to the Sonoran lands that were part of their heritage. Yet most of the social and political scientists who usually assist Indians in these cases were either ignorant or noncommittal. One sheepishly admitted that "Juan Stone's wealthy friends in the Southwest do a lot to support our humanities programs here."

Isidro's effort finally began to be appreciated by the Papago politicians in Arizona. They were intrigued by his attempts to document the aboriginal territory of the Papago, but were not quite sure where his inquiries could lead. Finally, they began to listen to him, not as politicians listen to political radicals, but as tribal elders have always listened to those moved by a vision. Isidro was relatively young, but they felt that he spoke for hundreds of generations of O'odham.

Are not all Papago one people, wherever they live, bonded together by a common culture, language, history, and a sacred sense of community? Hasn't a simple line on a map disrupted this sense of community? Hasn't the international boundary kept Papago families from visiting traditional sites of Papago religion? Isn't the Papago tribe *less than whole* if it continues to let an arbitrary political decision divide its legacy, and dispossess part of its people? The Papago met in May 1979 and passed several resolutions which Isidro and others had drafted.

At the Sells Papago Capital Center, the Tribal Council declared that the Treaty of Guadalupe Hidalgo and the Gadsden Purchase which divided Papago country were signed without consultation or the consent of the Papago people. They agreed that to counter this historic tragedy, they would consider enrolling the Mexican Papago in the Arizona tribe so that they could share all benefits, including the $26 million land claims award granted to the tribe by the U.S. government.

The Council also requested of the Mexican government that the aboriginal lands in Mexico be set aside and reserved exclusively for the Papago, or that they be ceded or transferred to the U.S. in trust for the Papago. Isidro and his collaborators had hoped that this resolution would embarrass the Mexican government into confiscating the deeds from Stone and others in order to set up a reservation south of the border. Yet they kept open a more pragmatic possibility: if Mexico did not act soon, they would approach the absentee landlords and buy the deeds back with Arizona tribal funds, at whatever price. They would then turn over the deeds to Papago who had retained their Mexican citizenship. But the Mexican government responded at last. It helped obtain small land reserves around two Sonoran villages that the Papago could use exclusively.

Finally, the Tribal Council addressed the problem of the borderline touching the reservation, more than 60 miles of jurisdictional headache. They demanded of both national governments that Papago be given free access across the international boundary, so that their people would never be accused of being "illegal aliens" again. They also made clear that both governments had been negligent in maintaining the fence and protecting residents along the border.

Isidro was well aware of the smugglers that frequently crossed the border near his homestead. Drug runners and "coyotes" who piloted wetbacks across the border had realized that U.S. agents patrolled the Papago reservation less vigilantly than any other area along the boundary. The runners had not only cut through the boundary fence; they had cut dozens of field and range fences on Papago lands, allowing cattle to roam and destroy crops. The drug runners sometimes shot at anyone in sight—not just official-looking gringos, but unassuming Indians too. Isidro had been offered $10,000 a month or 5,000 head of cattle if he would let a crime ring use his homestead as a front.

"I could have been a rich man several times over," he told me once. "But is that a life for a family man? How could I do that to my kids?"

In a meeting with U.S. Customs and other authorities, the Papago once expressed the danger to land and life that the border's proximity created for them. Who was ultimately to be responsible for patrolling it and for protecting residents from damage? One by one, the government agencies replied in their best bureaucratic jargon that they each had partial jurisdiction, but that it was the duty of the "particulars" living along the border to maintain the fences and to keep "aliens" from illegally crossing onto their lands.

Isidro stood up and roared, "THEN IF IT IS UP TO US, WE WILL TEAR YOUR BORDER FENCE DOWN!"

After the resolutions passed, Isidro began to concentrate on the land rather than its legalities. To keep the right to land in Mexico, you must work it. Land abandoned for more than two seasons can be claimed by squatters or *ejido* cooperatives, who can then stay on it as long as they use and improve it. While Isidro had been working in Arizona with resolutions and documents, he had been worried that his homestead might be confiscated, if not by Juan Stone, then by opportunistic *colonistas*. He has thus gone down every weekend, to plant fields and gardens when there was rain, to fix up the buildings and grounds when there wasn't.

The function of his wheat planting and the passing of the resolutions coincided. In "*gracias a Dios*," he began planning for a feast in honor of San Isidro, the agricultural guardian and his patron saint. In early June I stopped by Isidro's place in Sells, but he was not there. Isidro had retired from his research and political activities in order to spend more time farming in Sonora.

The next time I saw Isidro, the talk was of pinole, not politics. We spoke too of the best time to plant beans and corn. "To me, the most beautiful thing is the coming of the first summer thunderstorms. I stay outside and watch the sky. I know it is time for things to grow again."

PART VI

Environment, Technology, and the Peoples of the Southwest

More often than not, the Southwest has been romanticized in popular literature as a retreat from the pressures of modern, industrial society. These accounts make all the more incongruous the reality of the Southwest, which, despite its rich lore of uncomplicated life, is ironically the birthplace of the atomic bomb. The region also has the dubious distinction of being the vast proving ground of the nuclear development industry and the site of nuclear waste repositories. Scientific research and development is only the latest in a series of technological impacts to have come to the Southwest. By the end of the nineteenth century, the Southwest was already the home to massive extractive industries and economic exploitation. Economic activity in the area has been intense. Ranching, mining, agribusiness, timber harvesting, and hydroelectric power have all changed the way people live in and relate to the region. Most of these extractive industries are still in operation today.

The Southwest remains highly dependent on federal dollars, and at least since the Great Depression of the 1930s, its economic development has been tied to national politics and national legislation. Federal dollars in the form of government programs and defense contracts have spawned military bases, national laboratories, scientific and space exploration, missile testing, nuclear waste facilities, BIA boarding schools, rural assistance programs, and federal land management programs. The essays in this section are arranged to introduce readers to the idea of the Southwest as a major element in questions of national security and future development.

Albuquerque Learns It Really Is a Desert Town

Bruce Selcraig

For about as long as anyone can remember the good citizens of Albuquerque have been living a fantasy when it comes to water. Despite receiving only eight inches of rain a year, residents have grown up washing their cars in the street, playing golf on lush coastal grass and using some 250 gallons of water per person per day—nearly twice as much as folks in Phoenix or Tucson.

Yet, even in hindsight it's hard to blame them. Collectively, this high desert town of nearly 500,000, which gets its entire water supply from an aquifer, was led to believe by public officials that it sat atop an underground Lake Superior.

The aquifer allowed Albuquerque to provide its citizens with some of the cheapest water in urban America—over 60 percent less than what Santa Feans pay. Better still, not only was the aquifer enormous, so the conventional wisdom went, but it was perpetually replenished underground by the Rio Grande.

"Albuquerque behaved as it understood the commodity," Mayor Martin Chavez says in defense of his town's water ethic. "If you think you have an infinite resource, using all you want is not wasteful."

Civic boosters in pursuit of boundless growth delighted in the Duke City's good fortune. Housing permits were handed out like balloons at a bank, and new business was lured with the promise that water would never be a problem. Sure, there were warnings as far back as the early 1950s that alternative sources of water must be found, but there were always experts willing to sound more optimistic, and, besides, the realists couldn't be heard for all the bulldozers.

No less an expert than Steve Reynolds, the former (and now deceased) New Mexico state engineer for over 30 years, wrote in the *Albuquerque Tribune* in 1980 that the city could, comfortably, grow to a population of 1.5 million. "Albuquerque is probably better situated with respect to water," Reynolds said then, "than any large city in the Southwest."

If Reynolds were around today some citizens might like to serve his misguided words to him fajita-style.

Albuquerque's long-overdue wake-up call came in August 1993 when the U.S. Geological Survey released a report showing that Albuquerque was pumping out its groundwater nearly three times faster than it could be replenished.

Tests showed the underground water basin had dropped by as much as 40 feet between 1989 and 1992 and nearly 140 feet in some places over the past three decades. More important, the report shot down once and for all the notion that Albuquerque had a limitless source of water.

The Rio Grande, according to the USGS report, was not replenishing (or recharging) the city's aquifer at anything approaching a steady state. In 1993 the Albuquerque area pumped about 160,000 acre-feet of water from the aquifer, while the aquifer is being replenished by rainfall and mountain snowmelt at close to 65,000 acre-feet a year.

The landmark USGS report set into motion a predictable, but nonetheless fascinating, political dance:

The city's water experts said there was no immediate crisis, just a need for concern, and more definitive studies; the city council approved higher water rates and a voluntary conservation program; business leaders promised cooperation, but told everyone how little water their businesses used compared to homeowners; community activists predicted that conservation measures would fall hardest upon those least able to afford them; and, from a distance, a few sages surveyed the tumult and said, "We told you so."

"Albuquerque has been told for 20-plus years an approximate limit of its resource," says Tony Mayne, executive director of the Santa Fe Metropolitan Water Board. "And they have simply refused to believe it. They would have you believe the USGS told them one thing 20 years ago and a different thing last year. It ain't so. It just ain't so."

Suburbs spoke up for their water interests as did everyone from Indian pueblo leaders to car wash owners. There was some civic introspection about the city-sanctioned urban sprawl of the '80s and some wonderment that a desert town could not have had a water conservation program in place, but a great deal of the public reaction to the water "wake-up call" of 1993 focused on one very large company and its enormous thirst.

Chips in the Desert

On a mesa just northwest of Albuquerque sits a 200-acre complex of massive, square, beige-and-chocolate-colored buildings beneath a flock of gangly construction cranes. Grunting earthmovers and cement trucks plow up the mesa, as visitors churn through the temporary parking looking for office buildings named Jurassic Park and Godzilla.

Surrounding this futuristic compound is an almost perfect demographic portrait of changing New Mexico: on one side an evangelical church, cookie-cutter suburban homes, fast food outlets and shopping malls; on the other, beside the tranquil Rio Grande, a stylish bed-and-breakfast adobe mingles with horse stables, vineyards and old Impalas on cinder blocks. New immigrants from Dallas and Chicago walk their dogs past the few remaining vacant lots of sage and cholla that defiantly remind everyone they're still in the desert.

This is Intel, New Mexico.

When the world's largest independent maker of computer chips, the Intel Corporation of Santa Clara, California, came to this mesa in suburban Rio Rancho in 1980, the giant had but two dozen employees and gave hardly a clue that it would one day wield great influence in the Land of Enchantment.

Intel now employs 4,000 people in Rio Rancho, plans to hire at least another 500 next year and says it creates at least two spin-off jobs in the surrounding economy for every one inside the sprawling plant. Average plant salaries are $35,000—more than double the per capita income in New Mexico, the fifth poorest state. All of which made Rio Rancho the nation's fastest growing small city in 1993.

By far the state's largest private employer at one site—Wal-Mart ranks number 1 otherwise—Intel is a powerful constituency unto itself, rivaling most neighborhood groups or labor unions and crossing all racial, religious and political lines. New Mexico politicians would be certified fools to threaten those paychecks, and so, what Intel wants, Intel usually gets.

When Intel announced in 1993 that it wanted to build a new U.S. plant to make the new Pentium and next-generation P6 chips, New Mexico officials, longing to diversify from natural resource extraction and government jobs, unveiled the most lucrative come-hither campaign the state had ever seen. Their reward was Intel's $1.8 billion Fab 11, a project that would become the third largest industrial expansion in the world that year.

Beating Texas, California, Oregon, Arizona and Utah for Intel's affections, New Mexico laid out $57 million in property tax abatement, $36 million in waived new-equipment sales taxes and $20 million in manufacturing tax credits. Taxpayers would foot $1 million for training Intel workers, air pollution permitting would be streamlined and Sandoval County, in addition to floating a $2 billion bond issue for Intel, granted the chipmaker a lease on its mesa property you would have loved back in college: Intel may grant easements and build or raze improvements at will. It may sublease without the county's approval and it has the option to buy the Rio Rancho site for $1 at the end of the lease term.

An underlying assumption throughout this corporate courting process was that the Albuquerque area could provide all the water Intel could ever want. This is no small concern because Intel and all semiconductor companies freely admit they are, by the nature of their technology, world-class water hogs.

The six- and eight-inch-diameter silicon wafers Intel makes—they're later cut by diamond saws to yield the thumbnail-size chips that serve as the brains in personal computers—must be rinsed at least 20 times in hyper-clean water to remove impurities. Exactly how much water is used in these processes is something no company will divulge, but industry expert Graydon Larrabee, a former Texas Instruments fellow, says that among six companies he surveyed, an average of 2,840 gallons was used to produce one six-inch wafer and perhaps twice that for an eight-inch. If Intel's new chip factory makes about 30,000 eight-inch wafers a month, which Larrabee says is standard, the amount of water used could reach 6 million gallons a day. (For comparison, the daily use of a really gluttonous golf course is about 1 million gallons. Intel says it returns 85 percent of this water to the Rio Grande through Albuquerque's treatment plants; however, that water never makes it back to the aquifer.)

In April 1993—five months before the alarming USGS report—Intel applied to the New Mexico state engineer, who decides water allocation issues, for a new water-use permit that would allow it to use 4,500 acre-feet of water a year, or about 4 million gallons a day. An acre-foot is the amount of water it takes to cover an acre to a depth of one foot, or about 326,000 gallons. In addition to Intel's pumped water allotment, it would continue to use about 3.5 million gallons a day from Rio Rancho Utilities, which also pumps from the aquifer.

Intel's water request, arriving almost simultaneously with the aquifer alarm, quickly struck a nerve.

In the neighboring village of Corrales, just beneath the mesa on which Intel sits, residents had already complained of foul chemical emissions from Intel which they said caused skin rashes, nausea and headaches. (Intel installed $11 million worth of oxidizers to remove the odor.) Now the Corrales citizens, fearing that Intel's request for three new deep-water wells might affect their own shallower wells and the stately cottonwoods along the Rio Grande, joined with the Sierra Club, the New Mexico Environmental Law Center and others in formally opposing the Intel water request.

"Just a few feet of draw-down would put a lot of people's wells out of business," said village board member Lawrence Vigil. Tim Kraft, once Jimmy Carter's appointments secretary, and now a Corrales resident, said at a town meeting: "We've rolled out the red carpet, and now we're finding out our guest has bad breath and an unquenchable thirst."

Intel hydrologists say a solid layer of underground rock separates its 2,000-foot wells from the 200-foot wells of many Corrales residents, and so should not affect their flow.

The Debate Begins

In June 1994, after a year of study and a four-week hearing, State Engineer Eluid Martinez granted Intel 72 percent of its water application, but required Intel to drill monitoring wells to ensure that its pumping would not affect wells in Corrales. The Intel request became a catalyst for what Albuquerque had avoided for decades — a serious discussion of water problems.

"The Intel application raised a debate about what's good for the state," Martinez later told reporters. "It was a lot of water, but not more than would be used to irrigate 2,000 acres of farmland. Drying up a golf course or two would make that water available."

Doug Wolf, attorney for the New Mexico Environmental Law Center, is not nearly so sanguine about the Intel deal. "There's a real question," says Wolf, "about whether this is the right kind of industry for an arid state that's looking to the future."

Says Wolf: "Intel argues that because it provides so many jobs they should get whatever they want. The logical extreme of that is that water should go to big business, tourism, golf courses and exclusive, gated communities which destroy what we care so much about in New Mexico and will homogenize us into Scottsdale or some kind of industrial center like Baton Rouge."

Wolf's colleague, water policy analyst Consuelo Bokum, points out that New Mexico water law requires the state engineer to consider "the public welfare" in allocating water—as does Alaska's and others—but that the standard is rarely applied and remains largely undefined by the courts. The state engineer "punted" on the issue of public welfare, Wolf says, by simply assuming that any use of water that wasn't a clear waste was beneficial.

"If ever there was an argument for taking the public welfare into account," Bokum says, "it's in Albuquerque. The highest and best use of water has historically been defined as who has the most money, and anyone else be damned."

Squeaky Clean

"Watch your head," shouts Intel's Richard Draper as he leads me under the scalp-high, finger-thick metal tubes that course for 44 miles through the windowless bowels of Intel.

We're striding briskly past boilers and air scrubbers on a classic dog-and-pony plant tour where the company P.R. man could tell the clueless reporter everything is run by gerbils on treadmills and he would be none the wiser.

Intel is a bit overwhelming for those who don't speak in gigabytes—a palace of science akin to the innards of a nuclear submarine, only much taller and wider and cleaner.

We peer through two narrow, vertical windows in the doors of a "clean" room, where workers in white, air-filtered, Gore-Tex "bunny" suits control the robots that imprint the wafers with millions of electronic circuits. How clean, you ask, is a "clean" room? Well, no particle in the air can be larger than one micron. The width of a human hair is roughly 75 microns. Intel likes to say the rooms are 10,000 times cleaner than a hospital emergency room.

"I'm still pretty awed by what goes on in there," Draper says. "It's pretty 2001 stuff."

While Intel hardly needs anyone's sympathy—Rio Rancho did half of Intel's $8.7 billion gross in 1993, and Intel plans to build similar factories every year for the next six—it's not hard to see why the giant chipmeister feels unfairly picked upon by some in Albuquerque. Like 'em or not, Intel has never hidden the fact that it uses enormous amounts of water. Knowing that, New Mexico politicians tripped over themselves to offer Intel tax breaks and never expressed doubts about the water supply. Yet, through unfortunate timing with the USGS report, Intel—rather than dairy farmers and golf courses—became the convenient whipping boy.

"The blame game kicks in early in the conservation debate," Draper tells me back in his gray-carpeted cubicle office. "You've got to put in perspective how much water we really use. Industries use only 3 percent of Albuquerque's water.

Add Intel (which is not on Albuquerque's water system) and it's 6 percent. After our expansion it's 8 percent. Residential users make up 60 to 65 percent. We could stop pumping tomorrow and it would be a blip on the screen." Draper doesn't mention that Intel's presence has also created thousands of new water users and new demands on sewers, roads, schools and such.

Draper says Intel has spent $260 million on environmental safeguards at the Rio Rancho plant since the early 1980s and has contracted with New Mexico's Sandia and Los Alamos Department of Energy labs to improve its water conservation technology. Having been an Albuquerque TV reporter before coming to Intel, Draper wasn't surprised by some of the local anti-Intel attacks.

"Our expansion came at a time of debate about growth in New Mexico," he says. "We've had a rockier road in the last year than we would like. I think New Mexico is more complex than [Intel's leaders] thought. This isn't California or Arizona. There are different cultural and economic issues here."

That much is certain.

"No gracias Intel"

At a New Mexican restaurant in Albuquerque's downtown neighborhood, Jeanne Gauna, director of the South West Organizing Project (SWOP), heads for a back table and starts throwing punches at Intel before the chips and salsa can arrive. "How could they have not known about the water problems?" Gauna laughs. "All they know is chips, right? Come on, they're exploiting a poor state. That's such bullshit."

SWOP is a 13-year-old community group that has hounded Intel on chemical emissions, hiring practices and tax breaks, not to mention water. SWOP released a 60-page report on Intel's activities that suggests New Mexico's incentive package might cost taxpayers over $140 million more than expected, questions Intel's commitment to hiring New Mexicans and portrays the semiconductor industry as one that fouls the environment, exposes workers needlessly to dangerous chemicals and breaks promises to communities. Composed of veteran activists, SWOP also crashed an Intel party at a local hotel by unfurling a 30-foot banner that read: "No gracias Intel—Super Profits, Super Toxic Pollution—Real New Mexicans Pay Taxes!"

One might think that however tempting a target Intel presents, Gauna would tread lightly on the giant because it still holds out the hope of doubling her constituents' income. But, based on recent reports that suggest Intel has always planned to rely heavily on out-of-state workers brought to Rio Rancho, Gauna has never let up.

"I'm absolutely certain," says the 48-year-old grandmother with the fiery Basque eyes, "that Intel will never be a good deal for Albuquerque. We're not anti-development or anti-growth, but Intel has yet to prove that we will benefit when almost half of the jobs are going to people from out of state. The taxpayers have underwritten their entire development, yet our communities aren't prospering."

But if not Intel, who? Ten different ways I ask Gauna if Intel is so bad, what kind of industry and which company of Intel's size would be better.

She dodges, she weaves, she trots out the line about how New Mexico should grow chilies, not (computer) chips, but suggesting a real alternative proves difficult.

"If they would pay their taxes and pay for all the infrastructure," Gauna says, "just about any industry could come in, but we should not have to pay for their profits. Intel is not sustainable growth. Their industry is famous for boom-and-bust cycles. There's no guarantee those jobs we paid so dearly for will even be there in 10 or 20 years."

Fine points, but how *should* New Mexico grow out of its dependence upon government, the military and exploiting the land? As long as states will grovel for any corporate prize it will be hard for New Mexico to turn down companies that promise thousands of jobs and at least the hope of environmental stewardship.

For the Lords of Sprawl, however, it is a laughable debate. For them, attracting and keeping Intel has been the state's greatest economic achievement in years, and they welcome all the new homes, roads, malls and fast food emporia without a second thought. They see water conservation as a worthy topic for junior high school science posters, but never as a limit to growth and profits.

Albuquerque Mayor Martin Chavez can't afford to think that way. "If we don't act now about the water problem," Chavez told me, "we will have a crisis for which our grandchildren will condemn us." Chavez says he has already rejected the overtures of a California firm that wanted to relocate in Albuquerque but wanted a guarantee of 1 million gallons of water a day.

"Three years ago Albuquerque would've been shining their shoes," Chavez says, "but their attitude wasn't one of conservation, so we basically just said, no thanks."

Chavez now heads into a city-wide water education and conservation program designed to cut water use by 30 percent in 10 years. He's already pushed through an increase to monthly water bills and is preaching the new gospel to golf courses and gardeners alike. The city is also looking into injecting treated water back into the aquifer to replenish it, as some other cities do.

If Chavez is smart, say conservationists, he'll seize this historic opportunity to play the role of Head Water Miser to the hilt. Maybe he should walk the town handing out low-flow shower heads. People are willing to conserve if they see it as an equitable, community-wide effort; and Albuquerqueños, especially, know they must change their wasteful ways. But if they see water hogs being lured to the desert, they will know that politics and money still control their future—and Chavez will have squandered his chance.

In the Belly of the Beast

Barbara Kingsolver

The Titans, in the stories of the ancient Greeks, were unearthly giants with heroic strength who ruled the universe from the dawn of time. Their parents were heaven and earth, and their children were the gods. These children squabbled and started a horrific, fiery war to take over ruling the universe.

A more modern legend goes this way: The Titans were giant missiles with atomic warheads. The Pentagon set them in neat circles around chosen American cities, and there they kept us safe and free for twenty-two years.

In the 1980s they were decommissioned. But one of the mummified giants, at least, was enshrined for public inspection. A Titan silo—a hole in the ground where an atomic bomb waited all its life to be launched—is now a missile museum just south of Tucson. When I first heard of it I was dismayed, then curious.

What could a person possibly learn from driving down the interstate on a sunny afternoon and descending into the ground to peruse the technology of nuclear warfare?

Eventually I went. And now I know.

The Titan who sleeps in his sleek, deep burrow is surrounded with ugliness. The museum compound, enclosed by an unkind-looking fence, is set against a lifeless backdrop of mine tailings. The grounds are gravel flatlands. The front office is blank except for a glass display case of souvenirs: plastic hard hats, model missile kits for the kids, a Titan-missile golf shirt. I bought my ticket and was ushered with a few dozen others into a carpeted auditorium. The walls bore mementos of this silo's years of active duty, including a missile-shaped silver trophy for special achievement at a Strategic Air Command combat competition. The lights dimmed and a gargly voice rose up against high-drama music as the film projector stuttered, then found its stride and began our orientation. A ring of Titan II missiles, we were told, encircled Tucson from 1962 until 1984. The Titan II was "conceived" in 1960 and hammered together in very short order with the help of General Motors, General Electric, Martin Marietta, and other contractors. The launch sites are below ground—"safely protected from a nuclear blast." The missile stands 103 feet tall, 10 feet in diameter, and weighs 150 tons. A fatherly-sounding narrator informed us, "Titan II can be up and out of its silo in less than a minute, hurling its payload at speeds of over 15,000 miles per hour nearly halfway around the world. This ICBM waits quietly underground, its retaliatory potential available on a moment's notice."

The film went on to describe the typical day of a missile crew and the many tasks required to keep a Titan in a state of constant readiness. Finally we were told sternly, "Little remains to remind people that for 22 years a select group of men stood guard 24 hours a day, seven days a week, protecting the rights and freedom we enjoy in these United States." Day and night the vigilant crew monitored calls from their command post, "Waiting . . ." (a theatrical pause) "for a message that never came."

We filed out of the auditorium and stood in the hostile light of the gravel compound. Dave, our volunteer guide, explained about reinforced antennas that could go on transmitting during an attack (nuclear war disturbs radio transmissions, among other things). One small, cone-shaped antenna sat out in the open where anyone could trip over it. Dave told us a joke: they used to tell the rookies to watch out, this was the warhead. My mind roamed. What sort of person would volunteer to be a bomb-museum docent? The answer: he used to be a commander here. Now, semiretired, he trained cruise-missile operators.

It was still inconceivable that a missile stood erect under out feet, but there was its lid, an enormous concrete door on sliding tracks. Grate-covered holes in the ground bore a stenciled warning: TOXIC VAPORS. During accidents or miscalculations, deadly fuel would escape through these vents. I wondered if the folks living in the retirement community just downhill, with the excruciatingly ironic name of Green Valley, ever knew about this. Dave pointed to a government-issue weathervane, explaining that it would predict which way the poisonous gases would blow. What a relief.

We waited by the silo entry port while a Boy Scout troop emerged. I scanned little boys' faces for signs of what I might be in for. Astonishment? Boredom? Our group then descended the cool stairwell into the silo. Just like a real missile crew, we put on hard hats to protect ourselves from low-hanging conduits and sharp edges. Signs warned us to watch for rattlesnakes. The hazards of snakes and bumped head struck me as nearly comic against the steel-reinforced backdrop of potential holocaust. Or put another way, being protected against these lesser hazards made the larger one seem improbable.

A series of blast doors, each thicker than my body, were all propped open to let us pass. In the old days you would have had to wait for security clearance at every door in turn before it would admit you and then heave shut, locking behind you. If you turned out to be an unauthorized intruder, Dave explained, you'd get a quick tour of the complex with your face very near the gravel.

Some forty steps down in the silo's bowels we entered the "No Lone Zone," where at least two people stood guard at all times. This was the control room. Compared with my expectations, undoubtedly influenced by Hollywood, it seemed unsophisticated. The Titan control room was run on cathode-ray tubes and transistor technology. For all the world it had the look of those fifties spaceship movies where men in crewcuts and skinny ties dash around trying to figure out what went wrong. No modern computers here, no special effects. The Titan system was built, Dave said, with "we-need-it-now technology." I tried to get my mind around the notion of slapping together some little old thing that could blow up a city.

Dave was already moving on, showing us the chair where the missile commander sat. It looks exactly like a La-Z-Boy recliner. The commander and one designated enlisted man would have the responsibility of simultaneously turning two keys and engaging the missile if that call came through. All of us stared mutely at the little holes where those keys would go in.

A changeable wooden sign—similar to the ones the Forest Service uses to warn that the fire danger today is MEDIUM—hung above the controls to announce the day's STRATEGIC FORCES READINESS CONDITION. You might suppose it went to ultimate-red-alert (or whatever it's called) only a few times in history. Not since the Cuban missile crisis, maybe. You would be wrong. Our guide explained that red alerts come up all the time, sometimes triggered by a false blip on a radar, and sometimes (unbeknownst to crew members) as a test, checking their mental steadiness. Are they truly sane enough to turn that key and strike up nuclear holocaust? For twenty-two years every activity and every dollar spent here was aimed toward that exact end and no other. "But only the President can issue that order," Dave said. I believe he meant this to be reassuring.

We walked deeper into the artificially lit cave of the silo, down a long green catwalk suspended from above. The entire control chamber hangs on springs like huge shock absorbers. No matter what rocked and raged above, the men here would not be jostled.

On the catwalk we passed an eyewash facility, an outfit resembling a space suit, and a shower in case of mishaps involving toxic missile-fuel vapors. At its terminus the catwalk circled the immense cylindrical hole where the missile stood. We peered through a window into the shaft. Sure enough it was in there, hulking like a huge dumb killer dog waiting for orders.

This particular missile, of course, is impotent. It has been relieved of its nuclear warhead. Now that the Titans have been decommissioned they're being used as launch missiles for satellites. A man in our group piped up, "Wasn't it a Titan that blew up a few weeks ago, when they were trying to launch a weather satellite?"

Dave said yes, it was, and he made an interesting face. No one pursued this line of thought, although questions certainly hammered against the roof of my mouth. "What if it'd been headed out of here carrying a payload of death and destruction, Dave, for keeping Tucson safe and free? What then?"

Like compliant children on a field trip, all of us silently examined a metal hatch opening into the missile shaft, through which service mechanics would gain access to the missile itself. A sign on the hatch reminds mechanics not to use their walkie-talkies while inside. I asked what would happen if they did, and Dave said it would totally screw up the missile's guidance system. Again, I felt strangely inhibited from asking very obvious questions: What does this mean, to "totally screw up the missile's guidance system"? That the bomb might then land, for example, on Seattle?

The Pentagon has never discussed it, but the Titan missiles surrounding Tucson were decommissioned, ostensibly, because of technical obsolescence. This announcement came in 1980, almost a decade before the fall of the Berlin Wall; it had nothing to do with letting down the nation's nuclear guard. Make no mistake about this: in 1994 the United States sank $11.9 billion into the production and maintenance of nuclear missiles, submarines, and warheads. A separately allocated $2.8 billion was spent on the so-called Star Wars weapons research system. The U.S. government document providing budget authority for fiscal year 1996 states, "Although nuclear forces no longer play as prominent a role in our defense capability as they once did, they remain an important part of our overall defense posture." It's hard to see exactly how these forces are on the wane, as the same document goes on to project outlays of roughly $10 billion for the nuclear war enterprise again the following year, and more than $9 billion every year after that, right on through the end of the century. In Nevada, New Mexico, Utah, Texas, the Great Plains, and many places we aren't allowed to know about, real live, atomic bombs stand ready. Our leaders are hard-pressed to pretend some foreign power might invade us, but we are investing furiously in the tools of invasion.

The Pentagon was forced to decommission the Titans because, in plain English, the Titans may have presented one of the most stupendous hazards to the U.S. public we've ever had visited upon us. In the 1960s a group of civilian physicists at the University of Arizona worked out that an explosion at any one of the silos surrounding Tucson would set up a chain reaction among the other Titans that would instantly cremate the city. I learned about this in the late seventies, through one of the scientists who authored the extremely unpopular Titan report. I had months of bad dreams. It was not the first or last time I was floored by our great American capacity for denying objective reality in favor of defense mythology. When I was a child in grade school we had "duck and cover" drills, fully trusting that leaping into a ditch and throwing an Orlon sweater over our heads would save us from nuclear fallout. The Extension Service produced cheerful illustrated pamphlets for our mothers, showing exactly how to stash away in the basement enough canned goods to see the family through the inhospitable aftermath of nuclear war. Now we can pass these pamphlets around at parties, or see the quaint documentary *Atomic Cafe*, and laugh at the antique charm of such naiveté. And still we go on living in towns surrounded by nuclear choke chains. It is our persistent willingness to believe in ludicrous safety measures that is probably going to kill us.

I tried to exorcise my nightmares in a poem about the Titans, which began:

When God was a child
and the vampire fled from the sign of the cross,
belief was possible.
Survival was this simple.
But the savior clutched in the pocket
encouraged vampires to prosper ·
in the forest.

The mistake
was to carry the cross,
the rabbit's foot,
the spare tire,
St. Christopher who presides
over the wrecks:
steel cauliflowers

proliferating in junkyard gardens.
And finally
to believe in the fallout shelter.

Now we are left in cities ringed with giants.

Our tour finished, we clattered up the metal stairs and stood once again in the reassuring Arizona sun. Mine tailings on one side of the valley, the pine-crowned Santa Rita Mountains on the other side, all still there; beneath us, the specter of hell.

Dave opened the floor for questions. Someone asked about that accident at a Titan silo in Little Rock, Arkansas, where some guy dropped a wrench on the missile and it blew up. Dave wished to point out several things. First, it wasn't a wrench, it was a ratchet. Second it was a crew of rookies who had been sent in to service the missile. But yes, the unfortunate rookie did drop a tool. It bounced and hit the missile's sheet-metal skin, which is only a quarter of an inch thick. And which doesn't *house* the fuel tank—it *is* the fuel tank. The Titan silo's "blast-proof" concrete lid weighs 740 tons. It was blown 300 yards through the air into a Little Rock cornfield.

Dave wanted us to know something else about this accident: the guys in the shock-absorber-suspended control room had been evacuated prior to the ill-fated servicing. One of them had been drinking a Coke. When they returned they were amazed to see how well the suspension system had worked. The Coke didn't spill.

We crossed the compound to a window where we could look straight down on the missile's nose from above. A woman near me gasped a little. A man asked where this particular missile had been headed for, back in the days when it was loaded, and Dave explained that it varied, and would depend on how much fuel it contained at any given time. Somewhere in the Soviet Union is all he could say for sure. The sight of these two people calmly discussing the specifics of fuel load and destination suddenly scared the living daylights out of me. Discussing that event like something that could really happen. They almost seemed disappointed that it never had.

For years I have wondered how anyone could willingly compete in a hundred-yard dash toward oblivion, and I believe I caught sight of an answer in the Titan museum—in faces that lit up when they discussed targets and suspension systems and megatons. I saw it in eyes and minds so enraptured with technology that they saw before them an engineering spectacle, not a machine designed for the sole purpose of reducing civilizations to rubble.

Throughout the tour I kept looking, foolishly I suppose, for what was missing in this picture: some evidence that the people who ran this outfit were aware of the potential effects of their 150-ton cause. A hint of reluctance, a suggestion of death. In the absence of this, it's easy to get caught up in the internal logic of fuel capacities, circuitry, and chemical reactions. One could even develop an itch to see if this amazing equipment really works, and to measure success in purely technical terms.

The Coke didn't spill.

Outside the silo after the tour, I sat and listened to a young man regaling his girlfriend with further details about the Little Rock disaster. She asked him, "But that guy who dropped the, whatever it was. Did he die?"

The man laughed. "Are you kidding? That door on top was built to withstand a nuclear attack, and it got blown sky-high. Seven hundred and forty tons. That should tell you what happened to the guys inside."

She was quiet for a while, and then asked him, "You really get into that, don't you?"

"Well, sure," he said. "I love machines. It fascinates me what man is capable of designing."

Since that day, I've had the chance to visit another bomb museum of a different kind: the one that stands in Hiroshima. A serene building set in a garden, it is strangely quiet inside, with hushed viewers and hushed exhibits. Neither ideological nor historic, the displays stand entirely without editorial comment.

They are simply artifacts, labeled: china saki cups melted together in a sack. A brass Buddha with his hands relaxed into molten pools and a hole where his face used to be. Dozens of melted watches, all stopped at exactly eight-fifteen. A white eyelet petticoat with great, brown-rimmed holes burned in the left side stained with black rain, worn by a schoolgirl named Oshita-chan. She was half a mile from the hypocenter of the nuclear blast, wearing also a blue short-sleeved blouse, which was incinerated except for its collar, and a blue metal pin with a small white heart, which melted. Oshita-chan lived for approximately twelve hours after the bomb.

On that August morning, more than six thousand schoolchildren were working or playing in the immediate vicinity of the blast. Of most of them not even shreds of clothing remain. Everyone within a kilometer of the hypocenter received more than 1,000 rads and died quickly—though for most of them it was surely not quick enough. Hundreds of thousands of others died slower deaths; many would not know they were dying until two years later, when keloid scars would begin to creep across their bodies.

Every wooden building within two kilometers was annihilated, along with most of the earthquake-proof concrete ones, and within sixteen kilometers every window was smashed. Only concrete chimneys and other cylindrical things were left standing. Firestorms burned all day, creating howling winds and unmeasurable heat. Black rain fell, bringing down radioactive ash, staining walls with long black streaks, poisoning the water, killing fish. I can recite this story but I didn't, somehow, believe it until I looked at things a human being can understand: great handfuls of hair that fell from the head of Hiroko Yamashita, while she sat in her house eight hundred meters from the hypocenter. The pink dress of a girl named Egi-chan, whose blackened pocket held a train ticket out of the city. The charred apron of Mrs. Sato, who was nursing her baby.

The one bizarre, incongruous thing in the museum at Hiroshima, it seemed to me, was a replica of the bomb itself. Dark green, longer than a man, strangely knobbed and finned—it looks like some invention that has nothing to do with people. Nothing at all.

What they left out of the Titan Missile Museum was in plain sight in Hiroshima. Not a sound track with a politically balanced point of view. Just the rest of the facts, those that lie beyond suspension systems and fuel capacity. A missile museum, it seems to me, ought to be horrifying. It had better shake us, if only for a day, out of the illusion of predictability and control that cradles the whole of our quotidian lives. Most of us—nearly all, I would say—live by this illusion. We walk through our days with our minds on schedule—work, kids, getting the roof patched before the rainy season. We do not live as though literally everything we have, including a history and a future, could be erased by two keys turning simultaneously in a lock.

How could we? How even to pay our monthly bills, if we held in mind the fact that we are camped on top of a technological powder keg? Or to use Carl Sagan's more eloquent analogy: we are all locked together in a room filled with gasoline vapors, insisting that because *they* have two hundred matches, *we* won't be safe until we have *three* hundred.

The Cold War is widely supposed to have ended. But preparations for nuclear war have not ended. The Titan museum's orientation film is still telling the story we have heard so many times that it sounds, like all ultra-familiar stories, true. The story is that *they* would gladly drop bombs on us, if they weren't so scared by the sheer toughness of our big missiles. *They* are the aggressors. *We* are practicing "a commitment to deterrence."

Imagine you have never heard that story before. Look it in the eye and see what it is. How do strategic-games trophies and Titan-missile golf shirts stack up against a charred eyelet petticoat and handfuls of hair? The United States is the

U.S.

only nation that has ever used an atomic bomb. Dropped it, on men and women and schoolchildren and gardens and pets and museums, two whole cities of quotidian life. We did it, the story goes, to hasten the end of the war and bring our soldiers home. Not such an obvious choice for Oshita-chan. "To protect the rights and freedoms we enjoy" is a grotesque euphemism. Every nuclear weapon ever constructed was built for the purpose of ending life, in a manner so horrific it is nearly impossible to contemplate. And U.S. nuclear science has moved steadily and firmly, from the moment of its birth, toward first-strike capacity.

If the Titan in Green Valley had ever been allowed to do the job for which it was designed, the firestorm wouldn't have ended a world away. Surely all of us, even missile docent Dave, understand that. Why, then, were we all so polite about avoiding the obvious questions? How is it that a waving flag can create an electromagnetic no-back-talk zone? In 1994, half a century after the bombing of Hiroshima, we spent $150 billion on the business and technology of war— nearly a tenth of it specifically on nuclear-weapons systems. Any talk of closing down a military base raises defensive and reverent ire, no matter how wasteful an installment it might be. And yet, public debate dickers and rages over our obligation to fund the welfare system—a contribution of about $25 a year from each taxpayer on average, for keeping the poorest among us alive. How can we haggle over the size of this meager life preserver, while shiploads of money for death sail by unchallenged? What religion of humankind could bless the travesty that is the U.S. federal budget?

Why did I not scream at the top of my lungs down in that hole?

I didn't, so I'll have to do it now, to anyone with the power to legislate or listen: one match in a gasoline-filled room is too many. I don't care a fig who is holding it.

I donned the hard hat and entered the belly of the beast, and I came away with the feeling of something poisonous on my skin. The specter of that beast could paralyze a person with despair. But only if you accept it as inevitable. And it's only inevitable if you are too paralyzed with despair to talk back. If a missile can do no more than stop up our mouths, with either patriotic silence or desperation, it's a monument the living can't afford. I say slam its doors for good. Tip a cement truck to the silo's gullet and seal in the evil pharaoh. If humanity survives long enough to understand what he really was, they can dig him up and put on display the grandiose depravity of the twentieth century.

I left, drove down into the innocent palm-shaded condominiums of Green Valley, and then, unexpectedly, headed up the other side of the valley into the mountains. When I reached the plateau of junipers and oaks I pulled off the road, hiked into the woods, and sat for a long time on a boulder in the middle of a creek. Water flowed away from me on either side. A canopy of sycamore leaves whispered above my head, while they waited for night, the close of one more day in which the world did not end.

In a poem called "Trinity," Sy Margaret Baldwin explained why she would never go down to the site of the first atomic bomb explosion, which is opened to the public every year:

> I would come face to face with my sorrow, I
> would feel hope slipping from me and be afraid
> the changed earth would turn over and speak
> the truth to the thin black ribbons of my ribs.

The Box That Broke the Barrier

the swamp cooler comes to
southern arizona

Bob Cunningham

In Arizona, man's best friend is not the dog; it is the evaporative cooler. Imagine northern states without man-made heat in winter. The condition, in reverse, persisted in the arid Southwest until fairly recent times. Summers were unbearable. Weeks of high temperatures. Discomfort. Shortage of sleep. Accidents and errors. Personal frustration. Even miscarriages. Healthy migrants shied away, and permanent residents escaped to the mountains or the Pacific coast. Development, except for mining, lagged until the late 1930s. Industries would not go where production would slump through three to four consecutive months each year.

Then a new day dawned, and a key factor, if not *the* key factor, was a device which enabled virtually everyone to live and work through the torrid months. It cut interior temperatures better than fans or traditional cooling measures, and it cost far less than refrigeration. Once it was available, the great change began. The trickle of immigration became a tide, and year after year Arizona's rate of growth in population and production exceeded the national average. If discovery of gold in California caused the greatest westward migration in our history, the invention of the swamp cooler did almost as well.

How did it originate? The question is a tantalizing one, clouded by conflicting claims. Its evolution from a homemade gadget to a production-line commodity is a story in itself. Its rise to popularity over other cooling systems is homespun economic history, and its demands for seasonal attention engendered heartwarming neighborhood jollifications.

An evaporative cooler, or swamp box, is a louvered cabinet at a window or on a roof with panels of water-saturated open-mesh matting through which outside air is driven by an electric impeller and into the building. Direct evaporative cooling, exemplified by this combination, should be distinguished from simply moving air, which may make damp skin feel cool, and from mechanical refrigeration. Another form of direct evaporative cooling directs the airflow over a cooling tower or radiator without contacting moisture. The swamp box, however, leads all the rest in popularity in arid areas. Thanks to its low original and operating cost it cools most buildings in southern Arizona, including many homes with refrigeration.

The way it works can be described in technical or simple terms: direct evaporative cooling exploits adiabatic saturation; it transfers sensible heat from the air to latent heat in the water. If that explanation is hard to handle, try this:

> Evaporation of water requires heat. In the case of water evaporating from a kettle, the heat is supplied by a burner. When water evaporates from a wetted filter, the heat is supplied by the water and the air. [This] causes the temperature of the water and of the air to become lower. The air leaves "cooler and moister." This evaporative cooling system is best adapted to the arid regions where the hot dry air can be converted to cool moist air and the added moisture tolerated.[1]

Direct evaporative cooling apparently was used in principle in ancient China, Egypt, India and Iran. It is said that the method was also employed in Herculaneum and Pompeii where servants are depicted fanning air over water jars toward assembled dignitaries. In later years Leonardo da Vinci experimented with a fan-driven cooling system.

In our own Southwest the Spaniards found that natives draped a mesh of cactus fibers or grass over clay water jars (ollas) which, purposely under-fired, were slightly porous. Given any breeze, the dampened evaporative mesh kept the water relatively cool, inducing condensation which continued the dampening. Anglo settlers learned that some coolness was lent to the home by hanging the swathed olla in a doorway or window. Settlers later learned to hang wetted burlap at the top of wall openings. Part of the duty of a barber-shop sweeper, at least in Tucson, was to keep wetting a bug-bar curtain to achieve the same effect. Desert travelers wetted the felt covers of canteens or filled porous water bags, in both cases cooling the contents by evaporation.

The principle was used in many other ways. Freight crews on the Southern Pacific, for example, employed it by hanging gunnysacks over the cupola of the caboose. After tanking up his locomotive, the engineer would pull forward and pause while the trackside spout drenched the cupola drapery. Then the movement of the train forced air through the burlap, causing evaporation and cooling the otherwise oven-hot caboose. In many households a crate called a food box, surrounded by burlap or cheesecloth trailing in a trough of water, was exposed to the breezes. The netting kept itself damp by drawing up moisture like a wick and evaporation kept the food cool.

After electric fans were introduced, a generation of desperate Arizonans risked pneumonia by bedding in a damp sheet under the thrust of a fan. Tucson attorney Ralph Bilby recalls keeping a wet sheet in front of a fan to comfort his wife and first child, born June 18, 1917.[2]

Meanwhile more scientific approaches were being taken. On April 15 and 22, 1884, Boston's William V. Wallace was awarded U.S. Patents 297,039 and 297,476 for machines designed to cool by blowing air over wetted discs. In Europe other systems blew air over pre-cooled water.[3] Early automotive radiator systems gave impetus to indirect evaporative cooling, blowing air over cooled coils or tubes. None of these systems, however, stood up to the homely swamp box, when at last it was invented.

It may have originated in Phoenix, the brainchild of a man named Oscar Palmer. Basing his ideas on an interview with Palmer's son, Arthur William Gutenberg wrote in 1955: "In 1908 Mr. Oscar Palmer, Sr., built the first drip type evaporative cooler in Arizona. The cooler consisted of an electric fan mounted in a box. Three sides of the box were covered with chicken wire, the fourth open. Coal was placed behind the wire and kept wet. The fan propelled air over the wetted coal into the living quarters."[4]

In 1956 a Phoenix source affirmed that Palmer's Metal Works did devise such a contrivance in 1908 but described it with one significant difference. It had a "manually filled upper tank dripping water through holes onto burlap netting. An obliging breeze—when one happened along—furnished the 'fan.'"[5]

Later, of course, the electrically powered impeller became a critical component of the swamp box, but in 1908 electric fans were luxuries for the rich. Dentists offered a "complete and comfortable" set of false teeth for $10 while a fan cost $17. It took twenty-five years for a fan to become cheap enough for common use. Perhaps the birth date of the characteristically cheap swamp box, complete with electric fan, was set too early. Oscar Palmer relied on the breezes or his device cost too much for most people.

Householders did not wait for Oscar Palmer's invention to go into production. They began to combine the common food box and the damp-sheet-with-fan. Tucsonan Dick Hall wrote in his unpublished memoirs that between 1910 and 1917 his brother Harry put a fan in an apple crate, nailed a gunnysack over the outside, wet the sacking and "blew cool air around our house."[6] Undoubtedly others did the same.

Such primitive makeshifts shared a major shortcoming. The wetted material either failed to carry enough moisture to permit effective evaporation, with available draft, or retained so much that fan-blown drops spotted furniture and wallpaper. The soft material became soggy and subject to mildew. Excess water, drained through the bottom, left a messy pool that nurtured mosquitoes. To correct these drawbacks, men who were handy around the house kept trying to rig a contraption that would genuinely cool at least one room and that they could tolerate and afford. At home and in repair shops they experimented with different means of suspending the moisture, including blankets and burlap, charcoal and wood chips, generally settling on the wood shavings called excelsior. They tried using a single panel or pad, set between the fan and the house-opening. They went the other way, drawing air through pads on three to five faces of the cubicle and blowing directly into the house. They sought handier water controls. They worked without publicity and nobody gave them much notice. Boxes began to appear on buildings in the 1920s, but informants say they attracted no more attention than did odd birdhouses.

The pace of development was quickening, however. Former City Engineer Glenton Sykes recalled that in 1930 or 1931 an apprentice at the Taylor Metal Works in Tucson worked up a window box with an exceptionally effective combination of moist mat, fan power and water control.[7] According to historian John R. Watt, "the first mechanical direct evaporative cooler developed about 1932.... By 1933, thousands of homemade coolers had appeared in Arizona.... The University of Arizona conducted experiments to find optimum designs and circulated mimeographed instructions.... The idea spread widely."[8]

Hard times during the Great Depression contributed to the explosive production of swamp boxes. Jobs were scarce and many men had all the time there was to work at home. The cost of materials was low. Fans were now easily affordable. Additionally, more and more assistance was available to the do-it-yourselfers. Directions for making evaporative coolers were given out by newspapers; hardware and building-supply dealers offered kits. The result was described by Arizona's director of the Federal Housing Administration in a May 31, 1936, statement aimed to attract loan applications:

During the summer of 1935 literally thousands of Arizona homes were cluttered up with make-shift, homemade air-cooling devices. These were made of . . . wallboard, chicken wire, excelsior matting, an electric fan and a perforated trough to trickle water over the excelsior. They worked surprisingly well [but] did not properly condition the air, got stale and wore out and interfered with [window] lighting. Hundreds of Arizona residents have already replaced the make-shift box with standardized machines.[9]

Statistics confirm the invasion by the swamp boxes. For example, "In 1935 Phoenix had 1,500 of these window coolers. A year later, the Central Arizona Power and Light Co. counted about 5,000."[10] The Bureau of Reclamation put out 1,000 units in 1936 to alleviate the discomfort of its workers on dams.[11]

In spite of skeptics who pointed out that the boxes were often poorly assembled, poorly installed, poorly maintained and less than fully effectual, the surge of acceptance was not to be denied and people continued to make their own boxes. All that was required was building the cabinet and gathering and assembling the working parts. Not that it was easy. Archaeologist Emil Haury recalls that "stuffing the excelsior neatly into a semicircular wire cage and the whole contraption into a window tested my old-time religious restraints more than anything since plowing behind a rack of five mules."[12]

The market was essentially local and not yet ready for even small-scale manufacturing, but enterprisers sought continually to share in the action. Sheet-metal shops first got into the act by offering framed and top-covered weather-resistant cabinets in custom and popular sizes. Firms which could provide the other components tried to package them for assembly. Engineer Bob Lenon recalls that Imperial Hardware's Yuma branch proffered a wide selection of these components.[13]

A late-blooming Cinderella, the homely swamp box found footing for its grass roots amid industrialized competition. Engineers endorsed Carrier and other makes of refrigeration; dealers advertised their franchised brands. Contractors favored that patrician method of cooling, as, not surprisingly, did the suppliers of electricity. Radiator forms of indirect evaporative cooling were turned out by factories and heavily promoted by dealers.

Manufacturers began to displace some of the do-it-yourself swamp box volume by correcting shortcomings of the home-assembled models. "The engineered [model] washes the circulating air and is quiet."[14] The manufactured cooler is "more sightly, efficient, and durable."[15] Meanwhile, starting about 1937, most new buildings were provided with ducts to convey heated air to each room. A cooler installed on the roof could use the same ducts for cooling. This added to the demand for manufactured coolers, and by 1938 it was "estimated that direct evaporative coolers number[ed] ten times that of all other types in Arizona."[16] Although much of that volume was handled by just three Phoenix firms, each manufacturer retained the individualistic attitude of his small-scale start and personally strove to outdo his competitors by adding improvements while holding prices down.

Now that the evaporative cooler was a success and in assembly-line production, new voices were heard claiming credit for its invention. Loudest of these voices belonged to residents of Yuma which, as the hottest city in Arizona, might have been expected to take the first step first. Appropriately, in 1979, a journalist attributed the invention of the swamp box to a Yuma man: "Ingenious garage mechanic A. J. Eddy invented the evaporative cooler."[17] Another patriotic Yuman wrote: "In 1934 someone had the idea of what we now call the 'Desert' or 'Evaporative' cooler. Mr. Eddy built the first one in Yuma. He . . . determined what size of cabinet and pads were required for various sizes of fans, the advantages of certain types of fan blades, and developed a most efficient cabinet. . . . It changed the living conditions of the desert almost overnight."[18]

Tucson also had its claim to precedence, but nobody knows who really thought of the swamp box first. Likewise, it is almost impossible to date and attribute the advent of each improvement. We do not know who first combined a float-valved reservoir on top with a catchment on the bottom and an electric pump to recirculate the water—a combination which conserved water, did away with messy drainage and reduced need for adjusting the flow. Then there was the air filter, removable for cleaning, which was placed in a funnel-like cowling just back of the fan to keep bugs and dust from blowing into the cooled building and to dissipate odors emanating from the pads. Somebody invented three other items appealing to swamp-box users. One was insulation of the structure to be cooled. A second was the water softener which, when applied to the cooler's supply, greatly reduced the bad smell caused by the action of water-borne chemicals on the excelsior pads and at least postponed clogging of the drip holes and encrustation of the cabinet and fan assembly. Third was the dehumidifier. In various forms this device helped to keep interior humidity low enough for the cooler to be effective up to the brief peaks in the "monsoon" season.

The greatest improvement of all was the "squirrel run," consisting of a series of blades mounted in a circle, turning like a steamer's paddlewheel or a turbine and very much resembling Leonardo da Vinci's water-wheel cooler.[19] As a blower, it conveyed many more cubic feet of air per minute than a typical fan, enabling a box to cool more area by forcing more air over the evaporative pads and through a whole building's duct system.

By 1941 it was a rare structure in southern Arizona that did not use at least one cooler, perhaps nine out of ten of them being swamp boxes. All kinds of shops and warehouses—even bakeries, greenhouses, restaurants and poultry farms—found them profitable. A new and substantial regional industry had been born. Southern Arizona now operated without a summer slump. And that was only the beginning. Plastics, lighter and more resistant to corrosion than most metals, became standard for components from impellers to cabinets. Permanently lubricated motors required less space and care. Remote, even automated, controls were borrowed from other machines. A phased switch could start water dripping; a humidistat in the bottom of the box would start the blower when the mats were damp and ready, and these controls could also work in reverse, stopping the drip or the impeller if either malfunctioned. Slabs of mesh, made in standard sizes from mulched and treated paper, came to displace excelsior pads.

Aesthetic considerations were also served. Cabinets became less bulky and conspicuous, and some roof types were handsomely masked as cupolas, complete with weathervanes. A few were low and cylindrical with round, horizontal pads reminiscent of the 1884 wetted discs. Some were made of stainless steel, and some were finished in shades to blend with roof or wall. It was possible, after so many years, to be proud of one's swamp box.

It was not possible, however, to neglect it. Though less vulnerable to untreated Arizona water than was the radiator or indirect evaporative cooler and far less demanding than the refrigerative cooler, swamp boxes did need some attention. The handbook compiled by the University of Arizona in the early days advised that "pads of organic material should be dried weekly and seasonally flushed with a weak Clorox or Purex solution to avoid going sour and always before start up and after dust storms."[20] Few users were anywhere near so thorough. They treated their coolers, usually, with a wise and salutary neglect. Professional services grew more readily available with the thousands of boxes installed, but most people could maintain their own by following a printed checklist and working for a few hours each year, or they could learn from knowledgeable neighbors. In the fall they would shut the cooler down; in the spring, they would fire it up. The Rite of Spring was reported by Ted Craig in the *Tucson Citizen* on May 13, 1983:

Tomorrow is Swamp Box Day in Tucson. Tomorrow is the day when about 50 percent of the city's male population will be found on rooftops, sweating and swearing and making poor use of pliers, Budweisers, wire brushes, Coors, tar brushes, Michelobs, straightened coat hangers, and anything that might make those *N!!?/A evaporative coolers work. A lot of Tucsonians already have been on rooftops, many last weekend, some even earlier. There were some disgustingly efficient persons who cleaned up their swamp boxes back in the cooler months. . . . Then, a few days ago when the temperatures started edging toward the 90s, they merely flicked a couple of switches. . . . There's another type of guy—the one who doesn't sweat the swamp box routine, but just throws the switches when hot weather arrives. He lives by the conviction that, if it ain't broke, don't fix it. . . . He usually has the coolest house in the neighborhood—right up to the moment the bottom drops out and water pours through the ceiling.

Why is it called a swamp box? Not one of eight old-timers who have lived with the direct evaporative cooler since its infancy was certain, but all made similar guesses. Contractor Julian Hayden, who built a box that served him well for thirty years, speculated thus: "If it wasn't looked after, an early box became a miniature marsh. Bugs and fungus would grow in the wet pads or in the drainage under a window box. This would smell like a swamp."[21]

Smelly, inefficient and exasperating it may have been, but the swamp box broke the barrier that had blocked arid Arizona from its potential; it made the summers bearable and productive. It deserves its own museum.

Notes

1. Seicho Konzo, J. Raymond Carroll, and Harlan D. Bareither, *Summer Air Conditioning* (New York: Industrial Press, 1958), pp. 165, 168.

2. Bilby interview with Cunningham, May 23, 1984, Tucson.

3. Charles H. Harter, "The Cooling of Air in Summer," *Southern Engineer,* October 1910, p. 64.

4. Arthur William Gutenberg, "The Economics of the Evaporative Cooler Industry in the Southwestern United States" (Ph.D. diss., Stanford University, 1955), p. 23.

5. "Phoenix: World's Cooler Capital," *Arizona Days and Ways*, March 11, 1956, p. 104.

6. Dick Hall, "Sixty Years of a Misspent Life," typescript in Charles Leland Sonnichsen Collection, Arizona Historical Society, Tucson, p. 34.

7. Sykes interview with Cunningham, May 2, 1984, Tucson.

8. John R. Watt, *Evaporative Air Conditioning* (New York: Industrial Press, 1963), pp. 7–8.

9. *Tucson Daily Star*, May 31, 1936.

10. Jay Wagoner, *Arizona's Heritage* (Santa Barbara: Peregrine Smith, 1977), p. 309.

11. Gutenberg, "The Economics of the Evaporative Cooler Industry," p. 26. Also B.O.R. spokesman Walsh, phone interview with Cunningham, May 17, 1984.

12. Haury interview with Cunningham, May 10, 1984, Tucson.

13. Lenon interviews with Cunningham, May 8 and 16, 1984, Tucson and Patagonia.

14. James H. Collins, "Cooling the Desert Air," *Desert Magazine*, May 1939, p. 9.

15. L. G. Tandberg, "More Efficient Cooling for Desert Homes," *Desert Magazine*, June 1939, p. 32.

16. Martin L. Thornburg and Paul M. Thornburg, "Cooling for the Arizona Home," University of Arizona Agricultural Extension Circular 105, May 1939, p. 15.

17. Karen Thure, "Yuma Yesterday," *Arizona Highways*, November 1979, p. 9.

18. W. H. Westover, *Yuma Footprints* (Tucson: Arizona Pioneers Historical Society, 1966), p. 32.

19. Keith Allen Pieper, "Solid State Electronic Control of A. C. Motors in Evaporative Cooling" (master's thesis, University of Arizona, 1971), p. 7.

20. Thornburg and Thornburg, "Cooling for the Arizona Home," pp. 29–30.

21. Hayden interview with Cunningham, May 2, 1984, Tucson.

Urbanization Drains Reverence for Water

Ted Jojola

It's that time of the season again. *Mayordomos*, or ditch bosses, come out of hibernation. Way ahead of anyone else, they inspect irrigation ditches and assess this coming summer's work.

It's a rite of spring that has been carried on for centuries in this, the arid Southwest. Without irrigation, little of what we know as home would exist today.

When the first Spanish explorers came into the region, they found a Pueblo culture flourishing in the Rio Grande Valley. Around the immediate vicinity of Albuquerque, there were estimated to be 40,000 Indian "souls," principally of the Tiguex language group (today known as Tiwa).

Coronado's expedition of 1540 chronicled over 20 Tiwa villages among "fields of maize and dotted with cottonwood groves."

Like their cousins, the Hohokam, from whose ruins rose the present-day Phoenix, Arizona, they built extensive irrigation systems.

Today the only remnants of this extensive Tiwa culture are the pueblos of Isleta, Ysleta del Sur, and Sandia—and a whole bunch of ruins.

But the traditions of irrigation continued. Spanish colonists modified these traditions. The pueblos adapted new technologies and food crops. Eventually, from all this activity, evolved a distinctive philosophy of water.

For the farmer, water was and is considered the *sangre*, the life-blood. So it is no surprise that the main irrigation channels are still affectionately called the *acequia madre*, or mother of ditches; mother of all.

Albuquerque sprawls over the vast acres of what were once Pueblo and Spanish colonial farmsteads. Fertile fields that sustained generations of Nuevo Mexicanos and indigenous people are now paved over, victims of the city and its suburbs. And as a result of urbanization, we appear to have forgotten the basic relationship of life and water.

Occasionally, if one looks carefully, you can still discern the embankment of a ditch anywhere in the valley.

More often than not, they are lifeless vestiges of piled earth—choked to death with the trash and downstream effluent of uncaring urbanites.

And if you live downstream, like I do, then you are really reminded of that disrespect. Watergates overflow with trash; anything—the infamous orange barrels, automobile tires, oil cans, water heaters, soap scum, and bloated carcasses to name a few. It's not a pretty sight.

But in spite of this, water remains a magnet. In some parts of the city, ditches are the only multiuse lands left. They provide pathways for horses, dirt bikes, bicycles, and even joggers.

These are all activities that are prohibited by water authorities, but are nonetheless done with gleeful abandon.

Some years ago, after a rash of drowning incidents, the city of Albuquerque launched an educational campaign to keep children away from these ditches. You can still see the cartoon image of the Ditch Witch, complete with broom and witch hat, gracing the bumpers of thirsty cars.

Her message is simple, "ditches are dangerous, stay away." But given the Puritanical origins of that witch, a Salem witch, such danger can also be equated with evil. This meaning represents the antithesis of native and indigenous water traditions.

The releasing of water into the ditches is still a ceremonial rite practiced by many Pueblo and non-Pueblo communities alike. It is an occasion for celebration. And the message is hardly evil—rather it is "respect." We are reminded that water can take life as easily as it can give it.

I think urbanites like those of Albuquerque can still learn much from these traditional attitudes. Such attitudes of respect go straight into the heart of what is community.

If you regard the acequias as a nuisance, then they are bound to become deathtraps. Respect them and they will offer you a bounty that is irreplaceable.

Albuquerque continues to be one of the major cities of the Southwest that continues to turn its back on its riverways.

Ask the average Joe or Jane if they've ever been to the river and they will probably answer no. Ask them if they know what an acequia is and they will remain dumbfounded. That's sad.

The irrigation system is part of Albuquerque's heritage. The entire community should celebrate the opening of the watergates and not undermine their significance.

So if the city is serious about revamping its image, then it should look in its own back yard. I believe it's called maturity.

The Navajos and National Sacrifice

Donald Grinde
and Bruce Johansen

As Emma Yazzie approached her hogan from Shiprock, New Mexico, on Highway 550, the sky gradually changed color from the familiar pastel turquoise blue of the surrounding countryside to a murky, hazy brown. Herding sheep up a hill below her hogan, Emma might have called the muddy sky above her a Chicago sky—if she had ever been to Chicago. But she has never even been as far as Tucson or Phoenix, the cities whose industries have been largely responsible for the deathly smoke that cloaks her home and sheep.

Emma Yazzie was nearly seventy years of age in 1976. Ever since she was two years old, Yazzie had lived here, where during the early 1960s four smokestacks near her hogan began to billow the smoke signals of death. The four smokestacks belong to the Four Corners Power Plant, the largest single source of electric power—and pollution—in the western United States. After it was built, other power plants began to appear nearby, to sate the growing appetite for electricity. By contrast, throughout her entire life, Yazzie's consumption of electricity has been constant—at zero.

Chiseled by the wind, Yazzie's kind and weathered face exudes a rugged strength, the result of countless days spent herding sheep in the blazing sun of summer and during the blizzards of winter. A smile etches valleys into it when she talks of the past of clear skies, fat sheep, and goats which gave milk. However, Yazzie's face turns somber when she describes the power plant. Her melodic

Navajo words for the plant can be translated as: "This is the biggest, baddest disease ever visited on mankind." For thousands of years Yazzie's forebears woke up to a turquoise sky. Now, she wakes up to a brown sky smelling of burning dirty clothes and old tires. Some days the smoke funnels up the hill, over the poisoned lake and the chemical-coated grass, and into her hogan. She becomes sleepy and ill. A few hundred yards from the back of her home, a giant coal mining dragline scatters the bones of her ancestors, drawing from the earth the coal which feeds the plant's turbines and generators. In plush boardrooms in distant cities Yazzie's home is called a "national sacrifice area."

However, Yazzie will not move; she says that she will die here and that her bones will be returned to the earth, to join those of her ancestors. She does not say these things in a dramatic tone, to impress visitors. Rather, it is just the way things are done—the way of the creation. "The mother earth is very sacred to the Navajos . . . we replace what we take . . . we are born of the earth, and we return to rest," says Yazzie slowly and methodically.[1]

The draglines will not let the dead rest. Yazzie does not understand why people in the cities must use twice as much electricity as they did a generation ago. She has been to Shiprock, twenty miles to the southwest, and seen the artificial light, but she does not see much point to it. She is wise and dignified, and the Navajos listen to her. The power plant speaks a language of whistles and groans and mechanical voices, and it does not hear the wisdom of the earth nor the ages.

Yazzie speaks with her hands as she holds an imaginary lamb. "My sheep are dying. Their noses bleed. The baby goats do not grow up." She runs her left hand over the dusty earth, a foot above the surface, saying, "That's as big as they get now." Then Yazzie holds her hands an inch apart. "The wool is this thick now. It comes off in dirty brown balls. Before this disease—this thick." She holds her hands four inches apart. "And . . . I lose half the lambs. The ones which grow up are too skinny to sell. And the goats give no milk."[2] Before the power plant came, her lambs were fat, her sheep's wool was thick, and her goats gave milk. She lived relatively well, selling the wool or weaving rugs from it for the trading posts, producing lamb and mutton, and selling goat's milk. Now the sheep's thin, brown wool barely covers their skin. Before the year which the men at the power plant call 1963, Yazzie supported herself, but afterwards she got $80 a month from the government. The "free enterprise" system of rip-and-run resource exploitation has made her a "welfare Indian." When the government money runs out, she asks friends and relatives for food; when they are hungry, so is she.

While the affluent bask in electrically heated swimming pools in Phoenix, Yazzie goes hungry; ironically some of the coal which provides the electricity to heat the pools comes from the coal strip mine behind her hogan. She offers to take visitors into the huge, serpentine mine. "If you go alone, they will turn you back," she says. "They are afraid of me." Driving into the mine, Yazzie points to spots of brilliant green among the brown scrub land. "These are the reclaimed areas," she says. "Aren't they beautiful? But they won't last. They are drowned in water and fertilizer. And this kind of grass is not even native here. It will not survive." It is public relations grass, kept for touring government officials and television crews. At the bottom of the mine, Yazzie stands, her face to the sun, and points toward the dragline grabbing mouthfuls of earth. The shovel could hold several buses and cars. "That," she says, "is what I am fighting."[3]

Yazzie is shown standing at the bottom of one of the largest coal strip mines in the Western Hemisphere. Once the miners staked a road across her pasture for the trucks which rumble out of the mine toward the plant, without asking her permission. She pulled up the stakes, carried them to the mine manager's office, threw them on his immaculate desk, and raged: "You power plant people are watching us starve! You are making money off the coal in Navajo land, and you don't care for anything else! The earth is dying!" Occasionally Yazzie joined younger Navajos to protest coal development during lease negotiations in the tribal capital of Window Rock, Arizona. She smiles as she describes the bewildered expression on the faces of the riot police who confronted her.

Yazzie fought "progress," as defined by power plant developers and miners, whereby resources are mined from the earth, bought, sold, and used up. Plans in the middle 1970s called for at least three more coal-fired power plants in the Four Corners area. In addition, the developers wanted to build six coal-consuming plants which would make synthetic natural gas in the Burnham area, a few miles south of Yazzie's hogan. By 1990, that anticipated pace of development had not been maintained, but there was still plenty of coal dust and air pollution in the area. The coal-gasification plants are so dirty that no one can live within thirteen miles of them, and so risky and expensive that banks would not finance them without government guarantees. The developers wanted billions of dollars from the federal government to build the plants during the energy crisis years of the 1970s.

Conversation in Yazzie's hogan does not center on energy policy, however. Nor does it center on the technology of power production, on conservation, or on solar, wind, or geothermal power. Yazzie talks about what she knows and what she sees—the smoke signals of death, resistance, and survival; dying lambs and poisoned water, and the rape of the sacred earth. The flicks of millions of urban light switches sing Yazzie's death song.

Mining the "Mother Mountain"

Across a mountain range from Yazzie's hogan the giant coal shovels dig into another strip mine on Black Mesa, the Mother Mountain of the Navajo spirit. If the harmony of the Mother Mountain is destroyed, it is said, the Navajos, who call themselves the Diné, will die: survival of a people is tied to survival of the land. Yazzie, by refusing to move from her land, stands with the traditionals, whose Mother Mountain is Black Mesa. For energy developers, however, Black Mesa has become a tabernacle to another religion: that of power, progress, and profit.

The coal which gives Black Mesa its dark color has the consistency of hard, dry dirt. Until technology was developed to crush the coal and combine it with water, forming a dirty sludge which could be transported away in pipelines, the coal companies saw little value in it. As this technology was being developed, coal strip mining was becoming cheaper for the companies than underground mining in the East. Machines were developed which didn't complain about wages or working conditions, machines which never demanded pensions, went on strike, or got black lung disease. The western coal rush had begun; the companies were enticed westward not by the exhaustion of coal in the East but by the profit potential of open-pit mines in the West. The huge draglines float above the tabletop of the mesa, giraffe-like, their necks reaching three hundred feet into the air; their wheels propelling gigantic digging machines. The signs around the mine give the name of the company, Peabody. The coal becomes coal slurry, which, transported to giant smokestack-crowned monoliths in the desert, becomes electricity, which is carried in high-voltage transmission lines across the Navajo Reservation to Los Angeles, Phoenix, Tucson, and many other places outside the land of the Diné. The spidery, steel superstructures carrying the high-voltage lines stand in rank order, their cargo of kilowatts buzzing over Navajo homes, most of which have no electricity.

Across the countless ridges of mountains, across the plateaus and the deserts, in California the doctors of consumption have been at work developing new ways for people to use the power which comes out of the breast of the Mother Mountain. For example, the taste and waste makers have been test-marketing an electric toilet seat. Rusco American Bidet Corporation advertises that for a mere $175 to $195 its electric bidet will substitute for toilet paper a jet of electrically heated water and further claims that the bidet is "environmental" because it saves trees that would otherwise be used for toilet paper.[4] Of course, the inventors of such products do not seem concerned about where the electricity to run them comes from and the consequences of obtaining it. Those who are made to sacrifice so that such energy can be produced are seldom able to make use of such products. A majority of Navajo homes are automatically out of the market for the electric toilet seat because they have no running water. Most Navajo homes could also not make use of another California dream, the Mobot. The ultimate lawn mowing convenience sold for $700 in 1976, or slightly less than what the average Navajo earned that year.[5] Of course, most Navajos do not have lawns as Californians know them anyway, and the Navajos have been using automatic lawn mowers for centuries—they call them sheep.

In order to justify more production, the developers told the Navajos that there was an energy crisis—in the United States that per capita consumption of electricity had doubled between 1963 and 1975. Many of the energy developers complained that the grassroots Navajos just did not understand the energy crisis, but in about half the homes of the Navajo Nation, energy consumption remained constant: twice zero is zero.

To many Navajos, digging coal is sacrilegious and a form of energy colonialism. To them, the coal rush is only a transmutation of the gold rushes and land rushes which drove many Indians off their lands. It is an old story: the developers want the resources, and the Indians are in the way. The lure of profits demands growth, what Edward Abbey called "the ideology of the cancer cell."[6] That ideology puts the doctors of consumption to work, seeking more and more ways for the Alices in this technological Wonderland to consume electric power. The Navajos—their land, their heritage, their lives—are being consumed. The National Academy of Sciences ruefully calls their lands "national sacrifice areas."[7]

Everywhere the missionaries of power development go they promise to be "good neighbors," but the character of strip mining and power plants makes that promise impossible. Power development is as good a neighbor as an agitated skunk in close quarters, but with a difference: the damage it does is permanent. The National Academy of Sciences reports that no land has ever been successfully reclaimed after being strip-mined in the arid West; true reclamation takes centuries.[8] The conditions that Emma Yazzie lives with today are being prescribed as the future for many Navajos—all in the "national interest."

The "national interest" has paralleled the financial interests of some powerful Navajos, a select class which has been inculcated with a reverence for the yellow metal which drives white men crazy. Peter MacDonald, Navajo tribal chairman during much of the 1970s and 1980s, promoted resource development. The rents and royalties paid by the coal mining companies flowed directly to his tribal government. He was a businessman. The grassroots Navajos through whose hogans the dirty smoke flows called him "MacDollar." He lived in a luxurious ranch house, drove a Lincoln Continental, and drew a $30,000 annual salary as chairman of the Navajo Nation, where the average per capita income was about $900 in the late 1970s. In June 1976, tribal chairman MacDonald also assumed the presidency and controlling interest in Denay Insurance, a Window Rock–based company.

The Navajo tribal government is made up of a central administration (in Window Rock) and a tribal council, composed of members from 102 "chapters," or local governments. In the late 1970s, the tribal government system, which replaced traditional governance for the Navajos (and many other Indian nations), unfortunately attracted a group of Navajos with a taste for the kind of green that sheep do not eat. Art Arviso, assistant to MacDonald, was convicted of embezzlement; David Jackson, manager of the Navajo tribal fair, also was convicted of embezzlement. The list goes on: Larry Wilson, assistant manager of the fair, convicted of embezzlement; Stanley K. Smith, manager of Piñon Credit Union, convicted of embezzlement; Ernie Shorey, license examiner for the state of Arizona, convicted of embezzlement; Pat Chee Miller, director, Navajo Housing Authority, convicted of conspiracy to defraud; Mervin Schaffer, vice president, Jusco Construction Company, convicted of fraud; Regina Henderson, Navajo welfare worker, convicted of embezzlement; Doris McLancer, tribal court clerk, convicted of embezzlement; Laurita Williams, Navajo Election Board clerk, convicted of embezzlement; Ross Roll, tribal employee, convicted of embezzlement.[9]

Although MacDonald was relatively popular when he was first elected to head the tribal government, soon afterward he joined the ranks of the native elite in a very decisive way; he lived rather lavishly and promoted energy development—provided the price was right. Opposition to his policies began to grow, especially among the grassroots Navajos and on the northeastern quarter of the reservation, where much of the proposed energy development was to take place.

The Navajo Liberation Front

The Coalition for Navajo Liberation was born in 1974 and became most active in and near Shiprock. Navajo traditionalists from that area led a demonstration of about six hundred people on May 18, 1976, in Window Rock, the tribal capital. The marchers demanded MacDonald's resignation, and eighteen people were arrested. On August 25, 1976, traditionalists assembled again in Window Rock during a tribal council meeting where a coal strip-mine lease with El Paso Natural Gas and Consolidation Coal, a subsidiary of Continental Oil, was being negotiated. The majority of the demonstrators were from the Shiprock-Burnham area of the reservation, where most of the energy development was planned. Many of them stood to lose at least their land, probably their livelihoods, and perhaps their lives. At the Burnham chapter house residents voted 228 to 0 against coal gasification in 1976; in the same year the Shiprock Chapter rejected gasification proposals 129 to 0. The power to negotiate leases and mining plans, however, resided with the central tribal council and Mac-Donald, and thus the Shiprock Chapter voted 255 to 6 to demand MacDonald's resignation.

Opposition to gasification and the coal mining that it requires was so strong in the Burnham area that one tribal council member from the chapter offered to resign under pressure from area residents after he had supported an El Paso Natural Gas lease proposal during a debate held in August 1976. The closer to the grassroots level an energy development proposal came, the more strongly it was opposed. The tribal council itself has tended to support strip-mining leases while opposing the gasification and power plants which are inevitably proposed to consume the coal. In a letter to Congress written in 1976, 41 of the tribal council's 76 members opposed federal loan guarantees for gasification plant construction. The same council, however, approved the El Paso coal lease by 49 to 11 during August of the same year. MacDonald bragged that the El Paso coal lease was the best of its kind ever negotiated by an Indian nation or tribe. It was the best in terms of monetary value; the 55 cents a ton that was promised the Navajos was almost three times as much as the Crows and Northern Cheyennes had been offered on leases which later were suspended.

However, to traditional Navajos, especially those near Shiprock and Burnham, a lease was still a lease, even though the terms were good. To them, such leasing was a repeat of history, a trade of land and resources for money, an exchange which has almost always ended in Indian losses. Their opposition to the coal and uranium leases, as well as to the construction of electricity and gasification plants, was more than spiritual; it was a matter of economics, and ultimately a matter of life or death. Energy development would destroy the land and life that the Navajos had sustained for hundreds of years.

The Department of the Interior, which must approve all plans for energy development on Indian lands after tribal councils negotiate contracts, held hearings on the El Paso coal lease in March 1977. Cecilia Bitsui, a resident of the Burnham Chapter, reflected the beliefs of many of her neighbors when she said the following: "Do we have to wait until the whole land is destroyed before the tribal council says 'enough'? The people in Window Rock are only concerned with money. But no cash payment will replace what my family will lose. My children will not be able to herd sheep in Burnham and learn the ways of the Navajo as I did."[10]

The resistance to energy development runs long and deep. Fred Johnson, one of the founding members and early leaders of the Coalition for Navajo Liberation, told the U.S. Civil Rights Commission in 1974:

> Our clean waters are clouded with silt and the wastes of the white man; Mother Earth is being ravaged and squandered. To the Navajo people it seems as if these Europeans hate everything in nature—the grass, the birds, the beasts, the water, the soil, and the air. We refuse to abandon our beautiful land. To Navajos, land was something no one could possess, any more than he could possess the air. Land is sacred to the Navajos; it is part of the Almighty's design for life . . . "Mother Earth," because it is the mother of all living. To the whites, this is paganism as well as communistic, and it has to be eradicated. All the laws and federal regulations in existence cannot justify the criminal acts of tribal officials who knowingly deceive those who have placed their trust in them. . . . To protest is to speak out against, to let it be known that you don't like a certain action. . . . To protest is an act of intellectual commitment. To protest is to hate the inhumanity of another. To resist, we believe, is to stop inhumanity and affirm our own humanity. . . . The Coalition for Navajo Liberation intends to stop the land robberies known as the gasification plants, the T. G. & E. power line, the Black Mesa destruction of land, the Four Corners power plants and the Exxon uranium deal.[11]

Johnson, who was killed in the mysterious crash of a small airplane in early 1976, spoke forcefully about the dangers of strip mining and power generation, which could turn large areas of Navajo land into wastelands unreclaimable for perhaps hundreds of years. True reclamation involves more than simply filling in the mines and planting grass to cover the scars; it involves restoring the entire ecological community of plants and animals. A National Academy of Sciences (NAS) report states bluntly that this cannot be done in areas with less than ten inches of rainfall a year; the rainfall over most of the Navajo Reservation ranges from six to ten inches a year. The NAS suggests that such areas be spared development or honestly labeled "national sacrifice areas."[12]

Is "Reclamation" a Sham?

The amount of money a coal mining company spends on reclamation is not the crucial factor, asserts the National Academy of Sciences report. Nor are state or federal reclamation laws.[13] Reclamation is simply not possible until nature heals its wounds over several centuries.

Strip mining does more than scar the land. It also disrupts underground water flow and poisons the water itself. Coal seams in the arid West also act as aquifers—they carry water just as some metals conduct electricity. Underground water is a vital consideration in sparsely populated dry areas of the Navajo Reservation where a majority of Navajos rely on well water. Much of the soil in the Southwest (as well as on the northern plains) is high in alkaline salts. Usually the salts are leached out of the surface layers of soil and are concentrated below the topsoil. However, strip mining mixes the soil, resulting in high salt levels at the surface—which kill many plants. The process escalates as rain or irrigation water at the surface carries the freed salts into the aquifers, which feed wells and rivers. Every living thing then suffers from salty water. Strip mining also loosens surface soil, which is carried by rainfall and irrigation as silt and mud into rivers and wells.

No amount of corporate goodwill, no amount of money and effort, and no combination of reclamation laws will resolve the fundamental incompatibility of coal strip mining and nature in the arid Southwest.

Generation of electricity or natural gas from the coal only compounds the problems, which amount to a sentence of death for the land and a way of life. Fly ash, produced by burning coal, pollutes the air and water. Even if much of the fly ash is removed from power plant stacks before reaching the air, it is usually dumped in nearby landfills, where rainfall leaches chemicals into the groundwater.[14] Already the clouds of pollution sometimes obscure the turquoise sky around majestic Shiprock, which gives the Navajo town its name; more power plants will merely make the pollution denser. Between one hundred and two hundred pounds of fly ash can be released by the burning of a single ton of coal.[15] The burning of coal also releases sulfur dioxide, which is poisonous to people, plants, and animals. The sulfur dioxide reacts with water vapor in the atmosphere to form sulfuric acid, which returns to the earth as highly acidic rainfall.

In addition, coal burning releases nitrogen oxide, which combines with ozone and carbon in the air to produce smog. The pollution potential of coal gasification exceeds that of burning coal. According to research done by the National Indian Youth Council (NIYC):

> There will be at least two toxic air pollutants (lead and mercury) emitted from those [gasification] plants in such uncontrolled quantities that [they] may inflict permanent damage to all animal, plant and human life in the immediate vicinity of the plants. Expert testimony from a National Aeronautics and Space Administration physicist at recent environmental hearings revealed that all persons living within a 13-mile radius of the plants will have to be evacuated due to the dangerously high levels of lead and mercury around these plants. In fact, it is predicted that all workers in and around the plants will have to wear protective face masks for health and safety reasons. Another toxic emission (boron) is greatly feared by the planners of the Navajo Nation Irrigation Project because it could easily wipe out all of the crops grown there.[16]

The dangers to people, plants, and animals, as well as to the earth itself, do not end with the generation of electricity. The transmission lines which ride atop the spidery steel towers across the mountains to consumers carry so much electricity that they create a force field beneath them. Extra-high-voltage (EHV) transmission lines of the size planned for the Indian coal lands have given several people in Ohio severe shocks. One woman was knocked from her horse by such a force field; and a man working in his yard was knocked unconscious. The power company which owns the line advised the man to wear chains around his ankles to ground the current. Twelve of eighteen persons living near the Ohio EHV lines also have reported strong electrical shocks.[17] In addition, the transmission lines may create their own smog; electricity seeping from the lines combines with elements in the atmosphere to form ozone.[18]

Squandering Water in an Arid Land

Energy development also requires massive amounts of water from the arid lands of the Navajos. The use of water begins with the mining of the flaky coal of Black Mesa to form the coal slurry which is transported through pipelines. Water consumption continues with power generation, especially in coal gasification. One coal gasification plant requires about 10,000 acre-feet of water a year.[19] About 28 cubic feet of water per second, or 20,270 acre-feet a year, are required to cool the generating equipment of a 1,000 megawatt, coal-fired electricity plant. All of the water used in gasification is hydrolyzed into hydrogen and oxygen and lost to the arid Southwest. Some of the water used in electricity generation also evaporates; the remainder is returned to its source 10 to 15 degrees Fahrenheit warmer than it was before entering the plant.

To add insult to injury, the water demands and pollution generated by energy development pose a dual threat to an irrigation project which was included in the Navajo treaty of 1868. The first stages of the 110,000-acre project, near Burnham, began operating in 1976. If completed, the irrigation project could provide employment in the fields or in food-processing and marketing industries for 30,000 Navajos. However, the pollution and water demands of strip mining and of the gasification and coal-fired electricity plants may kill or severely damage the crops. The irrigation project has long been a dream of the traditional Navajos; its survival was a major reason why energy development was so bitterly opposed. The water required for the irrigation system, as well as for energy development, comes from the shallow, muddy brown San Juan River, which flows through Shiprock. The two projects are not environmentally compatible, and there is simply not enough water for both.[20] The Navajo Indian Irrigation project could provide the beginning of a totally Indian-owned and controlled economic base. Instead of always having to sacrifice their land and resources, Navajo people could develop and utilize their own land and resources in ways that would not destroy their homeland. ✢

Another factor in the water demand equation is the roughly 50,000 people who were imported to build and operate the complex of strip mines and power plants in and near the Navajo Reservation. Many brought with them habits of squandering water that they acquired in less arid climates. In the middle 1970s, Gerald Wilkinson, director of the National Indian Youth Council, said that those Navajos worried about the harm of uncontrolled strip mining are not totally against resource use. They want development to take place in a manner which does not disrupt the earth, human life, traditions, or the irrigation project. Wilkinson suggested that coal should be mined underground, using room-and-pillar techniques, if it is mined at all, and that the coal, once mined ought to be transported away from the Navajo Reservation for power generation. The Navajo Nation should also be a joint partner in any energy project. Only in this way could Navajo coal be mined without the penalties of energy colonization or the devastation implied by the designation "national sacrifice area."

The developers did not agree to such terms because they did not immigrate to the Southwest (and to the West in general) merely to mine coal. They came to strip-mine coal. If the coal companies wanted to mine coal underground, there was plenty of it in the East and the Midwest, much of it in abandoned underground mines. At present rates of consumption enough coal remains in mines already opened to last the United States seventy-five years. Converging trends in labor relations and technology, not scarcity of coal, have propelled the coal companies westward. A corporate policy based on bottom-line profit, instead of ecological and human needs or scarcity of coal, has brought coal miners to the West, where a million tons of coal a year can be mined with newly developed draglines using only twenty-five mine workers. A large force of underground miners paid at prevailing union rates would be much more expensive.

Nor have the miners of coal come to the West for the low-sulfur coal only because it will reduce pollution. While it is true that western coal is generally lower in sulfur content than eastern coal, it is also lower in heat value. More of it must be burned to produce the same amount of heat as eastern coal.[21] In addition, western coal acts as an aquifer, and so when removed from the ground it holds much more water than eastern coal. The water must be removed from the coal; the remaining product is lighter and, therefore, even higher in sulfur content. Consequently, by the time it is burned, western coal contains no less sulfur per pound than eastern coal.

In the long run, the energy the coal companies might provide by strip-mining the Navajo Reservation and much of the rest of the West may not even be necessary. It is probable that if people were not manipulated through advertising to use more energy, and conservation was promoted aggressively, per capita energy consumption from coal might stabilize or decline. Future coal needs could then be met from already opened mines or from careful underground mining in the East.

As for natural gas, several experiments are under way which may furnish substantial amounts of ersatz gas generated from methane, a clean-burning gas produced by the decomposition of organic matter.[22] For example, at Bay St. Louis, Mississippi, the National Aeronautics and Space Administration has harvested water hyacinths for distillation into methane. The hyacinths are one of nature's fastest growing plants. They thrive on raw sewage and have until now been considered a problem because they clog waterways in the South. Similarly, off the southern California coast scientists from the Naval Undersea Center and the California Institute of Technology have experimented with ocean farms of giant California kelp to be harvested, dried, and converted into methane. Ocean farms measuring 470 miles on each side could have supplied all of the United

States's 1976 demand for natural gas, according to Dr. Harold Wilcox, director of the project.[23] Both of these projects utilize a renewable resource to produce a clean-burning form of energy; they are ecological, in harmony a Navajo might say, with the "Right Way." Many other environmentally compatible energy resources could also be utilized, including solar power, wind power, and tidal power. There is no energy shortage; there is a shortage of will and imagination in dealing with an energy production system now wedded to fossil fuels.

Endnotes

1. Interview, Bruce E. Johansen with Emma Yazzie, at her home, eastern Navajo Reservation, August 14, 1976.

2. Ibid.

3. Ibid.

4. *Seattle Post-Intelligencer*, August 29, 1976, p. B-6.

5. "Gasification," *Akwesasne Notes* (Autumn 1976): 10.

6. Edward Abbey, *The Journey Home* (New York: Dutton, 1977), p. 183.

7. Thadis Box et al., *Rehabilitation Potential of Western Coal Lands* (Cambridge, Mass.: Ballinger Publishing, 1974), p. 85.

8. Ibid., p. 2.

9. *Navajo Times*, March 31, 1977.

10. Copy of remarks in the archives of the National Indian Youth Council, Albuquerque, New Mexico.

11. Speech of Fred Johnson to the U.S. Civil Rights Commission, archives, National Indian Youth Council, Albuquerque, New Mexico.

12. Box et al., *Rehabilitation Potential*, p. 85.

13. Ibid., p. 2.

14. James Cannon, *Leased and Lost: A Study of Public and Indian Coal Leasing in the West* (New York: Council on Economic Priorities, 1974), p. 17. Cannon's conclusions were confirmed in a follow-up report released by the council in 1978.

15. Ibid.

16. National Indian Youth Council, *What Is Coal Gasification?* (Albuquerque, N.M.: NIYC, 1976), p. 4.

17. Cannon, *Leased and Lost*, p. 18.

18. Ibid.

19. Ibid., p. 16. An acre-foot is the amount of water which will cover one acre a foot deep, or 326,000 gallons.

20. National Indian Youth Council, *Coal Gasification*, p. 4.

21. Western coals provide an average of 6,100–9,500 British Thermal Units per pound, compared with an average of 13,000 for eastern coals.

22. *Capturing the Energy of the Sun*, proceedings from the National Conference on Bioconversion as an Energy Resource, March 11–33, 1976, p. 249.

23. Ibid., p. 255.

PART VII

Making Culture

the future southwest

Just as there is controversy among archaeologists, geographers, and historians about the role that social, economic, political, and environmental issues played in the prehistory and history of the Southwest, so too are there divergent opinions regarding how these factors will influence the future. Despite the recent influx of high-tech and other "clean" industries that bring new employment opportunities to Sunbelt cities, a high percentage of the population in the Southwest has a markedly low per capita income as compared with other areas of the country. Additionally, like elsewhere throughout the world, burgeoning industrialization and other economic practices have led to the overutilization of once abundant natural resources. Some critical resources like water, that were scarce to begin with, are being depleted at an alarming rate. Another significant issue is the effect of changing demographics in the region. The nonwhite population will continue to grow, largely as the result of high immigration from Latin America and the Pacific Rim countries. Immigration and the ever-changing requirements of a global economy—as exemplified by global trade agreements such as NAFTA—will no doubt reconfigure how people make a living in the Southwest.

While some lament what has been described as "the death of tradition," those of us who have studied the region through its folklore and culture are more optimistic. We see that tradition is now, as it always has been, a dynamic process that is constantly being transformed. When we look to the region's past for indications of what the future holds, we see that an alteration in the transmis-sion of shared beliefs and values has not entailed the disappearance of long-held cultural practices. We are reminded by the contributors to this volume that in this regard Southwesterners are particularly adept, for their history is, to a great extent, a record of negotiating the difficult terrain of social, economic, and cultural change. The picture before us is constantly shifting and changing: the precise shape of the future is elusive, but we believe that the peoples long identified with the Southwest will always assert their presence and affirm the rights to view themselves as a fundamental element of the region's character.

Make-Believe and Graffiti

envisioning new mexico families

Virginia Scharff

I would like to begin this discussion of a half-century of change in the lives of New Mexico families with an ethnographic description, otherwise known as a personal anecdote. My anecdote is inspired by Fred Rogers, a man perhaps better known as "Mr. Rogers" of Public Television neighborhood fame. I am acquainted with Mr. Rogers because I have a six-year-old son named Sam, who has only very recently, and to my great dismay, abandoned the warmth of the Neighborhood of Make-Believe for the shrill environs of Nickelodeon. During the past six years, I have been comforted that, although my husband and son and I have lived in six different houses in four different Sunbelt states, Mr. Rogers hasn't moved. Sam has spent part or all of his weekdays with eight different day-care providers, under the supervision of heaven only knows how many care-givers or teachers. My husband, Peter, has held three different jobs, and I have taught at four different colleges. We had a second child, Annie, age eighteen months right now, and the only native New Mexican in the family. But Mr. Rogers hasn't changed jobs. He hasn't even left Pittsburgh, let alone the Neighborhood of Make-Believe. His livelihood and his neighborhood have been more consistent in my life than my own.

When I moved to New Mexico two and one-half years ago, to take a position in the University of New Mexico's history department, Peter agreed to quit his own professional job and be what sociologists and personnel officers call "the trailing spouse." Fifty years ago, there was neither any such designation nor any need for the term. First of all, notwithstanding the importance of the history of migration to New Mexico and the West, most people didn't relocate nearly so often or so far in the years before the Second World War. When they did, husbands virtually never "trailed" wives. Some historians of the American West have even described female migrants as "draftees in a male enterprise."

Of course, there were plenty of women who relished moving into the West in general, and to what is now New Mexico in particular (whether they came from north, south, east, or west of here), but that's not the point. The point is that families generally moved because male heads of households wanted, or were compelled, to move. Whether they liked it or not, few women had the luxury of refusing to migrate when their husbands or fathers or sons announced the decision to go. In the case of New Mexico since the seventeenth century, families moved in because of Spanish, Mexican, or U.S. government colonization plans, because of the movements of armies, and, after 1880, because of the coming of the railroad. Women and children, whatever their desires, were expected to go along with men's plans.

Family historians—like Lillian Schlissel, who followed a nineteenth-century family named Malik along a migration westward through death, trauma, and separation—have shown that moving is, to say the least, hard on families. But more broadly, humanities scholars, social scientists, corporate planners, and policymakers have barely begun to assess the increasing social and psychological costs and challenges of late twentieth-century mobility. The past fifty years, to be sure, have launched more families on the move, many of them into New Mexico. By 1990, only 54 percent of all New Mexico residents had been born in the state. In that year, a majority of residents of New Mexico's urban areas—which were the fastest growing parts of the state—had been born in other states.

My family arrived in 1989, to join that emigrant majority. As I began to explain, Peter came to Albuquerque without a job, which meant living on my professor's salary, which of course ruled out buying a house. Nothing odd in this; although New Mexicans and Americans had high rates of home ownership in the 1950s and 1960s, the percentage of Americans able to buy houses has declined substantially, across the nation, since 1973. Today, few single-income families in New Mexico or in the country can afford to become homeowners. Fortunately, Peter's skills made him a good candidate to milk New Mexico's cash cow—the government-sponsored science and defense industry, established with the advent of the Manhattan Project in 1940, now emanating from Los Alamos and Sandia Laboratories, from the military bases, and from defense subcontractors serving the bases and the labs. Thus, a few months after coming to Albuquerque, we became a two-earner family, both with professional jobs. Finally we were able to scrape up the money for a down payment on a house in a middle-class neighborhood in the near Northeast Heights, west of San Mateo Boulevard and south of Indian School Road. Finally, perhaps, we have settled in New Mexico, to live in a house of our own, and to pursue the American Dream of a safe, stable, secure family life. And so, in the spirit of Mr. Rogers's hospitality, I'd like to introduce you to some other New Mexico families by inviting you into my neighborhood.

Our house is of a design very common in Albuquerque—a two-and-a-half bedroom, flat-roofed, stucco-over-concrete-block box. It was built in 1949, and at that time it was on the northeast frontier of the city. The original owner, an Anglo mid-westerner now retired from the UNM English department, came over to our house one day last fall and showed us Kodak snapshots of the then-unobstructed view of the Sandia Mountains from our front porch. Another time, he arrived with a video camera and an Argentine poet who said that, decades ago, he had written some of his best poems as a guest in the house, and wanted to take a videotape of it home to Argentina to show his family.

The English professor, his wife, and their son lived in the house for twenty years, then sold it to an art-history professor, who lived in the house a few years and then re-sold it in about 1975. The new owner was a divorced mother of three, whom I will call Elizabeth (all names I will use here have been changed to preserve confidentiality). This female head of household, a New Mexico native, a Hispanic, a white-collar worker, raised her children in the house and sold it to us in 1990 for an amount slightly below both the national median home price and the median price for a house in Albuquerque.

Most people who buy homes move into their new residences when the house is empty. Ours, in a sense, came equipped with a family. Shortly after Elizabeth accepted our offer on the house, I went after work to pick up Sam at his childcare center, and ran into a staff member who said, "I heard you bought George's mother's house." It happened that Elizabeth's college-student son, George, worked in the child-care center, and he'd figured out that the people who'd bought his mother's house were the parents of Sam, a child he knew well. For his part, Sam was very excited at the prospect of moving into the room in which George had grown up.

We also learned, when we began to move in, that Mr. and Mrs. Parra, our neighbors to the south, were Elizabeth's parents. Her father, a retired railroad worker, and her homemaker mother had moved from Belen to Albuquerque when he retired and had bought their house in order to be close to their daughter and her grandchildren.

But that was only the beginning of our involvement with Elizabeth's kin. My daughter Annie was born that summer. Like most women in the United States with children under the age of six, I am (obviously) working for wages. And like most working mothers in the United States in general, and New Mexico in particular, I had no maternity leave. I went back to work three weeks after Annie was born and, amid plenty of anxiety about turning our tiny infant over to someone whom we planned, assuredly, to pay poorly, hired a student baby-sitter to come to our house and take care of Annie. As it happened, during the four months she worked for us, this young woman was also George's girlfriend.

Elizabeth's son George thus became a regular visitor to the house he'd lived in so long, splitting his time in our neighborhood between his old home, solely occupied by his girlfriend and our baby during daytime hours, and visits with his grandparents next door. In fact, Elizabeth's own brothers and sisters, along with her children, visited Mr. and Mrs. Parra every day. Sam liked to watch Mr. Parra work in the yard, and to ask him questions. On Christmas Eve, Mrs. Parra brought over presents for Sam and Annie, and on Valentine's Day she arrived with candy and cards. I began to feel the celebrated warmth, continuity, and strength of New Mexico's Hispanic families reaching out to touch our geographically manic, Anglo nuclear family.

The geographical proximity and emotional closeness of Elizabeth, her siblings, her parents, and her children exemplify what scholars have called "Chicano familism," which sociologists Maxine Baca Zinn and Stanley Eitzen define as "values emphasizing the family as opposed to the individual." This isn't to say that such families are without conflict or tension, just that they tend to hang together, to adapt to changing circumstances, and to be valued for concrete as well as abstract reasons. Elizabeth and her family represent some patterns typical of modern Chicano families, patterns including her own divorce (despite her devout Catholicism), her head-of-household status, and her employment in a white-collar, service-sector job. Her parents helped her bring up her children; as the Parras age, she and her siblings are taking care of them. But Elizabeth's kin also represent the optimistic end of the spectrum for Hispanic families. Her parents are able to live comfortably, if not opulently, on her father's pension, and to own their own home. They are in good health. Unlike most female heads of households, particularly Chicana single mothers, Elizabeth makes a living wage. Her children, soon to be college graduates all, are ambitious and upwardly mobile: more American Dream stuff, New Mexico style.

Professor Scharff's Neighborhood, middling though it is, is by no means representative of New Mexico families. Telling you about the people I live near will reveal nothing, for example, about the dilemmas of New Mexico's poor, who were more than 17 percent of the state's population in 1979. Still, my neighbors' households tell us something about the current state of the American Dream, a normative conception of middle-class family life forged during the 1950s, a period by all demographic accounts best understood as anomalous in American family history. You could go up and down our block and not find a single household that would conform to the pattern Americans enshrined as a family ideal on 1950s television shows, with a breadwinner father, homemaker mother, two children, one job, no divorces, no surprises. Across the street from us lives an Anglo couple with two teenagers. They come pretty close to the *Leave It to Beaver* model. He's a retired career military man, now working in the defense business, the primary wage earner. Still, she works as a teacher. An older couple, who often take care of their three-year-old grandson, live next door to them, on one side. On the other, a divorced working mother (she's a health-care professional) lives with her teenage son. Most people in the neighborhood own their homes; a few rent. There are Anglo and Hispanic families. There are numerous elderly people, couples, widows, widowers, divorced people. There are families with young children too, buying into the neighborhood as the original owners age. On our block, the two other families with small children both include mothers on their second marriages. Older half-siblings and step-siblings are sometimes resident, and sometimes live with their fathers. And so, if you're looking for the Cleavers in my neighborhood, I fear you'll search in vain.

This excursion into my neighborhood is intended to make the point that there is not now, nor has there ever been, such a thing as "the family" in New Mexico. I know that the word "diversity" turns to dust in the mouths of political conservatives nostalgic for some mythical time when native-born and immigrant Americans leapt into a population porridge kettle eager to be stirred down to a molten mush. Whatever the kinship patterns of these different groups of people, all were supposed to end up conforming to a narrowly defined ideal family life. But *diversity* is a precise and useful term for characterizing both historical and contemporary families of New Mexico. Even in the space of one block of a middling Albuquerque neighborhood, where the seeming uniformity of the population is expressed architecturally in houses of roughly equal size and value, households and their inhabitants' relations to one another vary in obvious

regards. The emotional, subjective, and even practical dimensions of those relations, and the material well-being of those inhabitants, may vary still more, and
still be familial to the core.

What all this means is that understanding New Mexico families will mean
putting this description of family life based on personal experience and observa-
tion in the context of broader social developments, while at the same time
accounting for the varied and subjective ways in which families meet the challenges of contemporary life. What, then, do we know about changes in New
Mexico families' lives in the past fifty years? And how might people have coped
with these changes?

Let me offer some fairly obvious and general observations, the kinds of
things most people understand intuitively, which are borne out by statistical
information. To begin with, during the period between 1940 and 1990, the
population of New Mexico has tripled, from 531,818 to 1,515,060. New Mexico
has also urbanized and suburbanized. In 1940, only 176,401 New Mexicans,
about one-third of all state residents, lived in places with populations over 2,500.
The population of Albuquerque at that time was 35,449, roughly the same as
present-day Laramie, Wyoming. By 1950, the population of New Mexico had
grown to 681,187; by that time, 341,889 people, or 50.2 percent of New
Mexicans, were living in urban areas. By 1990, Bernalillo County alone had
480,577 residents, almost as many as the entire state had had fifty years earlier.
In the interim, numerous suburban places (Rio Rancho, for example) had come
into existence.

What do urbanization and suburbanization mean to people in post–
World War II New Mexico? They mean lots of objective things, including
changes in the landscape, and in the means by which we navigate the spaces in
which we live. In California, of course, urbanization has taken a megalopolitan
form, so that people who live in greater Los Angeles, for instance, often find
themselves having to endure commutes of an hour or more each way as part of
the cost of living and working. New Mexico is not, of course, California, but we
would do well to take stock of the degree to which Californication has penetrated
our borders. New Mexico culture is car culture. Our roadscapes—Route 66,
Cerrillos Drive—tell much about us as urban people. Santa Fe, our City Different, is in one sense the City Generic writ large; it has *the nation's* highest per-
capita incidence of fast-food restaurants. We may despise the form of architecture I have come to call "Pizza Hut Moderne," but mobile, working parents have
certainly come to rely on Happy Meals and pepperoni pizzas as resources for
feeding the family.

Albuquerque is a city growing on the Los Angeles model. We live in single-family dwellings and low-density neighborhoods, travel mostly on increasingly crowded arterial freeways and, infrequently and with difficulty, on minimal public transportation. Our rush-hour traffic reporters have become local celebrities. Our real estate developers dream of "planned" bedroom communities that would exacerbate urban sprawl by excluding commercial development (whether for offices, factories, or day-care centers) and by making driving, driving, and driving a more and more time-consuming necessity for working people.

Our cities sprawl as they expand, without benefit of much in the way of public transit. Private automobiles are our main form of transportation; the carless are at a substantial disadvantage. In 1980, only 38,442 New Mexicans reported using public transportation to get to work; 378,719, nearly ten times as many, traveled to work in private vehicles, and of those, 292,001 drove alone. As of 1980, mean travel time to work for New Mexicans ranged between sixteen and twenty-two minutes, a number far below the mean times for larger cities, but certainly reflecting urban growth.

Urban historians, demographers, and transportation planners must learn to recognize that the popular commitment to increasing time in the car cannot be measured in travel time to work alone. Social historians have identified the separation of home and workplace, which accompanied the industrial revolution, as a critical development in American families' history. I believe we need to start talking about the spatial *dispersal* of families that has accompanied metropolitanization. A family of four today may well inhabit four or more different places in the course of an ordinary day. Reassembling the family unit, as a practical matter of negotiating time and space, has become an increasingly complicated task. At the simplest level, trips to grocery stores and schools and child-care centers have become part of the practical equation for New Mexico families, although we have yet to adjust our notions of city planning to this spatial and temporal reality.

If urbanization has spawned a reliance on the automobile, which can be construed as both access to independent mobility and dependence on a wasteful, polluting means of transportation, cities also offer their inhabitants greater access to other forms of technology that affect family life. In 1940, 41.5 percent of habitable dwellings in the state as a whole had no running water. Statewide, 20.5 percent of dwellings had no running water within fifty feet of the dwelling. Among urban dwellings in 1940, however, only 19.8 percent had no running water. Indoor plumbing accompanied city building. By 1950 only 7.5 percent of urban households lacked running water, and in the state as a whole 20.4 percent of households had no indoor plumbing. That year, 82.5 percent of urban households had kitchen sinks. Some may object that indoor plumbing is a bourgeois convenience, important chiefly in urban settings in which high-density living makes sanitation problematic. Nevertheless, no one would argue that abolishing the job of hauling water had no consequences for the (female) persons charged with doing domestic work.

These statistics about the dissemination of domestic technology translate into very real changes in the lives of New Mexico families. Urban women do not have to walk to wells or pumps and carry buckets over distances. That fact of life might have meant that New Mexico women spent less time in washing people, clothes, and household surfaces. Instead, it seems to have meant that housewives have been expected to, and have themselves striven to, wash more often. Generally speaking, new forms of domestic technology between 1920 and 1960 did not decrease the amount of time women spent doing housework, though they did change the character of the work, making it less physically onerous if not less psychologically and socially important. What has seemed to have affected women's housework is their labor-force status, a subject to which I shall return in a moment.

As with the matter of access to, and need for, new technology, urbanization also means that New Mexicans have greater access to and dependence upon formal education. New Mexicans now are attending elementary and high school longer, graduating more often, and going on to college in far greater proportions than they did in 1940. It remains true that those with the lowest rates of school attendance, and the fewest years in school, live in rural places, particularly among the Native American portion of the population.

Certainly, we can discuss the question of the value of formal schooling, particularly when state-funded and federally funded education has sometimes mandated training of dubious utility to poor people, or has sought at least as much to enact a repressive vision of assimilation as to teach skills. Still, I would argue that people who live in contemporary New Mexico can have more power over their lives by taking charge of the kind of information formal education can make available. And yet, though more New Mexicans are getting more schooling, New Mexico, sadly, lags behind most other states in the performance of its educational system. In 1980, 18.3 percent of all 16-to-24-year-olds in the state were not in school, and not high school graduates, placing New Mexico in the bottom ten states in that category. New Mexico schools were also crowded, with the state rated fortieth also in pupil-teacher ratio in 1980.

Education has become increasingly critical to New Mexicans because urbanization also forces people to rely more on cash, rather than land, to secure the necessities of life. Although the number of years spent in school does not translate neatly into dollar income or occupational mobility for workers (sex and race are more powerful forces in determining earnings), lack of schooling has a cost. In the years since 1940, New Mexico has become more like the rest of the nation in terms of the ways in which people make a living. Small-farm and ranch production remain part of the state's economic picture, but a diminishing part. Industrialization, and post-industrialization, have reshaped life in our state.

In the years since World War II, American economic growth has occurred primarily in jobs involving neither farming nor manufacturing. The prewar stereotype of the American worker was a blue-collar male who held some kind of manufacturing job, skilled or unskilled. The steelworker, the autoworker, the factory hand producing textiles in the South, or canned hams in Chicago, captured the imagination of both advocates and opponents of unionization. Union organizers focused their energies on such workers, with substantial success, particularly in the 1930s. Most New Mexicans, in those days, were not "workers" in this image, but, instead, farmers and ranchers.

Then came the war, which, as historian Gerald Nash has demonstrated, transformed economic and social life in the western United States. Manufacturing came west, in a big way, and so did bureaucracy. Defense contractors and installations lured job seekers and generated consumer businesses catering to, and employing, growing populations. The civilian and the military, the diplomatic and domestic, were inextricably bound in New Mexico's social development. The cold war rationale for an arms race—to safeguard American families from Communist aggression—had its own particular ironic spin in New Mexico. We glimpse that irony in the story of Los Alamos. In that paradigmatic place of Nuclear Age New Mexico, scientist professionals saw, in the magnificent canyons and mesas, safe places for children to grow up. And all the while, these paternal protectors of Trinity's children were themselves strewing the lovely landscape with the most toxic substances manufactured, so far, by human hands. In postwar New Mexico, we have reinvented the categories of safety and danger.

The war also catalyzed a permanent change in the composition of the labor force, as married women, including mothers, answered the need for workers in war industries and paved the way for ever-increasing female participation in wage work. The trend toward women's work-force participation correlated with the enormous growth in jobs in clerical, service, sales, and technical fields. In 1940, 78.4 percent of New Mexico men over the age of fourteen were in the work force;

21.6 percent were not, including 10.7 percent who were in school. That year, 18.7 percent of New Mexico women over the age of fourteen were in the labor force; 81.3 percent were not. Their rate of school attendance exactly matched that of men over fourteen, at 10.7 percent; 62.2 percent of women over fourteen were listed as "engaged in own home housework" (and, I might as well mention, 0.5 percent of men were listed as "engaged in own home housework").

By 1970, 74.0 percent of New Mexico men over the age of sixteen were in the labor force, indicating a very slight decline in male work-force participation accounted for, possibly, by the facts that some nonworking men were able to collect disability insurance, and that men's life expectancy (and pension benefits) had increased. New Mexico women's labor-force rates, on the other hand, had doubled in the thirty-year period, to 36.9 percent of all women over sixteen. At that time, some 29.7 percent of New Mexico women with children under the age of six were working for wages; among mothers of young children who were not married, 44.9 percent were working or looking for work. By 1980, almost forty thousand New Mexico mothers of children under six—42.5 percent of all mothers of preschool-age children in the state—were in the labor force. More than fifty-five thousand mothers of children between the ages of six and seventeen (57.2 percent of the total) were also working or looking for work.

In the past fifty years, the growth of bureaucracies like the state government, the University of New Mexico, and the national laboratories has provided jobs for women workers. Out of 140,269 persons employed in New Mexico in 1940, only 15,443 were listed as "clerical, sales, and kindred workers." Prophetically, of that number, more than a third—some 6,075, were women, comprising the largest category of female employment, although the most female-dominated job category in New Mexico in 1940 was domestic service, which employed 5,177 women and only 267 men. By 1970 the number of female clerical workers had more than doubled. That year, some 41,000 New Mexico women did clerical work, roughly one-third of all women workers in the state. Women also had entered service, sales, technical, and professional work in substantial numbers. Their wages, however, lagged far behind those of men in full-time occupations, with the average wage for a full-time employed woman stagnating at roughly two-thirds of that for the average full-time employed man.

It almost goes without saying that most New Mexico fathers work for pay; that's expected. What is worth repeating is that today most New Mexico mothers work for pay, whatever the ages of their children. Axiomatically, this makes a difference in family life, raising a series of questions. Some of them I have already discussed—the kinds of work women do, for example. Others are more complicated or troubling. How do families cope with the fact of maternal employment? Who does the housework traditionally performed by women? Are men taking on more household and parenting tasks now that women are taking on more bread-winning? How are families coping with speeded-up schedules and diminishing leisure time? Are mothers and fathers and children adjusting with grace and ease to new daily responsibilities that fly in the face of deeply felt ideas about motherhood and fatherhood, about masculinity and femininity, and about the responsibilities and rewards of belonging to a family? Sociologist Arlie Hochschild has written, "We're in the middle of a social revolution," and she has sensitively explored the myriad ways in which working couples face new dilemmas, with no help from politicians or government agencies. Hochschild has contrasted, with painful vividness, the potential for emotional satisfaction that family life might hold, with the frustrations of children forced to live at their parents' frantic pace and the burdens of what so many contemporary parents experience as "the second shift" at the end of the wage-work day.

Two-job families obviously have their problems, coping with the strains of pursuing the American Dream in a changing economic, geographical, and social landscape. But most married working mothers feel lucky compared to the growing number of women raising children alone, a situation increasingly common for mothers, still quite rare for fathers. In 1980, 23.0 percent, or nearly one-quarter of New Mexico children, lived in single-parent families. Single motherhood in itself is not necessarily a personal or social problem, despite negative media images and politicians' cynical or fatuous attempts to hold welfare mothers responsible for the federal deficit. At the very least, many women and their children are better off, physically and psychologically, living on their own than in the same household as an abusive man. But inadequate education and job training, and low wages in female-dominated occupations mean that few women can earn enough to support themselves and their children in comfort. Moreover, holding any kind of job generally requires that a mother have access to high-quality, affordable child-care, a service available to all too few Americans. Single mothers and their children are thus tragically likely to fall into poverty. They comprise the majority of the poor in the United States today. New Mexico, shameful to say, is among the nation's leaders in this regard. A Children's Defense Fund report estimated that in the years between 1983 and 1987 the average annual number of poor children in New Mexico was about 117,000. That meant that 27.5 percent of all children in the state in the mid-1980s lived in poverty. New Mexico ranked sixth from the top among all states and the District of Columbia in child poverty.

Whether never wed or divorced, single mothers in New Mexico, and their children, face heavy odds. New Mexico's divorced mothers can expect no help from either their children's fathers or the state. Fewer than 10 percent of mothers who sought child-support enforcement in 1988 received even one payment (ranking New Mexico forty-third among states in child-support enforcement). Unmarried mothers have even less hope of receiving state help in claiming nongovernmental support. In 1988, nearly one-third of all babies born in New Mexico were born to unmarried mothers. More than 10 percent of all New Mexico babies that year were born to unmarried teenagers. New Mexico's particular cultural background provides some benefits for some single mothers, particularly for Native American and Hispanic women, in the form of extended family-support networks exemplified, in my neighborhood, by Elizabeth and her kin. Such families continue to mitigate the problems of single motherhood for some women and children, despite urbanization and increased geographical mobility. But not all teenage mothers can count on such assistance. Compelled in most instances to interrupt their education, and to choose between earning a living and taking care of their children, most teen mothers face challenges that can defeat even the most loving families.

Many New Mexico babies are in trouble even before birth. More than 45 percent of New Mexico infants in 1988 were born to mothers receiving no prenatal care during the first trimester of pregnancy, and more than 16 percent of babies that year were born to women who received no care or late care; these figures put New Mexico squarely at the bottom of the nation in prenatal care. Such statistics reflect the larger fact that too many New Mexico families have no health insurance in an era of skyrocketing medical costs. Nationwide, according to the federal General Accounting Office, Hispanics are far more likely than other Americans to lack health insurance. An uninsured illness or accident can quickly plunge a family from relative comfort into a state of emergency.

Children are at risk in New Mexico, as are children across the nation, vulnerable to the difficulties and discontents of modern life. The Children's Defense Fund reported some horrifying statistics last year. In the United States in 1991, every thirty-five seconds a baby was born into poverty. Every fourteen minutes an infant died in the first year of life. Every fourteen hours a child younger than five was murdered. Every day, 135,000 children went to school carrying guns. Every night, 100,000 homeless children sought a place to sleep. Every month, at least 56,000 children were abused. And that year, nearly half a million youths gave up and dropped out of school—one every ten seconds of the school day.

We live in a nation, and a state, where all too many children are left exposed to poverty, neglect, and danger. Albuquerque is not Los Angeles, where the murders of children have become so commonplace that people seem somehow numb to the mass tragedy. But neither is it a safe place for many of its children. One way or another, these imperiled, breathing human beings will seek someone to care for them and some way to express their sadness and rage. Their tragic lives spill out at us from our morning newspapers. Consider, for example, the story of fourteen-year-old Clarence "Peewee" Kennedy, who, in January 1992, fired a shotgun into a crowd of high school students standing outside a Blake's Lota Burger fast-food restaurant in Albuquerque, critically injuring another fourteen-year-old. "These things just happened," Kennedy explained to an interviewer shortly after the incident. "But when you're in a gang, that kind of stuff happens." For Clarence Kennedy, his gang offered more protection, more satisfaction, and more pleasure than his family life could ever afford. "No matter what I do or what I say," he said, "I'm always going to be from my gang. I ain't never going to forget where I come from." He was afraid, however, to return from the state juvenile-detention facility to Albuquerque, where his mother lived. Rival gang members, he said, wanted revenge for the shooting.

Living, as we do, in a state that reveres the memory of Billy the Kid, it is wrongheaded, and perhaps self-righteous, to dwell overmuch on the deviance, or even the novelty, of Peewee Kennedy. But it is worth asking whether we can live with adolescent violence now, if indeed we ever could. Can we live in a world where gangs—"These things just happen"—replace families as nurturing institutions for poor children? Where even affluent families feel stretched, often to the breaking point, by the very facts of getting through the day? Where maintaining the nurturant, pleasurable dimensions of family life elude so many, and such diverse, New Mexicans?

The family may *never* have lived up to the ideal of being, in Christopher Lasch's wishful phrase, a "haven in a heartless world." But should we give up dreaming of a society that enables people to forge, and rely upon, bonds of affection? Politicians who insist that they are "pro-family" are assuredly responding to a widespread sense that the past fifty years has brought about a decline in Americans' ability to sustain satisfying family life. And yet, while the remarks I have made here demonstrate my own concern about challenges facing New Mexico's varied families today, I am not prepared to state, unequivocally, that more people had happy families fifty years ago than they do now. Indeed, our desire to return to some fictional golden age of the family, to reverse a purported historical decline, may be one of the most formidable barriers to solving the problems New Mexico's contemporary families encounter.

Attempts to impose conformity, to speak of "family" in the singular rather than acknowledge the strengths and problems of real and varied "families" in the plural, have been wrongheaded at best, pernicious at worst. Yet both "the family" and families themselves have always been contested terrain and have often focused political conflict in New Mexico. The image of the independent and happy fifties family—a family that survived and prospered on loyalty, discipline, and moral fiber without state "interference" or crippling federal "handouts"—is a myth that ignores the importance of such immense 1950s federal welfare programs as the G.I. Bill, which provided aid to veterans for college education and home-purchase loans. Nostalgia for this make-believe family has nonetheless shaped recent public policy regarding American family life in both the nation and the state.

In the past fifty years, the government of the state of New Mexico has issued only one report dealing with family life. This document, "The People Speak on Families," was published in 1981, as a report to then-Governor Bruce King by the Council for the New Mexico Conference on Families. That agency was created in response to a Carter administration call for state initiatives as part of a White House Conference on Families in 1980. The council, operating on a self-described "shoestring" budget, held hearings in different locations statewide, collected nearly one thousand pieces of testimony, conducted a state conference, and sent delegates to a meeting in Los Angeles.

Council members noted their desire to account for diversity among New Mexico families, to "examine the impact of economic and political forces related to poverty, unemployment, inflation and the energy crisis as they affect families in New Mexico," and to identify public policies "which may harm or neglect family life as well as . . . differing impact on particular groups, and to recommend new policies designed to strengthen and support families." These lofty goals are clearly based on a sense of urgency.

Such good intentions, to recognize families' diverse predicaments and to deal with them in a realistic manner, met up with the furious force of popular nostalgia on the road to the White House conference. When the time came to hold district hearings, self-styled "pro-family" groups representing the extreme wing of the New Right packed the meetings and dominated most of the recommendations reported out of both district and state gatherings. Thus, the state of New Mexico went on record with some rather interesting, and occasionally surreal, suggestions for meeting the complex and sometimes bewildering needs of contemporary American families. Confronting the question of how to define family at a time when New Mexico households often contained people unrelated by biology or by marriage, New Mexico took the position of trying to wish away all household groups that did not conform to a narrow definition of family. "The People Speak" report urged, "It should be the policy of the government to define the family as one of a relationship by heterosexual marriage, blood, or adoption." The report also suggested that the conference "strive to get laws to permit legal action against media for promoting other than heterosexual behavior."

When confronted with the predicament of the growing number of working mothers, New Mexico's representatives again narrowed discussion of an immensely complex and challenging contemporary social phenomenon, and put the significant question in the following fashion: "In what way do current policies on Equal Employment Opportunity harm the family?" They suggested a new system whereby heads of households would be given preferential treatment in hiring for all jobs, presumably as a means of keeping mothers out of the work force and in the home, thus disregarding the problems of thousands of New Mexico families dependent on two incomes. Faced with the growing need for good, affordable day care, the New Mexico conference officially opposed federal or state funding for day care.

The New Mexico conference's stated view on the issue of family violence reflected a longing for the bygone era of the "rule of thumb," when a man had the legal right to beat his wife and children with an instrument no bigger around than his thumb, without state interference. The official New Mexico position rejected any suggestion that government and society had an obligation to try to protect persons endangered by family members. Instead, the delegation asked, "How can we keep discipline of children outside of government and within the family?" Its answer: "Government should not support legislation that would infringe on parental rights of reasonable discipline."

Although the official positions adopted at district and state meetings clearly reflected the agenda of the New Right, the minority reports added to the document demonstrated the extent to which defining and supporting families lay at the heart of contemporary political battles. Some dismayed delegates, invoking "the ethnic diversity, cultural pluralism, and varying family values of New Mexico," submitted minority recommendations. A number of these minority reports took note of the challenges of varying family structures, the problems and possibilities created by geographical mobility, the horror of family violence, the demand for better child care, and the needs of working parents. For one set of conference participants, however, the majority report did not go far enough to warn against the dangers of such contemporary developments as maternal entry into the work force. These New Mexico citizens insisted that the important question facing the state in 1981 was, "How can public education, government, and state and local agencies inform women [sic] of the adverse effects of pursuing a career outside the home on her and her family?"

I wonder whether we can become a people sufficiently fair and imaginative to try to seek real solutions to the problems that families of all kinds face. I am one of the lucky ones. I am a denizen of Professor Scharff's neighborhood and a citizen of New Mexico. I enjoy the privileges of affluence, the rewards of a fascinating job, the joys of living in the American West, and the love of my family. I would like to believe that through love and understanding, and the material support our two incomes provide, my husband and I can provide our children with the security and self-esteem they will need to cope with a world that seems so often determined to live up to Lasch's description as "heartless." We New Mexico families are diverse, but we depend on each other. We are neighbors, fellow citizens, sharing a powerful government that can do good or evil, and a fragile landscape that can be beautiful and humane, or ugly and hostile. We don't yet see our common interest. We haven't fully realized the promise of a heritage of familism. We are not yet family. Seeking some form of safety, we are reinventing danger.

A couple of weeks ago I noticed the slash of spray-painted gang graffiti on a building a couple of blocks from my house. The owners painted it over, but it soon reappeared, and every day there seemed to be one more nearby building subjected to the spray-can treatment. Sometimes, I believe, we need to admit that the handwriting is on the wall.

Creating a Tradition

the great american duck race

Patricia Moore
and M. Jane Young

Racing ducks on land may seem incongruous to many, but in Deming, New Mexico, the Great American Duck Race is the town's most important celebration. There is a moment of near silence just before the clanging of the starting gate; then the crowd goes wild as eight ducks take off toward the finish line, their owners or renters urging them on. The race is over in a few seconds, but it's so close that the judges can barely discern the winner. Finally, they agree. The winner is "Peking Duck," who finishes the sixteen-foot dash in less than one second. A young boy wielding a net helps with the roundup of the ducks. When caught, the ducks are put in a tub full of cool water so that they can relax.

The next group gets ready to race—people walk around with ducks in their arms, petting them, talking to them, and occasionally sprinkling them with water. Eager children bring their favorite quackers, some of whom have no idea what to do when the gate opens. "On your mark, get ready, get set, go!" One of the ducks flaps his wings and then pauses in the middle of the runway, looking around curiously; the audience responds with laughter. He saunters towards the finish line and the announcer proclaims, "This is the slowest duck we've ever had; it took him thirty seconds to finish the course."

The ubiquitous Chief Quacker, with his team of volunteers, has labored all year to prepare for this event. He's "working the crowd" now, checking things out and making last-minute decisions, smiling because everything seems to be going smoothly. The weather is surprisingly cool for this time of year in Deming, and a gentle breeze brings with it a kaleidoscope of smells—cooking food of diverse types, dust, duck droppings, human sweat—all accompanied by the sounds of quacking, laughing, traditional Hispano and Anglo-American music, and the patter of the announcers who keep the crowds entertained. Visually, the scene is dominated by the red-brick courthouse, brightly colored vendors' tents and booths, balloons everywhere, ducks and duck images, and the casual summer clothing of old-timers, newcomers, and tourists. Stately cotton-woods and elms provide much-needed shade, and one can only assume that the grass will survive the traffic.

The mood is one of fun and adventure—if you get bored watching ducks race, you can observe, or take part in, other activities. The day begins with a mass ascent of hot-air balloons, and a footrace (the Great American People Race) provides a more serious counterpoint to the race-waddling ducks. There are carnival rides and pony rides for children, and there's a chili cook-off, a golf tournament, the Duck Royalty Dance, and horseshoe and washer throw competitions for adults. These traditional activities are embellished by duck images on street signs, T-shirts, caps, earrings, and food items. They are interwoven with other events that are either the outcome of a creativity that celebrates humor—the Tortilla Toss and the Outhouse Races, for instance—or an appreciation of the ridiculous that turns traditional events into duck-centered performances.

Perhaps the most important of the latter is the Duck Royalty Pageant, whose winners are "in-duckted" as royalty based on innovative costumes, their ability to waddle and quack, and their general fowl knowledge. "Just Hatched," "Little Waddlers," and "Darling Ducklings" are the categories for children's entries. In 1996, the seventeenth year of the race, the overall theme was "Remember When," an attempt to return to the early years of the Duck Race. The contestants tended to use "golden oldies" as a musical background to which they "waddled their stuff" in elaborate hand-made costumes.

The pageant has a carnivalesque quality to it, and the overall effect is hilarious, a collage of feathers, webbed feet, duck bills, wings, and made-up names such as Lady Duckiva, Duckahontas, and Groovy Granny Duck. The county mascot, Duck McPride, congratulates each winner. The young man inside the costume has only recently moved to Deming, but he says he loves "being" the mascot. "I put on the costume, and the duck takes over. It can do anything it wants to do, but mostly it tries to make people laugh and be happy." The mascot and pageant set the stage for a mood of community cohesiveness and humor.

Saturday morning's Tournament of Ducks Parade is THE parade in Deming each year. Lasting an hour and a half with more than eighty entries, the parade inevitably starts late. But it is awaited enthusiastically and patiently by visitors and Deming locals, who gather on the street corners and along the route and enjoy chatting and greeting friends. At last the Duck Royalty float appears with Duckahontas, the queen, who in everyday life is a shy medical technician born and raised in Deming. She entered the contest to represent the local hospital and was surprised to find that once the music started and the lights went up, she lost her inhibitions and danced and waddled her way to victory.

Floats sponsored by civic and commercial enterprises follow, and also high school bands, the football team, Mexican charros, the queen and court of the county fair, cowboys and cowgirls, the Border Patrol, and volunteer fire departments. A float featuring roping of a mechanical steer is followed by Shriners in their midget cars, low-riders, elaborately adorned cyclists, local politicians of various stripes — they all pass by. Children race to retrieve candies and to avoid being hit by water balloons thrown from some floats. Adults sit on lawn chairs or the curb and enjoy the variety and the chance to celebrate their community.

And the parade does just that — for Deming is a small ranching and farming community of approximately 12,500 people, about half Anglo and half Hispano. It was founded in the 1880s as the place where the Silver Spike was driven in — joining the two legs of the second American transcontinental railroad. The town is thirty-four miles from the border with Mexico and has a history as the home of military bases and camps, ranging from the days of Pershing's march against Pancho Villa through World War II. Today, Deming is characterized by a significant population of snowbirds during the winter months, attested to by its many RV and trailer parks. It is located just off Interstate 10, which runs east toward El Paso and west toward Tucson. Its businesses serve the many farmers and ranchers of the area (chilies and onions are two major crops).

Nearly half of Deming's current population has lived in the community less than five years. Even so, its residents describe Deming as a place "where everybody knows everyone else." This is a southwestern version of small-town America, sharing many of the realities of other such communities — from gangs and drug trafficking to meeting the demands of changing economic trends. But Deming has its own ethnic and historical character, and an unusual capacity to bring its people together to celebrate its strengths.

The first Duck Race was created by a group of businessmen who shared a cup of coffee in the morning and decided to enliven the rather boring life of the community. José "Butter" Milo, one of the six founding fathers, runs the J & J Printing Company in downtown Deming. He remembers that the group wanted to create something that everyone could have fun doing, and that no one would need a special membership for. "You wouldn't have to join a church, a political party, or any other kind of a group." They settled on ducks because one of the men had heard about duck races in Las Vegas once, and because they wanted to do something that really represented life in Deming. "We couldn't do horses, camels, or donkeys. In this area everybody had ducks in their irrigation tanks. We're a farming community. Ducks were everywhere." The group of six found-ers and their wives and friends did most of the work for the first three Duck Races, but it grew and grew and got beyond them. Eventually, they turned it over to the Chamber of Commerce. And for the past several years the race has been organized by GADR, Inc., an independent corporation that now has its own web site on the Internet.

In those first years they improvised and added new events—most of which came out of the traditional ways of life in Deming. There was the "Tortilla Toss" modeled after cow chip throwing. At first this was a wild event: participants made their own tortillas, and once a car fender was dented by a so-called tortilla that was more like a missile. After that they decided to use commercially pre-pared tortillas to avoid the possibility of injury. The "Outhouse Race" also seemed like another good way to transform something everybody had into something fun. So the organizers built outhouses and put them on wheels for an obstacle race held on a downtown street.

In the early years, they had a lot of fun thinking up all the ways they could make use of the duck theme. When a man actually named Robert Duck came along and began to win races, they were assured of publicity they had never imagined. The Duck Royalty Contest, with people dressing like ducks, was matched with a Best-Dressed Duck Contest in which ducks were dressed up like people and competed for prizes. This was a very popular event; adults and children spent weeks designing the costumes and making them. But animal rights activists from outside the community began to complain about the con-test, so the decision was made to drop it.

Although just about everybody in Deming felt that it was not abusive in any way, the consensus was that they couldn't afford the criticism—that kind of hostility didn't fit in with an event characterized by lighthearted fun. As Milo put it when he thought back over the origins of the race, "It was just a gag. It's unique. Everybody participates—children, adults, you don't have to be an ath-lete. Thursday through Sunday is a festive occasion."

Indeed, what began as a gag still is one. Deming is a community that once a year gathers around to make jokes and laugh about its own countrified, small-town ways of life. By doing so, it celebrates those same values. The Duck Race is really only the most successful of a variety of jokes that the community enjoys. For example, in this region where the rainfall is about eight inches per year and the only rivers are irrigation canals, a group of Demingites formed the Mimbres Valley Yacht Club, which met annually for a gala party—alongside a small sailboat parked near an irrigation canal. This ability to laugh at their circumstances—in a sense, at what outsiders might perceive as the community's impoverishment and powerlessness—is a great gift, one that Demingites have parlayed into a major occasion that attracts tourists and vendors from all over the country, and which brings economic benefit to their community. Aside from the dollars, though, the Duck Race allows the community to celebrate the virtues of small-town living, especially those of harmony, unity, and good old-fashioned hard work. Deming is a community whose people may sense that at some level their way of life is threatened, yet they have found a means of proclaiming the value of who they are and how they live together.

The ethnic cooperation exhibited in the Duck Race is remarkable in a region known more for ethnic diversity than harmony. Both Hispanos and Anglos hold leadership positions and participate actively in events. Ethnic division and discrimination are very real in this area where, every morning, in the early hours, young Hispano laborers wait along Deming's streets for an opportunity for work; but what is also real is the town's shared leadership and cooperation across ethnic lines—and that's what the Duck Race celebrates.

It brings together hundreds of volunteers who work hard to cooperate and yet sometimes disagree, thousands of participants from many places, varieties of traditions—Anglo and Hispano, rural and urban. It unites carnivalesque moments, children, parents, singles, seniors, musicians, racers, vendors, low-riders, horseback riders, the *migra*, and the fieldworker for a few days of fun and festivity. The complexity of life in Deming is mirrored in these events and has some similarity to the ducks themselves: ordinary, smelly, wriggling, often out of control, but fun. Sam Baca, Deming's mayor and onetime Chief Quacker, sums it up by saying, "People ask me, 'Why race ducks?' And I say, 'Why not?' "

Roads to Heaven

pilgrimage in the southwest

Steve Fox

Spring in the year 2000 was a blustery, bittersweet season for pilgrims in the Southwest. The month of April in particular was packed with pilgrimage. The most publicized pilgrim on the globe, frail, stooped, seventy-nine-year-old Pope John Paul II, was on TV making his Jubilee Pilgrimage to the Holy Land. Step by step, he emerged from peaceful grottoes into the bright glare of political battlefields. In Chinle, Arizona, at the mouth of Canyon de Chelly, members of forty churches and members of the Navajo and Mescalero Apache tribes arrived on a pilgrimage from Fort Sumner, New Mexico, four hundred miles to the east, where four thousand Navajo and Apache were imprisoned in 1863. Descendants of Col. Kit Carson handed over artifacts kept in the family ever since, and joined the clergy in asking forgiveness for "sins and atrocities" committed during "137 years of assailing Navajo culture."

In Nevada, fifty-four pilgrims walked the sixty-five miles from Las Vegas to the Nevada Test Site in the annual Good Friday observance staged by the Nevada Desert Experience. The nondenominational group had co-sponsored these candlelight marches and prayer vigils with Western Shoshone tribal officials for nineteen years at the place where 928 nuclear bombs were detonated between 1951 and 1992.[1]

At White Sands Missile Range, New Mexico, where the first atomic bomb was detonated in 1945, three thousand soldiers from thirty-four states and several foreign countries walked twenty-six miles with backpacks to observe the anniversary of the Bataan Death March. The event recalls how the entire New Mexico National Guard, mobilized in World War II as the 200th Coastal Artillery, was captured by Japanese forces and marched with others for ten days up the Bataan Peninsula, in the Philippines, with no food and water. Ten thousand of the thirty-five thousand men died.

And 250 miles north of White Sands, the Interfaith Pilgrimage for Peace carried holy dirt from the Santuário de Chimayó to Los Alamos. A woven pouch was brought to Chimayó from the northern Pueblos by young runners; filled at the Santuário, it was carried the twenty-seven miles to Los Alamos by relays of runners. On Good Friday, April 21, the largest pilgrimage in the United States converged on the Santuário—some sixty thousand, most walking up to twelve miles along winding roads choked with cars. The pilgrimage, always covered by TV news and freelance film crews, was marred this year by the murder of a pair of high school sweethearts from the valley as they walked Highway 76 before dawn on Good Friday morning. The headlines of that shocking event had hardly died down when the Cerro Grande Fire, a controlled burn that blew up in gale-force winds, roared through Los Alamos. Sixteen thousand upscale scientists and technical workforce were forced by the flames to evacuate to the working-class Hispanic and Indian towns of Española, Pojoaque, and Chimayó down in the valley. The largest fire in New Mexico history climaxed an unsettling spring by forcing pilgrims and technocrats into the same shelters with little more than the clothes on their backs. Flames destroyed the building holding the history of the Manhattan Project and then roared through sacred Pueblo lands, forcing firefighters to bulldoze firebreaks under the direction of archaeologists. Santa Clara Pueblo Governor Denny Gutierrez, reporting how Santa Clara Canyon was stripped by the flames, said, "That area is like a church to us. We can't put a price tag on it. I feel for Los Alamos and their losses, but homes can be rebuilt. For us, we'll never see that area again. It's a part of our life that has been destroyed."[2] Any trip into their canyon, with its ancestral dwellings, has echoes of a pilgrimage for the Santa Clarans.

Intention Brings Change

Being a pilgrim has always had political, as well as personal, aspects. To walk publicly in quest of change brings the status quo into question. While pilgrimage has very little to do with tourism, wandering, or leisure, it does have affinities with the protest march, the political demonstration, the fitness and ecology movements, and the modern task of finding oneself. What has made pilgrimage such an enduring activity is its links to the deep past. As McDonald-ization and secularization homogenize tradition and diversity, pilgrimage is the kind of reflective activity that reconnects people to questions and quests.[3] Sacred sites connect us to the healing earth. Being open and attentive on an intentional journey connects us to ourselves and to others. As Ambrose Bierce defined it, "A pilgrim is a traveler who is taken seriously."

Pilgrimage is a journey of spiritual intent that is long enough—or hard enough—to allow a person to change. Intent is everything: a pilgrim feels the need to change because something social or personal is not working. It is a two-way street: the physical journey reflects and empowers the inner effort to change. Pilgrimage is "walking the walk" of one's life. The American philoso-pher George Santayana stated: "Man and all other animals owe their intelligence to their feet. Thinking while you sit . . . the mind lapses into dreams. . . . Thinking while you walk, on the contrary, keeps you alert; your thoughts, though following some single path through the labyrinth, reveal real things in their real order; you are keen for discovery."[4]

In the Southwest, as all over the globe, pilgrimage has surged in the last thirty years. There are serious problems that demand serious effort to under-stand, challenge, and endure. Migration, subordination, meaninglessness, cul-ture clash, land disputes—all are common from Zuni to Kathmandu.

The Persistence of Indigenous Belief

Before state and national lines were imposed on the American Southwest, it was the Far Northwest—first of the Indian empire cultures of central Mexico, then of New Spain, then of Mexico. Before the Spanish came, the Sonoran and Chihuahuan Deserts and the Colorado Plateau were home to many peoples as hardy and well adapted to the climate as cactus. We don't know the names the earlier groups had for themselves; we now call them the Paquimeans, the Mogollon, the Mimbres, the Anasazi, the Hohokam. Later, more names: the Yaqui, the Tarahumara, the Mayo, the Pima, the Tohono O'odham, the Apache, the "Pai" peoples of the canyons.

Travelers, mostly men, covered vast distances on foot. They walked to shrines, ran in relays and games far exceeding our marathons,[5] and traded shell, gemstones, copper, seeds, feathers, even live macaws, from the valley of central Mexico to Mesa Verde, from the Pacific Coast to the high plains. The memory of these ancient pilgrims and travelers has settled into the petroglyph image of Kokopelli, the humpbacked flute player. Underneath the domesticated version popular in "Santa Fe Style," he's part hard-core fertility symbol, part mysterious trader, part the spirit of music, dance, and ritual.

The pilgrimage aspect of this age-old foot travel comes to light today when native pilgrims cross the many boundaries imposed by the political jurisdictions overlying their former homelands. Zuni Pueblo, for example, was forced in the 1980s and 1990s to reveal many details about its Summer Solstice pilgrimage that crosses from western New Mexico into Arizona every four years. This 120-mile round trip on foot and horseback down the Zuni River to the Little Colorado is the pueblo's most important pilgrimage, a visit to *Koluwala:wa*, where the Zuni came from and where their spirits go after death, and from which kachina spirits come to care for them. In court documents, the Zuni translated the marshy area's name as "Zuni Heaven." They were forced into a court fight over their right to make this pilgrimage because a BLM grazing leaseholder tried to stop them by ramming his truck into horseback-riding pilgrims. The Zuni won a new kind of "cultural easement" in federal court, guaranteeing them perpetual access to a fifty-foot-wide use corridor. This conflict has given another, earlier, story of conflict even greater symbolism: Tewa scholar Alfonso Ortiz and Zuni scholar Edmund Ladd have said that this Zuni Heaven pilgrimage was the setting for the first contact in what is now the United States between a European expedition and Native Americans, when Coronado blundered into the pilgrimage in June 1540.[6]

Other Pueblos have also revealed long pilgrimages across their spiritual geographies that cross modern boundaries. An Acoma Pueblo man told archaeologist Florence Hawley Ellis that his grandfather used to load up two burros with prayer-stick and turquoise offerings and take several weeks to visit a 240-mile circuit of shrines honoring Acoma's clan origins—visiting Chaco Canyon, Mesa Verde, Ute Mountain.[7] Many Pueblo people of several tribes make pilgrimages to Chaco Canyon. Fifteen years of study has convinced some archaeologists that the thousand-year-old road system radiating from Chacoan Great Houses was for regular pilgrimage use.[8]

Six Hopi priests took Jake and Susanne Page on a pilgrimage in 1981 to shrines far outside their current reservation boundaries. This happened after Jake, a writer for the Smithsonian, and Susanne, a photographer, had been working among the Navajo and Hopi for several years. There was initially some disagreement among the Hopi priests, but they worked it out; the motivation may have touched on the long-simmering Navajo-Hopi land dispute. In any case, the Hopi gave the Pages permission to publish text and pictures of this previously secret pilgrimage in a large-format book and in *National Geographic* magazine.[9] Traveling eleven hundred miles in four days by truck and foot, the pilgrims visited the edges of the Hopi *tusqua*, their homeland. They stopped and uncovered hidden shrines at sites of sacred power, salt deposits, and clan migra-tion routes from the New Mexico border to Navajo Mountain in Utah, and from the San Francisco Peaks to the Grand Canyon. They said, "We do this to conduct our lives in friendship and peace, without anger, without greed, without wickedness of any kind, among ourselves or in our association with any peo-ple."[10] The great difference between this and the mass, populist pilgrimages of Christians, Jews, Muslims, Buddhists, and Hindus is that only eleven living people—including two Anglos—had seen all the Hopi tusqua shrines when the Pages' book was written.

Perhaps the most important native pilgrimage to all U.S. tribes, because it set a precedent for federal recognition and return of traditional sacred lands, is the Taos Pueblo annual pilgrimage to Blue Lake. High above the pueblo in what is now the Wheeler Peak Wilderness, Blue Lake is "the most important of all shrines because it is a part of our life," said former governor Seferino Martinez in the 1960s. It is their lake of emergence and where their souls go after death— their heaven. President Theodore Roosevelt took the lake from Taos and gave it to the American public when his administration created the Carson National Forest in 1906. Pursuing the return of their shrine until it became the Pueblo's primary goal, Taos leaders gained allies in legal, literary, and arts circles until even the National Council of Churches, bipartisan congressional clout, and the Nixon White House wanted to give the lake back. In 1970, President Richard Nixon signed a bill giving Blue Lake back to Taos. Nixon handed the pen to Cacique Juan de Jesus Romero, whose Tiwa name was Deer Bird, and who had devoted most of his life to the struggle. Nixon said, "I consider this one of the most significant achievements of my administration." With great dignity, Deer Bird accepted the pen and said, "Now when I die, I will die in peace."[11] At the Pueblo, ringing church bells and freely shed tears greeted the announcement.[12] The last 764 acres of this Blue Lake pilgrimage path, called by Taos "The Path of Life," was returned to the Pueblo in 1996.

Although there have been several similar cases since, no other tribe has marshaled the broad support Taos achieved in 1970. However, Zuni Pueblo did win a $24 million settlement in 1982 for traditional lands taken from them. The Zuni prevailed in the Indian Land Claims Court largely through documentation that elders had names and prayers for shrine sites visited in pilgrimages far outside the modern reservation boundaries.[13]

Christianity Comes to New Spain's Far Northwest

Fifty-eight years after Coronado's encounter with Zuni, the colonizer Juan de Oñate brought settlers into the Colorado Plateau–Rio Grande provinces who embodied a fusion of European Christianity and indigenous beliefs. Oñate had married a granddaughter of Moctezuma, the Aztec emperor. Oñate's father, Cristobal, the founder of the silver mining center of Zacatecas, was born in the Basque village of Oñati, a day's walk from Europe's longest and most strategically important pilgrimage, the Camino de Santiago. The Camino runs from the Pyrenees across four hundred miles of Spain's northern countryside, ending at Santiago de Campostela in Galicia, on the Atlantic. According to legend, Campostela was where the bones of Saint James (Santiago) had been found in 900 A.D. Historians speculate that the church, under pressure from French nobility to help block the Moors from crossing the Pyrenees into France, used the legend of Santiago's remains to rally Christian resistance that finally pushed the Moors out of Iberia. The pilgrimage slowly died down during the nineteenth and twentieth centuries until it was resurrected in the 1970s by ecotourism, fitness walkers, and lovers of art history. Devout Catholics are now about a third of the perhaps 100,000 who walk the Camino each year.[14]

The Catholic culture's fusion with native traditions of sacred sites and pilgrimage is evident in many places in the Southwest, but its two avatars are the Santuário de Chimayó and its Holy Week pilgrimage north of Santa Fe, New Mexico, and the pilgrimage to Magdalena de Kino, Sonora, sixty miles south of the border twin cities of Nogales, on October 4.

Chimayó was originally a string of six *placita* (small plaza) settlements along the Santa Cruz River, which flows west from the Sangre de Cristo range to the Rio Grande. On at least three occasions after its founding in the 1690s after the Pueblo Revolt, Mexican and Pueblo Indians lived among the Spanish settlers, evolving one of the most thoroughly integrated Indo-Hispano cultures in New Mexico. Here, with scant contact with priests, the people became a stronghold of La Hermandad, the brotherhood of the Penitentes. Visiting bishops railed against Chimayó's rough folk religion and "idolatries" (read: Indian beliefs.) In 1804, the name Esquipúlas appeared in the baptismal records for the first time, and in 1813, a man named Bernardo Abeyta, also a Penitente leader, asked the church's permission to build a chapel over the spot where, for three years, his band of nineteen families had been venerating a crucifix that had appeared in the ground, carrying the image of the Black Christ of Esquipúlas. This image originated in southeast Guatemala, where Indios and mestizos made pilgrimages to eat healing earth in honor of a dark Cristo.[15]

The cross Abeyta said he found now hangs over the altar in the thirty-by-ninety-foot adobe chapel he and his neighbors built in 1813. But there are two other powers at the Santuário that have pushed Esquipúlas to the background—the Santo Niño de Atocha and the holy dirt. The Santo Niño appeared in 1856, the year Don Bernardo died. The family on the north side of the placita, the Medinas, brought back a *bulto*, or doll-like image, of the Santo Niño from Mexico and began attracting pilgrims to their own chapel across from the Santuário. The Santo Niño, or Holy Child, is an image of Christ that originated in Zacatecas and spread across the Hispanic world, even back to Spain. He is Christ depicted as a boy in medieval pilgrim's costume—staff, water gourd, broad-brimmed hat, and the scallop shell made famous by Campostela as the symbol of having trekked to the Atlantic shore. The story that grew up around this image is that Christians under siege from Muslims at Atocha, Spain, were saved from starvation and dehydration by Christ disguised as a pilgrim on the Camino. The Santo Niño is now the patron saint of pilgrims, lost strangers, and outsiders. People leave baby shoes at his image because he wears out his shoes going around at night solving people's problems. What a perfect Christ for eighteenth- and nineteenth-century New Spain! A roving troubleshooter in a land of refugees, migrants, captives, and fugitives.

The other healing power at Chimayó, as at Esquipúlas, Guatemala, is a handful of dirt—the most humble medium to convey spirituality, yet one symbolizing the nurturing of the earth itself. Bernardo Abeyta's story of finding the crucifix in a hole from which it refused to be separated repeats a myth widely believed in the European traditions—that a holy image, found by a humble person of the fields and taken to the nearest church or priest, returns each night to its hole as if to say, "I belong here. And so do you."

The story at the Santuário is that the hole from which an increasing number of pilgrims took a pinch or handful of sandy dirt miraculously replenished itself and was never empty. But it's a struggle even for the faithful to believe this today, since the priest assigned to the Santuário for the last forty years says, in his Barcelona Catalan accent, "Dirt don't heal! *Faith* heals!" But still, 184 years after that dirt had been made into adobes to enshrine itself and those who hoed and planted it, the metaphor of Chimayó remains powerful—the transforming spiritual idea for the largest pilgrimage in the United States. And the gathering of pilgrims has its own power. As a 1996 pilgrim said, "To me the miracle is the whole idea of just being able to be together with people and having everybody just be together in a spirit of prayer. Especially in these times and days in the world."[16]

Yet the heart of this holy place, to this Anglo observer-becoming-participant, is the ephemeral scores of little folded pieces of paper, ex-votos carrying pleas, prayers, and thanks to the saints who inhabit the sacristy, the side room usually identified in photos by the crutches and canes left there by pilgrims healed. The small sacristy is a gallery of sacred folk images—Santiago, patron saint of Spain and its war against Islam and infidels, on his horse; the Virgin of Guadalupe, Madonna of the New World and its darker people; Jesus as the Santo Niño and Sacred Heart; Saint Michael, Saint Anthony, and Saint Joseph.

On my first pilgrimage to Chimayó, trying to find my spiritual footing as a non-Catholic and newcomer, I was studying this gallery of painted saints at six o'clock on Good Friday morning, before the crowds became overwhelming. The paper prayers were stuck in the corners of every picture frame and in gaps in the glass cases housing Santiago and the Santo Niño, and in cracks in the plaster walls and low wooden vigas. Many were unfolded and fallen to the ground. "Please Nuestra Señora, bring our son home from combat. Carlos is our last child." "Santo Niño, come and take away the tumors from our Mom. She is caring for her two little granddaughters, we all need her." "Señor de Esquipúlas, por favor ayúdanos en este mundo de violencia." And on and on, a chorus of need beyond any Department of Health and Human Services budget increase or lucky lottery win to assuage. I stepped out into the growing morning light, found a bench, put my face in my hands, and wept. My own losses and disappointments made me feel those of la gente del norte. We were the same in our grief and hope. I knew why I had come.

Three other major pilgrimage sites line the Rio Grande/El Camino Real: the hills of Tomé, twenty miles south of Albuquerque; Tortugas, at Las Cruces; and El Paso. The latter two pilgrimages are made on Guadalupe Day, December 12.

In southern Arizona, which knows it is part of Sonora better than New Mexico knows it is part of Chihuahua, people go sixty miles south of the border to Magdalena de Kino. There, since the early 1800s, pilgrims have visited a trinity of San Franciscos: Saint Francis of Assisi, Saint Francis Xavier, and Friar Francisco Kino, who seem to have blended into one patron saint of the Pimería Alta.

Francis Xavier, born in 1506 near Pamplona, on the Camino de Santiago, was a missionary to India who died in 1552 and was canonized as the patron saint of missionaries. His day on the calendar is December 3. Father Eusebio

Francisco Kino was born in 1645 in the Italian mountains; he became a Jesuit and found his life's work as evangelist to the Pimería Alta from 1687 to 1711. That year he rode into Magdalena to dedicate a chapel to his patron, Francis Xavier, but became ill and died. He was buried under the floor of the chapel he had built for Xavier. In 1965, when Arizona selected him as the state's founding father to be depicted in Statuary Hall in the Capitol in Washington, D.C., Mexico sent a team of archaeologists to find and honor his remains. They did, and constructed a *plaza monumental* to surround his resting-place. So now a reclining statue of Francis Xavier lies in the 1830s church on the south side of the plaza, while the skeleton of Francisco Kino lies on the north side in its excavated grave several feet below ground level behind glass windows.

And permeating the whole region is the spirit of Saint Francis of Assisi, who was called to religious life in 1205, walked the Camino de Santiago, founded the order of monks that bears his name, and died in 1226. Franciscan brothers came to the Pimería Alta in 1767, replacing the Jesuits. Saint Francis of Assisi's day is October 4, and that is the day pilgrims come to Magdalena. Kino's bones are often identified with Xavier, and San Francisco is sometimes equated with God.[17]

Pilgrims in a Cold War and an Atomic Age

In the two families of pilgrimages discussed so far, pilgrims take comfort in the past. "For most," says Martin Robinson, "the sense of treading ground made holy by past events is crucial. . . . [T]he pilgrim becomes one with all who have gone before."[18] But the latest layer on the "Old Northwest" carries the ultimate laboratories and Ground Zeros where invisible particles make unimaginable mayhem. How can the wood and paper and shell of the past address this sorcery? Yet pilgrims now come to these places, too. Not holy places; not out of reverence for a visible past. Going to these sites evokes the whole world and generations unborn. Like the invisible particles, it is the unseen Future that Cold War pilgrims seek.

So, peace pilgrims and army vets who thank the bomb for shortening the war trek to Trinity Site, near White Sands, in April and October. Japanese *hibakusha*—radiation victims—and their descendants come to Los Alamos, White Sands, and the Nevada Test Site bearing origami cranes. Linking oldest to newest, the Western Shoshone open their reservation to participants in the Nevada Desert Experience, pilgrims protesting underground nuclear testing.

Most of the Shoshones' land—most of *Nevada* (87 percent!)—was taken by the military for weapons testing.

And so the Southwest contains many heavens and many hells. Roads to these heavens, and through these hells, web the entire region, and pilgrims, their hearts' eyes alert to every wisp of meaning, flutes and backpacks at the ready, walk them still.

Endnotes

1. *Las Vegas Review-Journal*, January 2, 2000, and April 22, 2000, on-line archive.

2. Governor Gutierrez spoke on the satellite-distributed program Native America Calling, originating from KUNM-FM, Albuquerque, May 22, 2000.

3. George Ritzer, *The McDonaldization of Society* (Newbury Park, Calif.: Pine Forge Press, 1993).

4. Quoted in Paul G. Kuntz, "Man the Wayfarer: Reflections on the Way," in *Itinerarium: The Idea of Journey*, ed. Leonard J. Bowman, p. 217 (Salzburg: Institut für Anglistik und Amerikanistik, Universitat Salzburg, 1989).

5. Peter Nabokov, *Indian Running: Native American History and Tradition* (Santa Fe: Ancient City Press, 1991).

6. J. Wesley Huff, "A Coronado Episode," *New Mexico Historical Review* 26 (April 1951): 115; Alfonso Ortiz, personal communication, March 15, 1990; Edmund Ladd, interviewed in *Surviving Columbus*, Peabody Award–winning documentary, 1992, first section.

7. Personal communication, Florence Hawley Ellis, March 1990.

8. W. James Judge, "Chaco Canyon—San Juan Basin," in *Dynamics of Southwest Prehistory*, ed. Linda S. Cordell and George Gumerman (Washington, D.C.: Smithsonian Institution Press, 1989).

9. *National Geographic* 162, no. 5 (1982): 607–29; Susanne Page and Jake Page, *Hopi* (New York: Harry N. Abrams, 1982).

10. Page and Page, *Hopi*.

11. Joe S. Sando, *Pueblo Profiles: Cultural Identity through Centuries of Change* (Santa Fe: Clear Light Publishers, 1998), pp. 93–105.

12. R. C. Gordon-McCutchan, *The Taos Indians and the Battle for Blue Lake* (Santa Fe: Red Crane Books, 1991).

13. T. J. Ferguson and E. Richard Hart, *A Zuni Atlas* (Norman: University of Oklahoma Press, 1985), p. xi.

14. Personal communication, Maribel Roncal, pilgrimage hostel proprietor at Cezur Menor and president, State of Navarra Camino de Santiago Association.

15. Stephen de Borhegyi, "The Cult of Our Lord of Esquipulas in Middle America and New Mexico," *El Palacio* 61, no. 12 (1954); Elizabeth Kay, *Chimayo Valley Traditions* (Santa Fe: Ancient City Press, 1987).

16. Raymond Jones, 1996. From the oral histories gathered in Sam Howarth and Enrique Lamadrid, *Pilgrimage to Chimayo: A Contemporary Portrait of a Living Tradition* (Santa Fe: Museum of New Mexico Press, 1999).

17. I am indebted to James S. Griffith, *Beliefs and Holy Places: A Spiritual Geography of the Pimería Alta* (Tucson: University of Arizona Press, 1992), pp. 31–66.

18. Quoted in Phil Cousineau, *The Art of Pilgrimage* (Berkeley: Conari Press, 1998), p. 96.

Sedona and the
New (Age) Frontier

Barbara A. Campbell

Oak Creek [Sedona] is Arizona turned idyllic. Here the mountains have married
the desert, and their union has been most fruitful. At one moment you are among
the firs and ice-cold waterfalls, and the next moment you are looking at sand and
cactus. . . . If you filmed the extravagant place, you would be accused of impudent
and careless faking. . . . [A]round the floor of the canyon, very sharp and bright in
the sunlight, were great twisted shapes of red sandstone, looking like ruined fairy-
tale castles and mysterious monuments. . . . I felt like saying that at last we had
arrived in Avalon and must stay here forever, vanishing from the world that had
known us. Why go on? . . . Here was the perfect haven. Why go on?

—J. B. Priestly "Midnight on the Desert"

The fairy tale, the Avalon, the haven, encompassing the idyllic, the mysterious, the extravagant: these are the words of one who has experienced the
geographical and environmental wonder that is Sedona, Arizona. While J. B.
Priestly's excursion into Arizona in the 1910s was for health reasons,[1] later
visitors to Sedona, such as the Surrealist artist Max Ernst in the mid-1940s,
came for the isolation and inspiration that the landscape and the Southwest
Amerindian tribes provided.[2] From the mid-1970s to the present, a different
kind of inspiration has brought people to Sedona—an embracing of Eastern
religion combined with nature-based worship systems, with a touch of popular
psychology added.

The Symbolic Frontier

"Frontier" has been commonly used to describe the fringe of civilization that adjoins undeveloped territory; "frontier" has also come to serve as a description of new thought or learning, an indicator of investigations still taking place. In America, the "West," or more specifically, the western "frontier" mentality, has transmigrated in many people's lives from a physical representation of frontier (no fences, no restrictions, infrequent social contexts) to a spiritual and material symbolism of a frontier (embracing Amerindian artifacts or beliefs, "mind" religion,[3] Old West folklore/antiquities).

In the past, the potential of the frontier was seen as physical freedom, "elbow room"; much of today's frontier is seen as spiritual, giving its adherents personal and emotional space in a society where physical space is at a premium. The "frontier" today is mainly a representation of freedom, a respite from the daily stress of modern life and an answer to life's perplexing questions for many people. Many of today's spiritual seekers find that the frontier is what Durkheim describes as "the supreme reality which no longer has anything of a divine personality about it," essentially becoming a reality "contained within man himself, or rather; man is but one with it, for nothing exists apart from it."[4] Yet, some New Age spiritual followers, in Sedona and elsewhere, incorporate a devotion to a divine being (such as Christ) into their quest for enlightenment. For many of these middle-class spiritual explorers, images of physical frontier such as Sedona have become intertwined with the perceived frontier of the vast expanses of the uncharted spiritual realm.

Sedona is a city physically between the earth's ancient history (the Grand Canyon) and humanity's bustling industry (the cities of Phoenix and Tucson) that has seen a dramatic increase in population—from 5,400 in 1971 to 14,800 people in 1993, a 274 percent increase over a period of twenty-two years.[5] The majority of the people who have moved to Sedona since the early 1920s have tended to be retirees and creative-artistic types, with both groups coming for the peace, tranquility, and solace that Sedona and the surrounding landscape provided. Sedona has inspired creative expressions from visual artists such as Ernst, writers such as Zane Grey (*Call of the Canyon*), as well as western-genre filmmakers.

White settlers have found the inspiration of the region in spiritual contexts as well. For example, a local resident in the 1950s decided to make a dramatic statement of Christian faith and created the Chapel of the Holy Cross within the red rock formations overlooking Highway 179.[6] Yet white settlers were not always so benign in their relations with the local inhabitants. In the 1930s, white Christian settlers tried to force the area tribes to *denounce* their "weird ceremonies" of snake dances and the like, and embrace Christianity; frustration mounted as some tribes would not convert; the Hopi "responded least of all to the white man's religion."[7] Ironically, in the late twentieth century Arizona has become one of many places in America where Amerindian and Middle Eastern naturistic beliefs coexist with traditional Judeo-Christian and capitalist beliefs. It is in Sedona, Arizona, that the nostalgia for the physical freedom of the western frontier circa the 1800s melds with the spiritual freedom of the nontraditional religions found under the umbrella term "New Age."[8]

The New Age Neiman-Marcus

The greatest New Age draw in Sedona is the "vortices" that are in the surrounding area. Vortices are described by the Sedona Chamber of Commerce as energy fields, some "magnetic" and some "electrical," that are mentally and spiritually stimulating, and have either an energizing or calming effect "on those who are sensitive" to them.[9] A New Age guide to these "power points," *The Sedona Vortex Experience*, describes a vortex as "a spiraling cone or funnel shape of awesome energy," which forms "behind any blunt object that has some fluid [motion] flowing over it, [such as] wind blowing around a house."[10] These "power points" are necessary because "advanced energy systems, coming in with the New Age, are forcing us to find new flexibilities. We must release old forms, embody the new energies, and transform our entire physical existence on this planet."[11] The most influential proponent of Sedona's "spiritual energy" came in 1986 with the publication of a popular New Age author's observations of the phenomenon. Dick Sutphen's book on Sedona and its vortex energies, *Sedona: Psychic Energy Vortexes*, has continually sold well since its publication.[12] From that point in the mid-1980s, the growing number of New Age devotees both within Sedona and in other communities began to focus their attention on these power points.

Taking this and similar information through the filter of mass media, Sedona has become a symbol of excess and indulgence where artifacts and metaphysics are intertwined and for sale. A writer visiting this "new-age Neiman-Marcus" jests about the presence of "an energetic, spiritual sales force" in Sedona that is trying to push "chakra lube jobs, high-frequency cornmeal, numerology lotto tickets, a second birth, [and] a third eye."[13] Another writes, "[Arizona's] inhabitants outdo even Californians in nuttiness. Newspapers abound in energy clinics, transformational joy breathing, solarial channeling, next-level empowerment and séances at the local crystal sanctuary."[14] While the phrasing may be in jest, the economic influence of the New Age movement on Sedona is not: the *Official Guide* for 1994–95 put out by the Chamber of Commerce listed three New Age bookstores, two New Age information centers, and fourteen providers of New Age products and services—for a city of less than fifteen thousand people.[15] It is the tourist trade, estimated at approximately three million visitors a year, that brings Sedona the majority of its income and notoriety.[16] By 1992, Sedona had sixteen companies for scenic tours by various means and "vortex tours," forty gift and jewelry stores, and a factory outlet mall.[17]

For residents and businesses alike, an "unspoiled frontier" theme is central in the Sedona myth and important to the Sedona economy. Joe Green, a local merchant, comments, "It may get dense [in downtown Sedona], but you can still go up in these mountains and find things no white man has ever seen."[18] Journalists are more than happy to feed the myth; one writer, on a canyon jeep tour, documents that "echoing across those Arizona cypress, juniper and pinyon, we heard the howls of one, two, three, perhaps a dozen unscripted wild animals. Coyotes."[19]

The influx of New Age pilgrims has overwhelmed the nature themes in the Sedona myth. Thousands of "pilgrims" come to the national forest surrounding the town to create rock arrangements known as "medicine wheels" that can be as large as 200 feet in diameter. Some of these "focal points" are removed by rangers and rebuilt by visitors up to twenty times per week.[20] Though considered "selfish" in forest ranger terms for damaging the national forest with rock formations, the majority of New Age wheel-builders have not been prosecuted due to conflict over religious freedom and the immense volume of New Age visitors, which reaches five thousand a month during the summer.[21] The encounters with nature increased dramatically after Dick Sutphen's *Sedona: Psychic Energy Vortexes* brought notoriety to Sedona and an increase in attention to the power of nature. One of many subsequent books and magazines on the subject, *The Sedona Vortex Experience*, delineates exercises that can be performed by New Agers in the wilds around Sedona, including "attunement exercises" to develop the awareness "of our own vast, multi-dimensional beingness."[22] These books and guides often refer to an Earth Mother, misinterpreting beliefs of various Amerindian tribes and combining them with the New Age vortex experience, which frustrates Amerindian groups longing for better recognition by the mainstream culture. One such misinterpretation is the medicine wheel phenomenon brought to the national forest—it is primarily found among the northern Plains nations and does not occur among the tribal nations living in the Southwest.

Site-Specific Representations

The increasing expense of foreign travel, the recent revivals of western novels and films, and the marketing campaigns of tourism offices have also increased Americans' interest in visiting places such as Sedona. Frank Clifford notes that "many of the same [western] writers who have been ringing the death knell for America's most mythic landscape have helped set in motion the century's last stampede of western tourists."[23]

The physical locations in the Sedona area have become objectifications of spiritual existence, pre-American and ancient history, and nature worship for tourists and New Age pilgrims, serving as site-specific representations of intangible and material contexts. I use the term "site-specific representations" to denote the location-specific object lessons given at such museum-like attractions as national monument sites, natural phenomena areas, and other places where the geographic location figures as prominently in people's experience as the material presented.[24] The West as a location figures no differently; Frank Clifford comments that "sometimes the romanticizing of the West can get so mixed up with the merchandising of it that you have trouble telling where one stops and the other starts."[25]

Jackie Donath describes the West in the minds of the American people as being "rooted in a generous affection, a construct of the imagination, a mystical landscape and period that defy the limits of geography and history."[26] It is this amalgam of nostalgia with mystical, ethereal spirituality that lends itself well to the New Age movement's intermixing of artifact and imagination. One travel writer falls into this confusing abyss in describing a state historical park south of Sedona, stating that "the dry, dusty look of the fort seems right out of the movies, and you fully expect John Wayne in cavalry dress to step from the commandant's house."[27] New Age ceremonies that utilize shamanistic rituals and drumming, along with reverence expressed for the Native American ways, have attracted many disillusioned white middle-class believers, causing one critic to note, "All that was missing was an Indian."[28] It is possible to speculate on the motives of the white middle-class believers, whose guilt is perhaps assuaged by these New Age ceremonies—a white person's guilt by association with the dominant culture, guilty because of the dominant culture's historical or current treatment of native or nonwhite cultures.

Conclusion

Sedona was founded, like many other towns in Arizona, predominantly by white settlers who brought in their own behaviors and way of life, often without ever knowing which indigenous peoples lived in the surrounding area. As the West expanded, so did Americans' fascination and folklore about "things out West." Visitors came by train and carload to explore and "tame" their own little piece of the frontier. For years, the attraction to such places as Sedona was precisely its isolation from urban growth and blight, as well as its connection to the western myth.

As Sedona came into the public awareness in the 1980s as a New Age religious hub, the media focus on this new amalgamation of Native American prayers and rituals, holistic healing, and popular psychology grew in astronomical proportions. The New Age movement brought the double-edged sword of tourism into Sedona, eliminating such problems as finding city services, but creating high housing costs, low-wage service-sector jobs, and urban growth that competes for the pristine space admired by those who first settled the city.[29]

In looking at Sedona, I am reminded of Durkheim's analysis of the idea of supreme reality found in Buddhism: "To find it, and unite himself to it, one does not have to search some external support outside himself; it is enough to concentrate upon himself and meditate."[30] The Sedona area embodies the dual nature of today's spiritual seeker who, like the Buddhist philosophy described above, believes in the frontier within oneself, yet also believes in the outward symbolism found in the objects and elaborate rituals of the New Age movement. Along with the freedom it espouses come ironic restrictions, such as the active disavowing of ritual and ceremony coming out of the Judeo-Christian traditions so dominant in American culture. The rituals and ceremonies chosen and elaborated on by the New Age followers themselves often take on an anti-Christian-establishment flavor, emphasizing the teachings of Jesus or the Bible over the doctrines of any specific denomination.

Sedona itself appears to be a symbol of objectification, a place where everything is made into material items or trinkets to possess physically rather than spiritually, appearing to go against the anti-establishment sentiments expressed in New Age ceremonies. Monuments, museums, gift shops, medicine wheels, crystals, western-style art, hats, clothing—all become objects representing an ideal, something that may not exist in this world; but by purchasing, photographing, or possessing these items, one can belong to an ever-present existence, a sort of spiritual continuum. Essentially, Sedona both rejects and embraces mainstream capitalistic culture, selling spirituality through crystals, mediums, and the like—becoming a suitably American, and thereby capitalist, religious form. While the vortex visitors and medicine wheel–builders continue to come to Sedona, along with the tourists, the naturists, the athletic-minded, the retirees, and the creative personalities, there is no doubt another spiritual frontier "out there" to be found, and Sedona may very well play a part in its discovery.

Endnotes

This essay was written as Independent Study 499 for Dr. Allan Axelrad at California State University at Fullerton in the fall of 1994, in response to the author's excursion through western Arizona the previous summer. The trip was originally prompted by the media attention and commentary on Sedona and the New Age movement since the late 1980s.

1. J. B. Priestly, "Midnight on the Desert," in *Grand Canyon, An Anthology,* ed. Bruce Babbit, pp. 105–6 (Flagstaff: Northland Press, 1978). Priestly was an Englishman on holiday in the 1910s in Arizona; the quote is taken from James K. Ballinger and Andrea D. Rubenstein, *Visitors to Arizona 1846 to 1980* (Phoenix: Phoenix Art Museum, 1980), p. 20.

2. Ballinger and Rubenstein, pp. 34, 160.

3. "Mind" religion refers to many of the belief systems developed to deal with internal expectations, personal growth, and harmony, unlike belief systems that address one's behavior and external expectations of such.

4. Emile Durkheim, *The Elementary Forms of the Religious Life,* trans. Joseph Ward Swain (n.p.: George Allen and Unwin, 1915; reprint, New York: Free Press, 1965), p. 48.

5. Estimated 1971 figures are derived from Thomas B. Leasure, *All about Arizona* (Greenlawn, N.Y.: Harian Publications, 1971). The 1993 figures are from Sedona–Oak Creek Canyon Chamber of Commerce, *Experience Sedona: 1994–1995 Official Guide and Membership Directory* (n.p., 1994), p. 61.

6. Marguerite Brunswig Staude had the chapel built in 1956; cf. *Red Rock Country Visitors' Guide,* June 1994, pp. 1, 11.

7. *The WPA Guide to 1930's Arizona*, foreword by Stewart L. Udall (Tucson: University of Arizona Press, 1989), p. 121.

8. According to J. Gordon Melton in his *New Age Almanac* (New York: Visible Ink Press, 1991), the current "New Age" developed in Western civilization in the 1960s and derives from earlier occultist or metaphysical religions skeptical toward Christianity, and with strengths coming from the scientific Enlightenment of the eighteenth century. Twentieth-century New Agers owe much to their eighteenth- and nineteenth-century metaphysical predecessors, such as Swedenborgianism, Mesmerism, Transcendentalism, Spiritualism, Christian Science, and Theosophy, to name a few (Melton, pp. 3–7). While the majority of the New Age movement developed from a skepticism for dominant Christian beliefs, a few recent developments in the New Age movement intertwine metaphysical beliefs and Christian theology.

9. *Experience Sedona*, p. 33.

10. Gayle Johansen and Slinnan Naom Barclay, *The Sedona Vortex Experience* (Sedona, Ariz.: Sunlight Productions, 1987), p. 3.

11. Ibid., p. 2.

12. Dick Sutphen, *Sedona: Psychic Energy Vortexes* (Malibu, Calif.: Valley of the Sun Publishing, 1986).

13. Jessica Maxwell, "Babagaboosh Is Calling," *Esquire*, November 1990, p. 43.

14. Simon Jenkins, "We Cannot All Sit and Commune with Nature in the Desert Wilderness," *Spectator*, April 16, 1994, p. 31.

15. *Experience Sedona*, 43.

16. Patricia Gober et al. "Job-Rich but Housing-Poor: The Dilemma of a Western Amenity Town," *Professional Geographer* 45 (February 1993): 12.

17. Christopher Reynolds, "Red Rockin'," *Los Angeles Times*, April 12, 1992, p. L1.

18. Joe Green, quoted in ibid.

19. Reynolds, p. L11.

20. Charles Leerhsen and Jeanne Gordon, "Wheels of Misfortune: It's New Agers vs. Forest Rangers in Arizona," *Newsweek*, June 10, 1991, p. 26.

21. Ibid., p. 26.

22. Johansen and Barclay, pp. 5, 7.

23. Frank Clifford, "Taming the West with Words," *Los Angeles Times*, July 19, 1992, p. L1.

24. John F. Sears addresses this type of "object lesson" in his book *Sacred Places: American Tourist Attractions in the Nineteenth Century* (Oxford: Oxford

University Press, 1989). Earl Pomeroy discusses the specific combination of tourism and the western myth in his book *In Search of the Golden West: The Tourist in Western America* (New York: Knopf, 1957).

25. Clifford, p. L23.

26. Jackie Donath, "The Gene Autry Western Heritage Museum: The Problem of an Authentic Western Mystique," *American Quarterly* 43 (March 1991): 83.

27. James T. Yenckel, "Seductive Sedona, in the Midst of Red Rock Country," *Washington Post*, November 19, 1989, p. E2.

28. Martin E. Marty, "Impure Faith: Borrowers and Wannabes," *Christian Century*, June 1–8, 1994, p. 562. Marty was quoting an article from the December 1993 *New York Times* by David Johnston.

29. Gober et al., passim.

30. Durkheim, p. 48.

Queen of Two Cultures

Leslie Linthicum

Radmilla Cody is smart, beautiful and has a 100-watt smile.

She speaks fluent Navajo; she easily turns flour and lard into nice brown fry bread and she knows her way around a sheep with a butcher knife.

Judges of the annual Miss Navajo Nation contest found the 23-year-old Arizonan to be the best example of Navajo life and culture and crowned her as the tribe's goodwill ambassador for 1998.

When Cody travels around the reservation, greeting crowds in her velvet, satin, turquoise and crown, she introduces herself in the traditional way; with her name followed by her clan affiliations, her mother's side first and then her father's.

"I am of the Red Bottom People," she says, "born for African-American."

The daughter of a Navajo mother and an African-American father, Cody is the first biracial Miss Navajo.

Her reign has opened wounds of racial prejudice on the reservation, but it has also sparked a discussion of what it means to be Navajo. A letter in the tribal newspaper critical of the judges' choice started it all, outraging many Navajos who wrote in support of Cody.

Raised on the Reservation

Cody, who was raised by her Navajo grandmother on the western edge of the reservation in a small community called Grand Falls, learned to speak the

Navajo language, to herd sheep, to weave rugs, to haul water and to cook over a kerosene stove. She knows the stories of the Navajo and can tell them in the Diné language.

She was raised by her grandmother because her father was absent and her mother was an alcoholic. Cody has no contact with her father and does not know where he lives. Her mother, now in recovery, lives in Flagstaff and the two are very close.

Cody was well prepared for the week-long Miss Navajo contest last September, which pitted her against six other young women in competitions of fry bread making and sheep butchering. Cody, who counted the family sheep as her childhood friends, found the butchering competition the hardest. Her fluent Navajo, a language that is being lost among younger tribe members, especially impressed the judges.

While she knew the nuances of the Navajo language, Cody was in high school before she learned anything about black history or black culture.

"I guess I never really considered it," she says, "being that I identified myself with my Navajo side."

But it is Cody's African-American features that have prompted controversy. In a letter published in the Navajo Nation's newspaper, the *Navajo Times*, a member of the tribe lashed out at the judges' choice of Cody as Miss Navajo.

"Miss Cody's appearance and physical characteristics are clearly black, and are thus representative of another race of people," Orlando Tom, of the Navajo community of Blue Gap in Arizona, wrote two months after Cody took the title.

Tom said tribal members who are of mixed race are a threat to the future of the tribe.

It is "the very essence of the genetic code which is passed down from generation to generation," Tom wrote, "that makes us who we are."

Tom suggested Cody focus on her African-American heritage ("she is a very pretty black lady," he wrote) and stay out of Navajo affairs.

Not "Half" of Anything

Cody was stunned when she read the letter. At 23, she had come to terms with being a curiosity among both blacks and Navajos and she had entered the Miss Navajo contest to make a statement that biracial people should not be judged as "half" of anything.

"Instead of looking at you as a human being and just another person, they want to look at you for the color of your skin," Cody says. "And if you are half-black, they push you into that position where you feel you have to try to fit in when you're with either group."

It wasn't until Cody entered elementary school that she heard the taunt "*zhini*," the Navajo word for black. She was in high school in Flagstaff when she first heard blacks and other non-Indian students talk about "drunk Indians."

"When I read that letter I actually felt like I was a child again," Cody says. "I was dealing with all the feelings I had dealt with growing up, dealing with racial slurs from the black side as well as the Navajo side."

Tom lives in the hills outside Blue Gap, an isolated community just north of the Hopi reservation. He does not have a phone and could not be reached to talk about his reasons for singling out Cody or for his response to the flood of responses to his letter—many from mixed-race members of the tribe and all in support of Cody.

Eunice Muskett, part Navajo and part German, wrote from her home in Nakaibito, New Mexico, with a message for Cody: "You are a positive role model for our daughters and grand-daughters in your strength to overcome ignorance and prejudice where it should not be in the first place."

Another tribal member wrote: "I am proud of who I am (Navajo-Black.)" Another tribal member who is Navajo and Puerto Rican responded, "We are Navajos too, and proud of it. We are not the enemy."

Daphne Thomas from Leupp, Arizona, wrote that "ethnic blood cleansing has no place in the Navajo society because the Navajo way teaches that beauty is everywhere."

After weeks of letters in support of Cody and in disagreement with Tom, Sean Walker, a representative of the NAACP in Gallup, wrote to the *Navajo Times* to say "it is encouraging that many people of the great Navajo Nation do not share his opinions."

Welcomed by Many

Cody, whose schedule includes appearances at schools and meetings on the reservation as well as representing the Navajo Nation at intertribal functions, is welcomed wherever she goes with thundering applause and gaggles of autograph-seekers. She keeps a punishing schedule of two, three or four appearances a day.

Although she decided to enter the competition with the goal of showing that Navajos of mixed race "should be taken seriously," judges made no mention or issue of her race during the competition, which requires contestants to be enrolled members of the tribe. And Cody usually makes no mention of the criticism of her selection as Miss Navajo or of her racial makeup.

Cody, who was working as a home and school liaison for the Native American program in the Mesa schools before she became Miss Navajo, usually sings the "Star Spangled Banner" in Navajo, describes her early life with her grandmother and the week-long contest and tells children to work hard in school and be proud of their Navajo heritage.

But Cody talked about her background and her experiences with racial prejudice during appearances last month at an NAACP banquet in Gallup and before the Navajo Nation Council to discuss changing the council session's opening day so it does not fall on Martin Luther King Jr. Day. And in a recent speech at the Black History Month program at Navajo Preparatory School in Farmington, Cody told a standing-room-only audience of students that she has weathered the storm by relying on the advice of Dorothy Cody, her grandmother.

"I have always had my grandmother there who was my back-bone then and who is still my back-bone," Cody told students. "She said, 'I don't care what anybody says. You be proud of who you are. People may share ignorant thoughts, may make ignorant comments, but you never forget who you are or where you came from.'"

Opening Doors

Cody's first contact with blacks came when she left the reservation as a high school junior, moved into an apartment in Flagstaff with her mother and enrolled in Coconino High School. It was then that her ignorance of black history and culture also became apparent.

She saw a black student wearing a T-shirt emblazoned with a large "X" and assumed it was simply a fashion statement.

"I thought it was just another letter of the alphabet," Cody remembers. "I said, 'you have an X on your T-shirt. I guess I'll go and get me an R for Radmilla.' His facial expression was, like, 'What planet are you from?'"

"I had not the slightest idea who Malcolm X was. The only person I was aware of as a black leader was Martin Luther King and that was just briefly."

She has since made it a point to learn about black history, especially as the events of this year have put her in the position of a spokeswoman for black Navajos.

Cody, who has been taking classes at community colleges in Arizona, plans to enroll at Arizona State University when a new Miss Navajo is chosen this September and her reign ends. She plans eventually to go to law school and specialize in tribal law.

Although the letter episode has been painful for Cody, she has been heartened by how it has sparked discussions about racism and by tribal members' responses.

"In a way," she says, "it was probably good that he wrote the letter. It's brought up a lot of things."

Cody did not expect her reign to be ordinary.

"I went into this competition with a goal, a goal that not only was I going to open eyes, but I was going to open doors." Cody says. "You run for Miss Navajo Nation. It's not just a hand wave and a smile."

Mythical Dimensions/Political Reality

Rudolfo Anaya

Many of us who live in the Southwest have developed a mythical dimension that enables us to relate to the land and its people. This dimension keeps us close to the land and its history. We value the indigenous myths that evolved on this continent. Now the tremendous economic changes that came with the Sunbelt boom that began in the 1960s have not only altered the landscape, they have altered the way people relate to the land and each other, and there is a danger of losing this dimension. Many of us are asking what happens when we lose our mythic relationship to the earth and allow only the political and economic forces to guide our way of life.

I take much of my identity from the values and tribal ways of the old Nuevo Mexicanos, from their legends and myths and from the earth, which they held sacred. In this essay I turn my attention to the processes of world politics and economics that are altering the Southwest so radically. The growth of the Sunbelt has altered our perception of our landscape: the personal, the environmental, and the mythic. The old communities, the tribes of the Southwest, have been scattered, and they have lost much of their power. If we do not take action now, that creative force of the people which has nourished us for centuries may be swept aside.

Our future is at stake. We who value the earth as a creative force must renew our faith in the values of the old communities, the ceremonies of relationship, the dances and fiestas, the harmony in our way of life, and the mythic force we can tap to create beauty and peace. We must speak out clearly against the political and economic processes whose only goal is material gain.

It is the individual's relationship to the tribe and one's response to the elements and the cosmos that give shape to our inner consciousness. These relationships create meaning. They have shaped the Indian and Hispano Southwest, just as they have shaped part of the Anglo reality and myth. But the old communal relationships are changing as the new urban environments change our land. The diaspora that began in the 1940s has continued, the once-stable villages and pueblos are emptied to create a marginalized people in the ghettos of the new urban centers.

Many of us no longer live in the landscape our parents knew. We no longer enjoy that direct relationship with nature which nurtured them. The Southwest has slowly changed, becoming an urban environment. We no longer live in the basic harmony that can exist between humanity and the earth. A new and materialistic order has become paramount in the land, and we have little control over this intrusion. By and large, the land that nurtured us is now in the hands of world markets and politics.

True, some of our neighbors survive in mountain villages and pueblos, on ranches and reservations. These folk remain an historical link to our mythic dimensions. They keep the values and communal relationships of our grandparents, and they struggle against the destructive development that characterized the past.

Urban Sunbelt population growth; renewed attention to the oil, gas, and mining industries; the construction of air bases and weapons laboratories; and a high-tech boom with its dream of a new economy are some of the elements of the politicizing process that our generation has seen become reality in the Southwest. The full force of that change has been felt in our generation as the New York and world money markets gained control over and exploited the resources of this land.

The signs of the web of the political world are all around us. Visit any of the large cities of the Southwest and you see unchecked growth, a plundering of land and water, and a lack of attention to the old traditional communities. Immense social disparity has been created overnight. We have lost control over our land. The crucial questions for us are, Have we been defeated? Have we let go of our old values?

Because I am interested in and understand the power of literature, I have to ask what this means to writers from the Southwest. For some it means a retreat into formula: the cowboy-and-Indian story is still being churned out. Some writers armed with computers simply make that formula longer and more ponderous to read. For others the retreat means moving out of the city to the suburbs or if possible to the villages or the mountains. The Indian and Chicano way of life is idealized as the refusal to deal with the new, engulfing economic and political reality grows. Some draw closer to the Indian and Hispanic communities, to the old tribes of the land, seeking spiritual warmth from, and reconciliation with, these earth people. Others create new tribal centers: Zen centers, mosques, and monasteries in the desert, hippie communities. Some writers just drink and quarrel more, subconsciously surrendering to the old Western movie plot in their withdrawal.

In my lifetime I have seen this tremendous change come over the land. Most of my contemporaries and I have left our Hispanic communities and became urban dwellers. The people, the earth, the water of the river and of the *acequias* (the irrigation canals), and the spiritual views of the tribal communities that once nurtured me are almost gone. The ball game has changed, and it is appropriate to use the ball-game metaphor, because the original game of *la pelota* in Mesoamerican history has a spiritual orientation, a deep meaning for the tribe. Now it is played for profit. In our most common ceremonies and rituals we see the change, we see the new view of the West.

Politicizing the Southwest has meant corralling people in the city. Reckless developers take the land for the false promise of the easy life where homogenized goods and services can be delivered. Work in one's cornfield has become work for wages, wages which can never keep up with ever-spiraling taxation. The pueblo plaza or village post office where the community once gathered to conduct both business and ceremony has become chaotic urban sprawl. The center has been lost.

What does this mean to me — I who have now lived longer in the city than in the rural landscape of my grandparents, I who have seen this drastic change come over the land?

When I was writing *Bless Me, Ultima* in the early 1960s, I was still tied to the people and the earth of the Pecos River Valley, the small town of Santa Rosa, the villages of Puerto de Luna and Pastura. The mythic element infuses that novel because it is a reflection of the world I knew. Now the West has lost its natural state, and development after development sprawls across once-empty desert. Growth and change are inevitable, but that which is guided only by a material goal is a corrosive element that has insidiously spread its influence over the land and the people. How can I write and not reflect this process?

Who has taken charge of our lives? We are now informed by television, the daily dose of news, the homogeneous school system, and other communication media that are in the hands of the power manipulators. Many ancient ceremonies and dances are still intact along the Rio Grande, but even the people who sustain these ceremonies are affected by the bingo parlors and quick cash. My city is hostage to those who control the flow of the river, and the quality of that water will continue to be affected by the chemical and nuclear waste it washes away. This reality must affect our writings.

The Chicanos, Indians, and old Anglos who worked the land are now a labor force to serve the industries that the world economic and political system imposes on us. The time is disharmonious; no wonder we gather together to discuss the changing landscape, and the changing human-scape. We know we have been manipulated, and in the resulting change we feel we have lost something important.

Our people have been lulled into believing that every person can get a piece of the action. We set up bingo games as we pray for rain, and we train our children to take care of tourists even as they forget to care for the old ones. We begin to see the elemental landscape as a resource to be bought and sold. We do not dream the old dreams, we do not contemplate the gods, and less and less do we stand in front of the cosmos in humility. We begin to believe that we can change the very nature of things, and so we leave old connections behind, we forget the sacred places and become part of the new reality—a world reality tied to nerve centers in New York, Tokyo, London, and Hong Kong.

The old patterns of daily life are forgotten. The cyclical sense of time that once provided historical continuity and spiritual harmony is replaced by atomic beeps. The clock on the wall now marks the ceremonies we attend, ceremonies that have to do with the order of world politics. It is no wonder we feel we are being watched, our responses recorded. We are being used, and eventually we will be discarded.

But there is hope. The sensitive writer can still create meaningful forms that can be shared with the reader who is hungry for a mythic sensibility. We still have the materials and beliefs of our grandparents to work into poetry and fiction. Reflection in our writings need not become mired in paranoia. The old relationships of the mythic West need not be reduced to a formula. Technology may serve people; it need not be the new god. If we flee to the old communities in search of contact with the elemental landscape and a more harmonious view of things, we can return from that visit more committed to engaging the political process. We can still use the old myths of this hemisphere to shed light on our contemporary problems.

We, the writers, can still salvage elements of beauty for the future. We can help preserve the legends and myths of our land to rekindle the spirit of the old relationships. We can encourage the power of creativity that takes its strength from the elemental and mythic landscapes. The problems we face are not new: prior generations of Mesoamerica dealt with many of the same problems.

In exploring the legend of Quetzalcoatl while writing *The Lord of the Dawn*, I was astounded at the close parallels between the world of the ancient Toltecs of Tula and our own time. Then, as now, men of peace and understanding struggled against the militaristic and materialistic instincts of the society. Both the historical king and the deity known as Quetzalcoatl came to the Toltecs to bring learning in the arts, agriculture, and spiritual thought. Under the benign rule of Quetzalcoatl, the Toltecs prospered. But much of their prosperity was taken by the warrior class to conduct war on the neighboring tribes. Toltec civilization rose to its classic apex, then fell.

In the end, Quetzalcoatl was banished from Tula. The materialists of the society, who waged war and conducted business only for profit, had their way. The deity who brought art, wisdom, and learning was banished, and the Toltec civilization fell. The influence of Quetzalcoatl was later felt in the civilizations of the Aztecs and Mayas, for every society seeks truth and the correct way to live.

Even now, the story of the Toltecs and Quetzalcoatl speaks to us across the centuries, warning us to respect our deep and fragile communal relationships within and among nations, and our meaningful relationships to the earth.

The past is not dead; it lives in our hearts, as myth lives in our hearts. We need those most human qualities of the world myths to help guide us on our road today.

My novel *Albuquerque* addresses some of these questions. The city where I live, like any other city in the Southwest, reflects the political processes that have permeated our land. The novel is about change, the change that has come during our lifetime. In it, some of the principal characters are driven by the desire to control the land and the water of the Rio Grande. Others, members of the old tribes, take refuge in withdrawal in order to survive urban poverty. They withdraw to their circles of belief to wait out the storm.

We, the writers, cannot wait out the storm; we have to confront it. For us, the bedrock of beliefs of the old cultures provides our connection, our relationship. From that stance we must keep informing the public about the change that has come upon our land.

The battle is of epic proportions. We are in the midst of one of those times from which will emerge a new consciousness. The environment seems to reflect this struggle between evil and good; it cries out to us. We see it scarred and polluted. The people of the old tribes cry out; we see them displaced and suffering. Even the elements of nature reflect the change: acid and toxic chemicals pollute the water, nuclear waste is buried in the bowels of the earth. These are the same signs the Toltecs saw hundreds of years ago as their society faced destruction.

We, too, face a measure of destruction. The goal of material acquisition and a homogeneous political process supporting that goal have taken hold, driving us deeper into the complex nature of materialism. Is it any wonder we look back to legend and myth for direction?

We are poised at the edge of a new time. We have the opportunity to look again into the nature of our hemisphere. We can see that the struggle for illumination is not easy. It was not easy for the Toltecs, and we know now that as they gave up their old knowledge and turned to materialism and material gain, they destroyed their society.

Will we preserve our old values or let them die? Will we rediscover our relationship to the earth? What of the communal relationships that are so fractured and split in our land? Is there time to bring peace and harmony to our tribal groups?

The first step in answering these questions is to realize that we have turned away from our inner nature and from our connection to the earth and old historical relationships. We have allowed a political and economic consciousness from without to take control. How we engage this consciousness not only describes us but also will inform future generations of our values. Our writings will say where we stood when this drama of opposing forces came to be played out on our land.

Jefe, todavía no saben . . .

Jimmy Santiago Baca

Jefe,
todavía no saben . . .

Under color of race
on your death certificate,
they have you down
as White.

You fought against that
label
all your short life, jefe,
and now they have you down
as White.

They had you down
when you lived, down
because you were too brown.

Dead on arrival
when you tried to be White.
You were brown as empty whiskey bottles,
and your accent was brown adobe dirt
you shattered bottles against.

Dead now,
you are White.
Under specify suicide or homicide,
I scribbled out accident and wrote in
Suicide—
scribbled out White and wrote in
Chicano. Erased caused by aspiration of meat
and wrote in
trying to be White.

Birthplace Blues

Margaret Regan

In these days of the El Niño rains, the land at the eastern foot of A Mountain is even more desolate than usual.

A damp wind blows across the barren flats, ruffling the colonies of weeds that thrive atop the buried trash dumps. The breeze sails on over the Santa Cruz, a river so dead it's wet only when it rains, then hits the tacky motels on the other side before disappearing into the ungainly elevation of the freeway. And if the river is dead, so is the land. Beyond wild grasses and a few scraggly trees, there's hardly a living thing to be seen on this beaten-down patch of dirt. Everywhere, though, there are shards of glass, survivors of countless beer parties, and the noise of the glass crunching underfoot punctuates the monotonous roar of the highway.

Welcome to the birthplace of Tucson.

"There's a spirit in that piece of earth," says Daniel Preston, vice chairman of the San Xavier District of the Tohono O'odham Nation. "The spirit of my ancestors that have prayed and used the land in a respectful religious way."

Nowadays one would be hard-pressed to find a respectful spirit toward the big tract of riverfront land just west of downtown, south of Congress Street. Tucked between the sacred mountain and the once flowing river, this exhausted patch of earth is an urban eyesore, home only to a bus barn and a bunch of landfills that were closed in the 1960s. There's a small neighborhood, though, Barrio Sin Nombre, that still clings to its western edge, and its inhabitants are the latest in a long line of people who have lived on this spot for at least 3,500 years.

For more than three millennia, Chuk-shon, Place of the Black Spring, sustained human life. It was a desert oasis, full of cottonwood trees, marshes and ponds, a place where wildlife was abundant and where nomadic desert dwellers had the luxury of not worrying about water. Those who lived here over the centuries—archaic people, Hohokam, Pima, Spanish, Mexicans, Apaches and Anglos—drank from the spring and the river, and they used river water to irrigate their fields in the fertile floodplain. As late as the turn of this century, 15 different species of ducks were recorded among its reeds. The site is remarkable and possibly unique.

"For 3,000 years, there's been continuous human use and occupation at the base of Sentinel Peak," says Linda Mayro, cultural resources manager for Pima County. Some historians believe it may be the longest continually occupied site in North America.

Yet less than a century and a half after the United States became steward to this land, the river's run dry and its lush shores have been denuded and trashed. Long gone are the cottonwoods and the ducks. An 18th-century adobe Convento abandoned by Spanish priests crumbled to dust, making way for trash dumps. A 20th-century brickyard came and went. (Preston says the remains of his ancestors, quarried from the site's mud, went into the bricks.) A boxing gym and a supermarket followed the brickyard into oblivion. A homeless camp at the southern end, on the A Mountain Landfill, was emptied out by force by city workers. Apart from a recreational river park snaking along the dry channel, the forlorn survivor on the vast tract of 90 acres is the Citizen's Auto Stage bus barn.

In the late 1980s, the whole place—archaeology, history, ancestors and all—was scheduled to be buried forever under a new four-lane highway. Clever protestors, including some guerrilla activists who concocted a makeshift shrine by night and orchestrated a highly publicized religious ceremony by day, sent the road plan down to defeat. Nothing much has happened there since. Meantime, day in and day out, the buses bounce past the ancient graves.

"My parents are back in this earth," Preston maintains. "People putting trash on it put trash on my parents."

Lately Tucson has begun to think again about its trashed birthplace. The long-hoped-for Mission San Agustín del Tucson Cultural Park, a history and archaeology interpretive park planned since 1991, is at last gaining momentum, with the city and Pima County working to acquire the final patches of privately held land at the tract's center, along Mission Lane. A group from the nearby Kroeger Lane neighborhood has enlisted a team of architecture students and professors to help design a proposed park on the A Mountain Landfill, which the city owns.

And Preston delivered his mournful remarks by invitation at a meeting last month of the Santa Cruz River Project Citizens' Advisory Commission. This group of eight local bigwigs and neighborhood leaders, appointed last October by City Manager Luis Gutierrez, will make a recommendation for what to put on Rio Nuevo South, the 44 acres of city-owned land at the northern end of the tract.

This piece of long-vacant land may well prove the trickiest to develop. Burdened by landfills and archaeological treasures alike, it's nevertheless enjoyed a flurry of proposals in recent years. A baseball park, a campus for the "new university"—the school that became Arizona International Campus of the University of Arizona—and even a Colonial Tucson theme park have all had their champions during the 1990s. Right now city leaders say they're determined to come to a decision, and soon. The commissioners have been holding hearings to entertain any and all proposals for Rio Nuevo South. (Their larger mission is to come up with ways to better the dispiriting condition of the dry river.) Eventually, maybe even this summer, they'll tell the city council what they think is the best use of the land.

Gutierrez, a Tucson native, explains that the mission of the commission is fourfold.

"The mayor and council have directed that the city look to use the property in a sensitive and careful way," Gutierrez says. Any new project for Rio Nuevo South has to "enhance the revitalization of downtown, to provide direct benefit to the adjacent neighborhood in the form of job opportunities, and to reflect the history and culture of the community."

It's a tall order, certainly, but developers sniffing around for opportunities have not failed to materialize. After all, as Carol Carpenter, a downtown specialist in the city's Office of Economic Development, points out, it's rare to find such a huge tract of land ripe for development so close to the heart of a growing city.

"There's no doubt," she says, "that the development community wants this 44 acres in the worst way." Plus, the value of whatever goes in there can only be enhanced by the cultural park that will go in at its southern flank.

Dreams are not in short supply. Among the contenders:

• A local consortium wants to build a complex of three or four museums, abetted by some shops, restaurants and parking. It would include newer, bigger versions of the Arizona Historical Society museum and Flandrau Planetarium/Science Museum, both of which are cramped in their present locations by the University of Arizona. There would be room for another small museum, to be determined, and possibly an outdoor performance center that could be used by the Tucson Symphony Orchestra and other arts groups. Its flagship and big tourist draw, promoters hope, would be the Museum of the American West, a brand-new enterprise that hopes to get its goodies on long-term loan from the Smithsonian Institution. (More on that later.)

- Then there's the California developer called Dunhill Ltd. whose officials imagine a dense, upscale retail/entertainment complex with concealed parking structures. Complete with a hotel, three department stores, a multiplex cinema, even housing, the Dunhill project is a high-end attraction whose labyrinthine bridges and archways look ominously reminiscent of the failed La Placita downtown. David Hoyt Johnson, a downtown resident and arts administrator, compares the design's treatment of public space favorably with Horton Plaza's in San Diego; a rival developer dismissed its upper-crust ethnic chic as "Barrio Nordstrom."

- Some cheerful oceanographers pushing for a Sonoran Sea Aquarium seemed to win over the skeptical commissioners at the March meeting with a highly entertaining slide show full of loggerhead turtles and crabs with coral on their backs. Shannan Marty told the commissioners that the nonprofit aquarium would concentrate solely on the 10,000 species inhabiting the Sea of Cortez. "Having an aquarium would make Tucson the gateway to Mexico," she said. Occupying only two acres, the aquarium could join forces with one of the other developers.

- Jack Camper, president of the Tucson Metropolitan Chamber of Commerce and a member of the commission, promises to regale his fellow commissioners at a future meeting with plans for a River Walk, inspired by San Antonio's successful attraction of the same name. Tucson's version would consist of a channel dug in the bed of an old rail line east of the river; the channel would cross the real riverbed and extend over into Rio Nuevo South.

- More hopefuls will take to the podium at the meeting next week, Wednesday, April 15. Bob Shelton, the man who developed Old Tucson as a tourist attraction in 1959, has downsized his old proposal for a Colonial Tucson theme park. Reinvented as San Agustín Square, it would be a more modest 15,000 to 20,000 square feet of artsy shops and restaurants, highlighted by an outdoor amphitheater suitable for tourist-attracting sound and light dramas about Tucson's history. Shelton says he's been talking informally with the museum group for about a year about joining forces. "It's led to some quiet dialogue. We're continuing to talk. There's no commitment. We're exploring the possibilities."

- Pat Darcy and Pete Villaescusa, a pair of local brokers, will present a plan by Daystar of Woodland Hills, California. Darcy, a former Cincinnati Reds pitcher who once pushed for a baseball stadium on the site, said Daystar specializes in inner-city development. Right now the company is constructing an entertainment and retail complex in downtown Bakersfield, California.

Clearly these projects are costly, and various ideas have been tossed around about public funding, at least for the nonprofit museum complex. At the moment, though, says Albert Elias, the city staffer who's moderating the meetings, no one's nailing anybody down to financial specifics. A few developers have criticized the city for not issuing an official request for proposals, but Elias says RFPs will come after the city council votes on the direction they want to go. One thing, though, should be paramount to anybody with designs on the site: "Whatever happens in Rio Nuevo South has potentially a great impact on the Convento site and the park," Elias says. "We have some unanimity here. We don't want Disneyland. We want only what's culturally appropriate and respectful."

While everyone else has been loudly debating the merits of the assorted ideas, Daniel Preston, the Tohono O'odham leader, has been consulting a higher authority. He returned to the Place of the Black Spring.

"I went over to the area and said a prayer to those relatives," he told the Santa Cruz commissioners. "I told them even though all those bad things happened to them there, I hope we can turn a negative into a positive. Whatever it is that's going to be built out there, I want to see the spirit of my relatives kept. I hope one of your religious people can say prayers over your project."

They may just need to.

Credits

The editors are grateful to the authors and publishers for their permission to reprint copyrighted material. We have made every reasonable effort to identify and locate the copyright for each item we include in our anthology. In particular we would like to acknowledge the prior publication of the items listed below.

Anaya, Rudolfo. "Mythical Dimensions/Political Reality," from *The Anaya Reader*. Copyright © 1995 by Rudolfo Anaya. Published by Warner Books. Originally published as "The Myth of Quetzalcoatl in a Contemporary Setting: Mythical Dimensions/Political Reality," *Western American Literature* 23, no. 3 (November 1988). Reprinted by permission of Susan Bergholz Literary Services, New York. All rights reserved.

Anzaldúa, Gloria. "To live in the Borderlands means you," from *Borderlands/La Frontera: The New Mestiza*, by Gloria Anzaldúa. Copyright © 1987 by Gloria Anzaldúa. Reprinted by permission of Aunt Lute Books, San Francisco.

Baca, Jimmy Santiago. "Jefe, todavía no saben . . . ," from *Martín and Meditations on the South Valley*, by Jimmy Santiago Baca. Copyright © 1986 by Jimmy Santiago Baca. Reprinted by permission of New Directions Publishing Corp.

Cabeza de Baca, Fabiola. "Milo Maizes," from *We Fed Them Cactus*, by Fabiola Cabeza de Baca. Copyright © 1994 [1954] by Fabiola Cabeza de Baca. Reprinted by permission of the University of New Mexico Press.

Campbell, Barbara A. "Sedona and the New (Age) Frontier," *American Papers*, Journal of the American Studies Student Association, California State University at Fullerton (pp. 41–45). Copyright © 1996. Reprinted by permission of the author.

Chávez, John. "The Chicano Homeland," from *The Lost Land: The Chicano Image of the Southwest*, by John Chávez. Copyright © 1984. Reprinted by permission of the University of New Mexico Press.

Cormier, Steve. "'You Don't Know Cows Like I Do': Twentieth-Century New Mexico Ranch Culture." Copyright © 1999 by Steve Cormier. Printed by permission of the author.

Cunningham, Robert D. "The Box That Broke the Barrier: The Swamp Cooler Comes to Southern Arizona," *Journal of Arizona History* 26, no. 2 (1985): 163–174. Reprinted by permission of the author and the *Journal of Arizona History*.

Fainaru, Steve. 1998. "Mexican Children Get Hard Lesson: New Laws Cut Them from N.M. Schools," *Boston Globe*, March 1, 1998. Reprinted by permission of the *Boston Globe*.

Fox, Steve. "Roads to Heaven: Pilgrimage in the Southwest." Originally published as "Sacred Pedestrians: The Many Faces of Southwest Pilgrimages," *Journal of the Southwest* 36, no. 1 (spring 1994). Reprinted by permission of *Journal of the Southwest* and the author.

Garreau, Joel. "MexAmerica," from *The Nine Nations of North America*, by Joel Garreau. Copyright © 1981 by Joel Garreau. Reprinted by permission of Houghton Mifflin Company. All rights reserved.

Gaspar de Alba, Alicia. "Lent in El Paso Texas," from *Three Times a Woman: Chicana Poetry*, by Alicia Gaspar de Alba, María Herrera-Sobek, and Demetria Martínez. Copyright © 1989. Reprinted by permission of the Bilingual Review Press, Tempe, Arizona.

Griffith, James S. "Baroque Principles of Organization in Contemporary Mexican American Arizona," from *A Shared Space: Folklife in the Arizona-Sonora Borderlands*, by James S. Griffith. Copyright © 1995. Reprinted by permission of the Utah State University Press.

Grinde, Donald, and Bruce Johansen. "The Navajos and National Sacrifice," from *Ecocide of Native America: Environmental Destruction of Indian Lands and Peoples*, by Donald Grinde and Bruce Johansen. Copyright © 1995. Reprinted by permission of Clear Light Publishers, Santa Fe, New Mexico.

Harjo, Joy. "3 AM," from *Southwest: A Contemporary Anthology*, edited by Karl and Jane Kopp. Copyright © 1977 by Joy Harjo. Published by Red Earth Press. Reprinted by permission of the author.

Herrera-Sobek, María. "Sunday Mass," from *Three Times a Woman: Chicana Poetry*, by Alicia Gaspar de Alba, María Herrera-Sobek, and Demetria Martínez. Copyright © 1989. Reprinted by permission of the Bilingual Review Press, Tempe, Arizona.

Heyck, Denis Lynn Daly. "Interview: Jesus Martínez and Ricardo Murillo," from *Barrios and Borderlands: Cultures of Latinos and Latinas in the United States*, edited by Denis Heyck. Copyright © 1994. Reprinted by permission of Routledge, Inc., New York.

Jojola, Ted. "Urbanization Drains Reverence for Water," *Albuquerque Journal*, March 20, 1994. Reprinted by permission of the author.

Kingsolver, Barbara. "In the Belly of the Beast," from *High Tide in Tucson*, by Barbara Kingsolver. Copyright © 1995 by Barbara Kingsolver. Reprinted by permission of HarperCollins Publishers, Inc.

Linthicum, Leslie. "Queen of Two Cultures," *Albuquerque Journal*, June 29, 1997. Reprinted by permission of Albuquerque Publishing Company.

Lummis, Charles. "The Golden Key to Wonderland," in *They Know New Mexico*, edited by Atchison, Topeka, and Santa Fe Railway (Chicago: Rand McNally). Copyright © 1926 by Charles Lummis.

Meinig, Donald W. "The Southwest: A Definition," from *The Southwest: Three Peoples in Geographical Change, 1600–1970*, by Donald W. Meinig. Copyright © 1971 by Oxford University Press, Inc. Reprinted by permission of Oxford University Press, Inc.

Meléndez, Gabriel. Excerpts from "Sombras de la Jicarita," *Blue Mesa Review* 2 (1990): 111–116.

Moore, Patricia, and M. Jane Young. "Creating a Tradition: The Great American Duck Race." Based on a paper presented by Moore and Young at the Annual Meeting of the American Folklore Society, Pittsburgh, Pennsylvania, October 1996.

Mora, Pat. "Legal Alien." Reprinted by permission of the publisher of *Chants* (Houston: Arte Público Press, University of Houston, 1985).

Nabhan, Gary Paul. "Raising Hell as Well as Wheat—Papago Indians Burying the Borderline," from *The Desert Smells like Rain: A Naturalist in Papago*

Indian Country, by Gary Nabhan. Originally published by North Point Press, San Francisco. Copyright © 1982. Reprinted by permission of Farrar, Straus and Giroux, New York.

Ortiz, Simon. "Dry Root in a Wash," from *Going for the Rain: Poems*, by Simon Ortiz. Copyright © 1976 by Simon Ortiz. Published by Harper & Row, New York. Reprinted by permission of the author.

Paz-Martinez, Eduardo. "Romancing Mora." Copyright © by Eduardo Paz-Martinez. First published in the *Santa Fe [New Mexico] Reporter*, July 15–21, 1992. Reprinted in *In Discovered Country: Tourism and Survival in the American West*, edited by Scott Norris. Copyright © 1994. Albuquerque: Stone Ladder Press. Reprinted by permission of the *Santa Fe Reporter*.

Pego, David. "We're Not Extinct." Originally published in the *Austin American-Statesman*, September 1, 1996, D1, D6, D7. Copyright © 1996 by the *Austin American-Statesman*. Reprinted with permission.

Regan, Margaret. "Birthplace Blues," *Tucson Weekly* 15, no. 6, April 9–15, 1998. Reprinted by permission of the author.

Scharff, Virginia. "Make-Believe and Graffiti: Envisioning New Mexico Families," from *Contemporary New Mexico: 1940–1990*, edited by Richard W. Etulain. Copyright © 1994. Reprinted by permission of the University of New Mexico Press.

Sekaquaptewa, Emory. "Hopi Indian Ceremonies," from *Seeing with a Native Eye: Essays on Native American Religion*, edited by Walter Holden Capps. Copyright © 1976 by Walter Holden Capps. Reprinted by permission of HarperCollins Publishers, Inc.

Selcraig, Bruce. "Albuquerque Learns It Really Is a Desert Town," *High Country News*, December 26, 1994, 1, 10–11. Reprinted by permission of the author.

Suina, Joseph. "And Then I Went to School: Memories of a Pueblo Childhood." Copyright © 1985 by Joseph Suina. Originally published in *New Mexico Journal of Reading* 5, no. 2 (1985): 34–36. Reprinted by permission of the author.

Swentzell, Rina. "Remembering Tewa Pueblo Houses and Spaces." Copyright © 1990 by Rina Swentzell. Originally published in *Native Peoples* 3, no. 2 (1990): 6–12. Reprinted by permission of the author.

Tapahonso, Luci. "Ode to the Land: The Diné Perspective." Copyright © 1995 by Luci Tapahonso. Originally published in *New Mexico Magazine* (August 1995): 60–64, 67–69. Reprinted by permission of the author.

Tapahonso, Luci. "Raisin Eyes," from *Sáanii Dahataal: The Women Are Singing*, by Luci Tapahonso. Copyright © 1993 by Luci Tapahonso. Reprinted by permission of the University of Arizona Press.

Toelken, Barre. "Seeing with a Native Eye: How Many Sheep Will It Hold?" in *Seeing with a Native Eye: Essays on Native American Religion*, edited by Walter Holden Capps. Copyright © 1976 by Walter Holden Capps. Reprinted by permission of HarperCollins Publishers, Inc.

Weigle, Marta, and Peter White. "Sky Looms: Texts of Transformation and Sacred Worlds," from *The Lore of New Mexico*, by Marta Weigle and Peter White. Copyright © 1988. Reprinted by permission of the University of New Mexico Press.

About the Contributors

Rudolfo Anaya is the author of the critically acclaimed Chicano novel *Bless Me, Ultima* (1972), which tells the story of Antonio, a young New Mexican who is mentored by Ultima, a wise *curandera*. In recent years, he has authored a number of children's books and a series of murder mysteries set in the Southwest. Anaya lives and writes in Albuquerque.

Gloria Anzaldúa grew up on a ranch settlement called Jesús María in South Texas. Anzaldúa obtained her B.A. at Pan American University and earned an M.A. in English and Education from the University of Texas at Austin in 1972. She is the author of the path-breaking work *Borderlands/La Frontera*. She has lived in California since 1977.

Jimmy Santiago Baca is a poet, screenwriter, and writer living in Albuquerque. He is the author of *Martín and Meditations on the South Valley* and *Black Mesa Poems*, both works published by New Directions Press. Baca, who authored the screenplay for *Bound by Honor*, heads his own production company and is working on several film and media projects.

Fabiola Cabeza de Baca-Gilbert (1894–1991) was born into a family of merchants and stock raisers at the family ranch in La Liendre, New Mexico. She was one of a group of pioneer Hispana educators who taught in the rural schools of New Mexico. Her most celebrated work, *We Fed Them Cactus* (1954), is a mix of her memories and the stories she heard growing up in the Hispanic settlements of the Llano Estacado of eastern New Mexico.

Barbara Campbell holds a Master of Arts in American Studies from California State University, Fullerton. Her research deals with American religion with a particular emphasis on the careers of women leaders like Aimee Semple McPherson. She is currently a stained-glass artist and writes both fiction and nonfiction.

John R. Chávez is a Professor of History at Southern Methodist University in Dallas, Texas. The focus of his research and teaching is on Mexican American history. He is the author of *The Lost Land: The Chicano Image of the Southwest* and *Eastside Landmark: A History of the East Los Angeles Community Union*. His most recent work is a comparative history of regional ethnic minorities in North America and Western Europe.

Steve Cormier holds a Ph.D. in American Studies from the University of New Mexico and teaches History at the Albuquerque Technical/Vocational Institute. He developed and taught the first course on ranch history and culture at the University of New Mexico in 1988 and has published several articles on the topic. He is also a former cowboy and a touring folk singer.

Robert D. Cunningham was born and raised in Evanston, Illinois. He worked his way through Northwestern University and the Depression and went on to jobs with advertising agencies. He moved to Arizona for his wife's health. After completing an M.A. in Archaeology he turned to casual writing and has placed his work in historical publications.

Denis Lynn Daly Heyck earned her B.A. at the University of Texas and holds a Ph.D. from the University of London. She is the author of *Life Stories of the Nicaraguan Revolution* and *Barrios and Borderlands: Cultures of Latinos and Latinas in the United States* (1994). Daly Heyck employs oral interviews and testimonial accounts to record the fluid and complex social history of Hispanic America.

Steve Fainaru is an investigative reporter for the *Boston Globe*, where he has worked since 1982. His reports about the U.S.–Mexico border came as a result of his three-year stint as chief of his newspaper's Latin American Bureau, based in Mexico City. The story we reprint here is the outgrowth of dozens of interviews with people living along the border, many of whom noted a persistent disconnect between public policy being made in Washington and the reality of their daily lives. Fainaru is currently based in New York City.

Steve Fox has been studying pilgrimages for eleven years, seeking the sacred at many Pueblo feast days from the early 1970s on. He has been going on "official" pilgrimages for seven years. He manages public programs for the New Mexico Endowment for the Humanities.

Joel Garreau began his career as a reporter for the *Washington Post* and has become a leading writer on environment, place, and society. Using regionalism as a frame of reference, Garreau has authored stories of place dealing with the urban and rural population corridors. The excerpt we reprint here is taken from his study of cultural regions in the United States, *The Nine Nations of North America* (1981). He is also the author of *Edge City: The New Frontier* (1991).

Alicia Gaspar de Alba is a native of the El Paso/Juárez border, and her work inhabits the border between academic scholarship and creative writing. She is the author of *Chicano Art, Inside/Outside the Master's House* (University of Texas Press, 1998). Her poetry and short stories have been anthologized in several collections. Her first novel, *Sor Juana's Dream*, was released last year. Alicia holds a Ph.D. in American Studies and teaches at the University of California at Los Angeles.

James S. Griffith is the author of *A Shared Space: Folklife in the Arizona-Sonoran Borderlands* and *Beliefs and Holy Places: A Spiritual Geography of the Pimería Alta*. Griffith teaches at the University of Arizona, where he has been the director of the Southwest Folklore Center.

Donald Grinde, a Professor of History at California Polytechnic State University, is a member of a small tribe indigenous to the Savannah River Valley of Georgia. His published works include *The Iroquois and the Founding of the American Nation* and *Exemplar of Democracy*. Professor Grinde is married to a Navajo and maintains a residence on the Navajo Reservation in northern Arizona.

Joy Harjo was born in Tulsa, Oklahoma, and is an enrolled member of the Muscogee Nation. She is a graduate of the Institute of American Indian Arts in Santa Fe, and holds a B.A. from the University of New Mexico and an M.F.A. from the University of Iowa. She is the author of six books of poetry and has received several notable awards for her writing. Harjo plays the saxophone and performs internationally with her band, Poetic Justice.

María Herrera-Sobek has a Ph.D. in Hispanic Languages and Literatures from the University of California at Los Angeles. She is the author of three books and several collected editions on Chicano and Chicana literature. Herrera-Sobek's poetry has appeared in various anthologies of Chicana literature. She is the associate editor for the *Norton Anthology of U.S. Latino Literature* and holds the Luis Leal Endowed Chair at the University of California at Santa Barbara.

Bruce Johansen teaches Communication and Native American Studies at the University of Nebraska at Omaha. He has written on Native American and

Chicano history. His books include *Wasi'chu: The Continuing Indian Wars* and *El Pueblo: The Gallegos Family's American Journey*. He is coediting, with Donald Grinde, the forthcoming *Encyclopedia of American Indian Biography*.

Ted Jojola is a Professor in the Master's Program in Community and Regional Planning at the University of New Mexico. He is an enrolled member of the Pueblo of Isleta.

Barbara Kingsolver has received wide acclaim for her novels and works of nonfiction on Southwest subjects. Her published works include the novels *Animal Dreams, The Bean Trees,* and *Pigs in Heaven* and the nonfiction titles *Holding the Line* and *High Tide in Tucson*. A native of Kentucky, Kingsolver divides her time between Tucson, Arizona, and a farm in southern Appalachia. She contributes regularly to literary anthologies and periodicals on a wide range of topics, particularly in the areas of social justice and the environment.

Leslie Linthicum, a native of the Midwest, has been reporting on people and events in New Mexico for the past fifteen years. As a reporter for the *Albuquerque Journal,* she writes about the people who contribute to the unique mix that is the Southwest. She lives in Alameda, New Mexico, with her husband and daughter.

Charles Fletcher Lummis (1859–1928), who was called the "first and greatest Southwesterner," began his literary career as a correspondent for the *Los Angeles Times*. His dispatches to his publisher about his 3,507-mile trek from Cincinnati to Los Angeles became the basis of his 1892 book *A Tramp across the Continent*. In a career spanning some thirty years Lummis published an impressive number of writings, which record his observations of the cultures of the Southwest.

D. W. Meinig is the author of *Southwest: Three Peoples in Geographic Change, 1600–1970,* which was first published by Oxford University Press in 1971 and laid an important foundation for later works in Southwest studies. While Maxwell Professor of Geography at Syracuse University, Professor Meinig published and lectured widely on landscape and geography.

Pat Mora is the author of several works of poetry as well as nonfiction and children's literature. She is a native of El Paso, the city to which her grandparents came during the Mexican Revolution. Pat Mora held the distinguished Garrey Carruthers Chair in Honors at the University of New Mexico in 1999. Her latest book is *My Own True Name: New Selected Poems for Young Adults*. She has worked to have April 30 recognized as Día de los Niños/Día de los Libros, a celebration of children, books, and cultures.

Gary Nabhan is a graduate of Prescott College in Prescott, Arizona. He is the co-founder of Native Seeds/SEARCH and the Director of the Arizona-Sonora Desert Museum in Tucson. Nabhan is a MacArthur Fellow and has published six books and a number of technical articles on ethnobotany, nutrition, and plant conservation.

Simon Ortiz was born in 1941 at Acoma, New Mexico, considered to be the oldest continuously inhabited settlement in the United States. He has published nearly a dozen books of poetry. His work has been widely reviewed in Native American publications and he remains one of a handful of Native American poets published by a major publisher.

Eduardo Paz-Martínez is a freelance writer and former Mexico City bureau chief for the *Houston Post*. He has been a contributor to the *Boston Globe*, the *New York Post*, the *Santa Fe Reporter*, and other papers.

David Pego is a Saginaw Chippewa tribal member who was born near his tribe's reservation in Michigan. He is a former editor and reporter who now works as the Newspapers in Education director for the *American-Statesman*.

Margaret Regan has been a reporter since 1990 for the *Tucson Weekly*, where "Birthplace Blues" first appeared. Her stories on the arts, culture, and urban development have won her numerous journalism awards; "Birthplace Blues" won a prize for feature writing by the Arizona Press Club. Regan holds a degree in French from the University of Pennsylvania.

Virginia Scharff is an Associate Professor of History at the University of New Mexico. Her publications include *Taking the Wheel: Women and the Coming of the Motor Age* and *Coming of Age: America in the Twentieth Century* (Houghton Mifflin, 1998). Scharff has served as a consultant on numerous documentary films and writes fiction under the name of Virginia Swift. Her first novel, *Brown-Eyed Girl*, was published by HarperCollins in April 2000.

Emory Sekaquaptewa is a Research Anthropologist for the Bureau of Applied Research at the University of Arizona. He has written extensively on Hopi lifeways and culture. Part of his work has been to produce a series of children's readers. He is the translator and editor of *Coyote and Little Turtle: A Traditional Hopi Tale* (1994).

Bruce Selcraig, since his days as a cub reporter in the 1970s, has written extensively about cultural and environmental issues in Mexico and the Southwest. He is a former U.S. Senate investigator and staff writer for *Sports Illustrated*. Selcraig now writes for the *New York Times Magazine, Harper's, Sierra*, and *High Country News*, among others. He lives in Austin, Texas, with his wife and two children.

Joseph Suina is an Associate Professor in the College of Education at the University of New Mexico. He is a Councilman for the Pueblo of Cochiti and has published in the area of Indian education and literacy for Indian children. He serves on the boards of several cultural and educational organizations, among them the New Mexico Endowment for the Humanities and the Cochiti Community Development Corporation.

Rina Swentzell was born in Santa Clara Pueblo. She now lives in Santa Fe, where she has many grandchildren. She holds advanced degrees in Architecture and American Studies from the University of New Mexico.

Luci Tapahonso was born in Shiprock, New Mexico, and was brought up in traditional Navajo ways. Tapahonso received her B.A. and M.A. in English from the University of New Mexico. She is on the faculty of the English Department at the University of Arizona. Her books include *Sáanii Dahataal: The Women Are Singing* (1993) and *Blue Horses Rush In: Poems and Stories* (1995). Simon and Schuster recently published her latest children's book, *Navajo ABC: a Diné Alphabet*.

Barre Toelken is a Professor of English and History at Utah State University and is the Director of the Graduate Program in Folklore. He is past president of a number of regional and national folklore societies including the American Folklore Society. His publications include *The Dynamics of Folklore* and *Morning Dew and Roses: Nuance, Metaphor and Meaning in Folksongs*.

Marta Weigle is the University Regents Professor and Chair of the Department of Anthropology at the University of New Mexico. Interested in the Southwest and women's studies, tourism, and oral tradition, she also coedited *The Great Southwest of the Fred Harvey Company and the Santa Fe Railway* with Barbara Babcock and *Spanish New Mexico* with Donna Pierce.

Peter White received his Ph.D. from Pennsylvania State University in 1976. He has taught English and American Studies at the University of New Mexico since 1977. He has published on early American literature, technical writing, and the folklore of New Mexico. He has a long-standing personal and academic interest in folk music. Currently, White serves as the Interim Dean of Undergraduate Studies at the University of New Mexico.

About the Editors

A. Gabriel Meléndez is Chair of the Department of American Studies at the University of New Mexico. He has contributed short stories and poetry to several collections of Chicano literature. His book, *So All Is Not Lost* (1997), documents cultural journalism in Mexican American newspapers in the Southwest. His contribution to this anthology is from an unpublished novel on the Mora Valley in northern New Mexico, the author's place of birth.

Patricia Moore has a Ph.D. from the University of New Mexico, where her dissertation research was an ethnographic study of Hispano devotional art and its meanings in the lives of contemporary people. She coauthored with M. Jane Young the article on the Deming duck race that is printed here.

Patrick Pynes is a native Texan but grew up in the Panama Canal Zone, Mexico City, and Tegucigalpa, Honduras. Since receiving a Ph.D. in American Studies from the University of New Mexico in 2000, he has been living in Flagstaff, Arizona. During the past several years he has been teaching and doing research for Northern Arizona University's Center for Sustainable Environments, Department of Applied Indigenous Studies, and Master of Arts in Sustainable Communities graduate program. Outside of academia, Pynes is a professional gardener and beekeeper. Since 2001, he has been Gardens Manager for historic La Posada Hotel and Gardens in Winslow, Arizona. He has three daughters: Carson, Zia, and Shannon.

M. Jane Young is Professor of American Studies and Regents' Lecturer for the College of Arts and Sciences at the University of New Mexico. Her research interests include material culture and folk art, ritual and festival in the Southwest, and gender studies. She is the author of *Signs from the Ancestors* (1988) and the coeditor of *Feminist Theory and the Study of Folklore* (1993). Of special interest to her is the Great American Duck Race of Deming, the subject of the essay she coauthored with Patricia Moore for this anthology.